Faces of the
Old Testament

Faces of the Old Testament

Joseph A. Callaway

Smyth & Helwys Publishing, Inc.®
Macon, Georgia

ISBN 1-880837-56-0

Faces of the Old Testament

Joseph A. Callaway

Copyright © 1995
Smyth & Helwys Publishing, Inc.®
6316 Peake Road
Macon, Georgia
31210-3960
1-800-568-1248

Library of Congress Cataloging-in-Publication Data

Callaway, Joseph A.
    Faces of the Old Testament / by Joseph A. Callaway.
    viii + 208 pp.   6" x 9" (15 x 23 cm.)
    ISBN 1-880837-56-0
    1. Bible. O.T.—Biography.
    2. Bible. O.T.—History of Biblical events.
    3. Bible. O.T.—History of contemporary events.
    I. Title.
    BS571.C27   1994
    22a.9'22—dc20
    [B]   94-27687
                                                         CIP

Contents

Acknowledgments

When Joseph A. Callaway died in 1988, he left behind a legacy of outstanding archaeological achievement, a multitude of grateful and well-taught students, and an unpublished manuscript that he had written more than a decade earlier.

Friend of the family and campus minister Becky Matheny encouraged Joe's wife, Sarah, to have the manuscript published. Becky also submitted the work to Scott Nash of Smyth & Helwys for consideration. Gerald Mattingly, a Callaway protegé and college professor, further encouraged the book's publication and devoted considerable time to reviewing much of the archaeological information to ensure that the book remained up-to-date. Maxwell Miller of Emory University, an eminent archaeologist himself, offered guidance for the chapters on Adam and Prehistoric Humans and Israel and the Liberation of Canaan. The latter chapter on Israel and Canaan posed special problems since Callaway had rethought his position in light of new evidence and had intended to rewrite the chapter. Another of his students, John Laughlin of Averitt College, who was indebted to Callaway for his own involvement in archaeology and who was familiar with the position Callaway was moving toward, agreed to write a new chapter on this crucial period in Israel's history. Nancy Stubbs of Mercer University keyed the manuscript onto computer disk, and Jackie Riley of Smyth & Helwys guided the book through the editorial process.

Throughout the movement from rediscovered manuscript to book, Sarah Callaway has been involved, striving to ensure that the archaeological data was up-to-date and that her husband's aim of using that data to retell the familiar Old Testament story in a fresh and enlightening way would be realized.

The Faces
of the Old Testament

Life in ancient Israel, as in our time, had many faces. It was spirit as well as substance, always throbbing impatiently at the frontiers of history. In the written word, history follows experience and interprets it. In a sense, the written word mummifies experience and seeks to make it look life-like, but the written word is as different from life as the cold, hard leather of a mummy's skin is different from living flesh.

As written word, the Old Testament follows at the heels of experience. Like life, it has many faces. There is the face of accomplished deed, historical fact that life must accept. There is the face of ideas, which keeps pace with deeds but has its own history. Ideas are as historical as deeds but are clothed in different flesh. They live in symbols, always just beyond the written word, always eluding mummification.

Then there is the face of spirit, the offspring of ideas and deeds, and more elusive of capture than either of its parents. Spirit lives in the soul and must be felt to be understood. It is the haunting beat of Hebrew poetry often lost in translation, or the surge of emotion that articulates the prophet's soul and inspires him, or the feeling of the pious Jews for their land and the holy city of Jerusalem.

In stark deed, subtle ideas, and the elusive reality of spirit, life lies behind the book. The Old Testament therefore is the story of this life in all of its dimensions and with all of its many faces.

The Face of Accomplished Deed

A small stone monument stands across the site of the old Mandelbaum Gate road from the American consulate in Jerusalem. It is simple, an in-scribed slab cemented in field stones gathered from the spot on which it stands. Carved on its face are twenty-three names in Hebrew, in twin columns like a new tablet of the Ten Commandments. The first name is Silmah, a young soldier who died in the battle for Jerusalem in June 1967. The other persons fell in the same battle.

Similar monuments may be seen beside roads and on hillsides around east Jerusalem, each consisting of a single or double column of names, usually draped with wreaths or flowers and evergreens. These names are the men Israel lost at Jerusalem in the Six-Day War. Their names, engraved in stone, were the first local historical records of the war.

The people of Israel visit all of the monuments. Sometimes whole classes of children from local schools gather around the monuments and listen to the story of the war and learn of those who died in the fighting. They see the results of accomplished deed and feel the price paid in lives lost. No longer does the Mandelbaum Gate exist, and no longer does Silmah sit at dinner with his family.

Stories of the Six-Day War were immediately sold in paperback books. At public meetings and discotheques, citizens sang sentimental songs about the capture of Jerusalem. Half-hour movies of the lightning conquest and revised roadmaps and travel guidebooks that include the captured territories became available. Burned-out trucks littered the side of mountain roads in the Golan Heights. Life and events conspired to drag Jerusalem and Palestine into a devastating fit of anger and violence in June 1967, and history took a new turn.

The face of accomplished deed is what history sees now in Jerusalem. When events are understood in the broadened perspective of world events, serious books will tell the story of the Six-Day War with a different emphasis on causes and effects. Instead of shots at Nahal Oz triggering off the strike at Egypt, the cause of the war may be laid at the door of the two great powers of that day: the Soviet Union and the United States, who were thought to play chess with smaller nations. The story will reach a tentacle back into Jewish history and seek nourishment for the state of Israel in the soil of the Old Testament. When the book catches up with life, it will have all of the faces of Old Testament history, beginning with the stark reality of accomplished deed.

Across fifteen centuries, from Abraham to Paul, the sheer fact of accomplished deed shaped the Old Testament. Abraham migrated from the Euphrates valley to the land of Canaan and left stories of his exploits that fed the spirit of Israel in the new land. A significant part of Israel escaped from slavery in Egypt and settled in the hill country of Palestine, establishing a claim to the land. The monarchy was established, shaping the messianic hope of Israel for centuries until the days of Jesus. Wars with Assyria and Babylon displaced the population. Divorced from the land and the state, Israel fought its own war of hopes and ideals, with the result that some of the faithful ones looked for a restoration of the political kingdom and others looked for a spiritual kingdom.

Life was always interesting and complex at the frontiers of history, and the book tagged along, huffing and puffing to keep up. Life always stayed ahead of the book, however, blazing the trail of history with the sheer facts of accomplished deed. Nowhere is this more evident than in the Assyrian historical annals that picture Jehu bowing with tribute before Shalmaneser III; or the naked statement of Sennacherib that he destroyed forty-six cities of Judah, shut up Hezekiah of Judah in Jerusalem like a bird in a cage, and carried 200,150 captives off to Assyria.

The Face of Ideas in the Old Testament

I saw a beautiful display at the Israel Museum entitled "Jerusalem in History and Vision." An entire floor of the vast museum was devoted to historical objects, arranged artistically and symbolically, that were intended to convey the idea of the city that makes it significant for the Israelis.

On one side of the room was a fenced area containing three snow-white Jewish ossuaries, limestone boxes that were used for the burial of bones of the deceased. On the end of one ossuary, the name "Simon the Temple Builder" was scratched in Hebrew. In the simple stone box were the bones of a man who helped build the temple of Herod the Great and the remains of the so-called "Wailing Wall," the last remnant of the temple complex.

There are many ossuaries from the time of Herod, but this one was different because the name of a man infused the temple and its walls with personality, the personality of a fellow Hebrew. Therefore, an idea was communicated that was much more subtle than the naked fact of the ossuary. To rob the ossuary of Simon, the person, would be to rob it of life, to take the spirit out of history and reduce it to a mechanical thing. The exhibition fleshed out the historical fact of the capture of Jerusalem with the idea that the city belongs to the Jews and the idea is a part of history.

I viewed another display that was more elusive. A scale model of the hills on which Jerusalem is built rested on a table waist-high against a wall. The Mount of Olives stood high on the east, separated from the temple mount by the deep Kidron valley. Around the southwest side of the old city was the Valley of Hinnom, which intersects the Kidron at the south tip of Ophel, the site of the city of David. The model presented the Kidron valley as cutting too deeply between the Mount of Olives and the temple mount. The hills were constructed too steeply as well. The east side of Ophel has a forty-degree slope, but the slope on the model was seventy-five degrees.

The hills and valleys were all exaggerated to portray an idea about the city. Because Jerusalem is built on hills, in the model the hills were made higher and the valleys cut deeper to emphasize the terrain. With this idea fixed in the mind, any reference to Jerusalem in the newspapers or in the Bible causes a subconscious picture to rise to the surface, that of a city built on hills and surrounded by deep valleys. The picture is connected to an idea.

On the wall behind the display model was a five-foot wide photograph of a bare, rocky hillside. The hill was fairly steep, with about thirty degrees of slope. Boulders from head-size to three feet across studded the hillside, and the space between was filled with straggly grass and weeds. Was this truly representative of Jerusalem?

It was a part of the idea of Jerusalem that the display intended to convey: the ancient city of David with bare, rocky hillsides waiting to be built into a city. The idea can take the modern Israeli on a magic carpet back to the city of the Jebusites over 3,000 years ago. The Israeli spirit is made to drink of the heady enthusiasm that led David to take the city and make it his capital. Yes, this was Jerusalem, the Jerusalem of an idea.

On the other hand, the photograph was of a hillside in the country, south of Jerusalem. It was not literally Jerusalem. One can drive in the country and see the actual hillside with its boulders and straggly grass. This photo was not Jerusalem, literally, but part of an idea of Jerusalem that over 2,000,000 Israelis have. It was a part of the Jerusalem that has captured the imagination of Israel and is a part of history. The idea was catching up with the historical event that took place in the Six-Day War, 5-10 June 1967.

A literalist could have browsed through the museum hall and seen nothing but a grotesque plaster model of the hills on which Jerusalem is built, along with the strange background of boulders and weeds. If this is all one saw, however, that person missed one Jerusalem in history—an important face of history.

This face of history is in the Old Testament also. It is prominent especially in references to Jerusalem and the temple. From reading the

Psalms, one gets an exaggerated idea of the city of David. Actually, the city that David captured on Ophel covered about eight acres, a place large enough for 1,500 to 2,000 inhabitants. In reality, thousands of colorless, nameless little towns across America are larger than David's city, but the exaggerated idea of the city of David is historically important. Because the people of the Old Testament placed so much hope on Jerusalem, it became, for them, the most important city in the world. We dare not literalize Jerusalem and see only a small eight-acre city spread like a saddle across a long, narrow, backbone ridge. If we do, we miss the most important Jerusalem of history.

In addition to the technique of exaggeration, the Old Testament brings together unrelated literary "pictures" to describe an idea. The traditions in Genesis 1–11, from the creation story to the tower of Babel, are of this kind. In quick succession, like the flicking frames of a motion picture, are the graphic literary pictures of Adam and Eve, Cain and Abel, Noah, and the mob around the tower of Babel. These are unrelated stories, each of which can be traced along its literary genealogy to different settings in different places. They are brought together in Genesis 1–11 to depict the biblical idea of the role and nature of humanity.

After reading Genesis 1–11, persons who lack imagination may envision a quite unrealistic world, one that flies in the face of all learning and historical fact. If they only see Adam and Eve and their posterity, they have missed the most important face of history in those chapters. The idea of humankind that lies just under the surface of the principal characters is the golden thread that ties the stories together, and this is the idea that the Bible hitches its imagination to in the unfolding drama of redemption.

The face of history in ideas requires that we think with the people of the Old Testament. We dare not try to make Americans of the ancient Hebrews. We cannot force them to think as Americans. The Old Testament will not take the shape of our level of learning or ways of understanding. The ancients lived in their own world, unaware that America existed, and the revelation came into their world through the media of their own understanding and language. We must knock on their door to find it.

Americans have difficulty thinking with the ancient Hebrews for two reasons. First, we are incredibly arrogant. Our first impulse is to make biblical people think and speak English. We do not realize that the ancient people had their own language and symbols that developed in a completely different culture. For instance, how many church building programs have been promoted with the text, "Where there is no vision, the people perish" (Prov 29:18)? Actually, the word "vision" in this verse means revelation from God, a common term used of Isaiah's prophecy (1:1), but descriptive of his inaugural call in 6:1ff. Vision has a completely different implication from the American usage meaning foresight and planning for the future.

To admonish a congregation to exercise foresight in planning and building is not wrong, but to find this practical meaning in the proverb is to impose our own use of the word "vision" upon the Bible and rob the word of its inspired meaning. Its value and relevance are bound up with its own meaning, drawn from the experience of the people behind the book. If we impose the experience of our life and ways of thinking upon the book, then the book becomes a sacred relic, dead as a piece of driftwood but endowed with magic because of its origin.

To find the living people of the book in truth and, therefore, the life of the book, we must go to them. We must meet them in their houses, see the food they ate, feel the heat and cold and dryness of their climate, read the literature that preserves their ideas and symbols, worship in their sanctuaries. We must knock on their door.

Just as we must acknowledge the different culture of biblical people, we must recognize that the Bible is very complex. It is a legacy of the religious experience of a people and has all of the natural dimensions of experience. To study the Bible requires that we engage in dialogue with its people. We must be aware of their kinds of schools, scientific knowledge and outlook, political and religious factions, moral and ethical standards, and understanding of God in the light of their own customs.

When we read the Bible, we engage in conversation with people, not God. The book is clothed in the thoughts and forms of those people who lived out its story. I do not feel conscience-stricken to argue with those people or to speak up for my own opinion. When Ezra read the law to his people in Jerusalem and expected them to sit on the ground in a cold rain in November until he finished his sermon (10:9) (while he probably stood under a shelter), I feel cold shivers run up my back—and I do not admire Ezra. I think he would lose his congregation much more quickly today than he did on that uncomfortable November day in Jerusalem.

I admire Amos who had courage to confront the corrupt priests and socially insensitive people of his day in their own place of worship. He had boldness and prophetic insight, but I suspect he would be difficult to live with, both then and now. His bias for rural ways of life and despair of finding anything good in urban life would cause serious problems in most churches today. I can communicate with Amos, even when I feel that he was biased against city life. Furthermore, through communication with Amos, I find a revelation of God in his witness. It was not an oppressive, enforced kind of witness but the free interchange of ideas, allowing one the right to think.

The complexity of the Bible lies in its faithful witness of the experience of its people. We should not fear its complexity, even if some of our simplistic dogmas about authority and revelation have to be reconsidered. After all, they are our dogmas, not God's. We developed and wrote them. If they make Bible study intellectually oppressive, perhaps they should no longer stand between us and the people who wait to meet us in the pages of the book. Ideas flourish in complexity and dialogue, and we need to bring our ideas into the forum of biblical thinking with complete candor if we expect the Bible to become a dynamic influence in our day.

The Face of Spirit in the Old Testament

I stood on the highest point of the ancient ruin of 'Ai, east of Bethel, and feasted my soul on the view to the east and south. It was unexpectedly beautiful. With my back toward Bethel, I looked down the Wadi Auja to the Jordan valley a few miles distant. Perched on the left side of the wadi (deep, dry stream bed) was Rammun, biblical Rimmon, the last village at the edge of the wasteland leading to the valley. Tucked just out of sight behind a hill on the right was Mukhmas (biblical Michmash), and beyond it and behind a hill in the edge of the valley was Jericho, whose springs fed a large patch of green in the wide-open valley. Geba was visible on a ridge across from Mukhmas, and directly south were the two landmark towers on the Mount of Olives, not more than ten miles away. In front of the hill that hid Jerusalem was Anathoth, close by the conical hill of el-Ful, perhaps the location of biblical Gibeah. Facing el-Ful across a wide valley toward Bethel was Er-Ram, or biblical Ramah. I marveled at the panorama of biblical sites, a veritable roll call of important villages in the Old Testament, until I became aware of a strange feeling.

Spread around my feet in a radius of little more than ten miles and near enough that I could almost reach out and touch it was a significant part of the Holy Land. Two places, Jerusalem and Bethel, are mentioned more than any other cities in the Bible. I became aware when I saw how small the region was that all of it could be tucked inside my home county in Georgia. And the villages were so small! How unbelievable that this little parcel of relatively dry and very rocky earth could have left such a mark on the world!

I realized in a way I never before experienced that the spirit of the people who lived there made the difference. This awareness of spirit has to be felt, often in chance encounters that are surprising. I had this same feeling when I picked up the Jerusalem telephone directory, a volume much smaller than those of a hundred American cities. I had to look again for the Jerusalem number I wanted when I became aware that the directory was for *all Israel*, from Dan to Beersheba to Eilat!

Occasionally one stumbles upon the face of spirit in the Old Testament history. These chance encounters open up the soul of a people in ways that are felt and remembered. Persons have not really encountered the Old Testament until they have met in the way the incredible spirit of its people, not even if they have memorized half of its verses.

One example is Elijah, the spokesman for a faithful remnant of Israel who had not bowed the knee to Baal. We are acquainted with Elijah's encounters with King Ahab of Israel and his contest with the prophets of Baal on Mount Carmel. Countless sermons have made Elijah almost a superhuman hero because of his unwavering spirit and faith, unreal and detached from the kind of world we know. I do not disagree, but the usual picture is too simple to be real. Elijah's spirit fed on something besides the prayers of his own soul. I think I found the answer one night in Jerusalem.

Every visitor to Jerusalem remembers the unusual appearance of the Hassids, the orthodox Jews who wear a long black coat, a wide black hat or a fur hat, and long curls of hair hanging from the temples in front of the ears. The appearance is unmistakable and unforgettable. These people live in Mea Sherim in north-central Jerusalem. My discovery was occasioned by a conversation with a brilliant, hard-driving, young tank commander who remarked that Israel would be better off without the Hassids. Their other-worldly appearance and peculiar way of life were an embarrassment to the twenty-six year-old man.

One night in Jerusalem when friends from Hebrew University were present, I raised the question of these orthodox Jewish men and their role in Israel. I inquired if they fought in the Six-Day War. I learned that all but about 5,000–7,000 of the ultra-orthodox ones participated in the fighting. These spent their time in prayer and reading the scriptures. One friend observed that the latter would have been useless in a battle anyway and that the people would rather have left them at their prayers, which seemed to offer a sense of security. In a very peculiar way, the spirit of Israel fed on their prayers and total dedication to God.

Since Israel is a relatively new nation, and Hebrew is the spoken language, I raised the question of language continuity from biblical times. Where did Israel learn its Hebrew language? The Hassids, who study the ancient traditions in Hebrew and pray in Hebrew, have kept the language alive. The nationalism of the new state required the Hebrew language, so the state fed on the spirit of these people. Behind all of the remarkable deeds and ideas of the modern state of Israel is a substratum of spirit that has its roots in ancient Israel, physically evident in the anachronistic-looking Hassids. The state would not be better off without them; they are a part of the soul of the state.

Elijah was associated with a militantly orthodox faction of Hebrews in his day, a devoted band that had not bowed the knee to Baal. When he felt that he stood alone, he was reminded that 7,000 persons remained orthodox. They nurtured the spirit that flourished again when Ahab's baalism was defeated. Elijah fed on a hidden stratum of spirit that reached wider than he thought and deeper than he recognized, even to the sources of Moses' inspiration. A core of the faithful remained indomitable, more than conquerors because they refused to be conquered, and Elijah walked briefly across the state of history as their spokesman. He was a hero, but a real one attached to other real people who preserved the orthodox spirit of Israel.

The Old Testament has many faces and dimensions. It cannot be reduced to a simple historical event because it reflects life in all its dimensions. In some sections of the Old Testament, the historical pilgrimage of ideas is even more dominant, and more important, than the literal event. When we come to these passages, we will do well to allow life to emerge again from the pages of scripture in whatever forms it is accustomed to take.

Chapter 1

Adam and Prehistoric Persons

For many centuries Adam was our only prehistoric human. We lavished upon him every gift of the imagination because he fulfilled a deep human need for legitimate ancestry, both physical and spiritual. He was our claim to authenticity, our status symbol, and nothing he could do would make us want to disown him.

Therefore, we have had problems adjusting to the presence of other prehistoric people who have been resurrected from the dust by archaeologists and paraded into the presence of Adam. We are confronted with real persons. In the household of our intellect, another bedroom must be added; and Adam must learn to live with them.

Adam

We meet Adam in Genesis 2. One bold, sweeping statement introduces him: "Then the Lord God formed man from the dust of the ground, and breathed into his nostrils the breath of life; and the man became a living being" (v. 7). He is placed in a special garden in Eden, somewhere in the east, where a tree of life stands in the midst of the garden and a tree of the knowledge of good and evil is close by. A counterpart or helpmate to Adam is then fashioned from one of his ribs, and she is called Woman. Their adventure in the garden with the serpent and the forbidden fruit is common knowledge.

One question concerns us: Who is Adam, and where do we find his ancestry? Archaeologists have raised this question because they discovered prehistoric humans and dated them. We can visit the cave on Mount Carmel where the buried remains were found of a human who lived approximately 50,000 years ago. The skeletal remains of this man suggest some kind of kinship with the two-million-year-old *Homo habilis* of East Africa. We can also visit the Rockefeller Archaeological Museum at Jerusalem and view the bones of a man buried on Mount Carmel 10,000 years ago. His features resemble those of many other humans, known by

their bones and artifacts, who developed primitive tools for food production and established the first villages in Palestine. We can visit Jericho
and view the heap of ruins marking what appears to have been a sanctuary built around 8,000 B.C.

Have the archaeologists also found Adam? The answer is yes, but he
has been found in a different setting, and his relationship with prehistoric
man is not as simple as we would like it to be. The Bible itself points the
way to Adam. It gives direction in identifying and locating him. We note
first that he is a peculiar kind of individual. The New Revised Standard
Version translates "Adam" in Genesis 2 as "the man," a correct rendering
of the Hebrew *'adam.* "Adam" is a transliteration, merely transferring the
phonetic sounds of the Hebrew word into English, and not a personal
name. Thus Adam in the Bible seems to be a representative man, all of
mankind poured into one individual. A colleague of mine put it this way
in a statement to some first-year students: "You don't know me from
Adam; but if you know Adam, you know me."

The ancestry of Adam is different in kind from those ancient humans
whose bones have been preserved and discovered. Adam, as individualized humankind, lives in the world of thought, not ruins of cities; and his
ancestry is found in literature and art, not caves or burial places in the ancient Near East. Adam feeds on symbols, not bread. Indeed, the fruit that
he ate is often painted as actual fruit, because most symbols have roots
in concrete, literal things. That fruit evokes meaning that cannot be contained in an apple, however. His bite of forbidden fruit sent shock waves
of guilt through unborn generations of the human race, and the terrible
truth about Adam's rebel heart created an emergency in the normally
serene abode of God. Adam is a man; but as symbolic man, he encompasses in a compact and intelligible form every human, including prehistoric and modern people.

A different kind of skill is needed to excavate Adam. For instance,
how would one get a Carbon 14 date of the tree of life? It is a palm tree
in ancient art, but it is the tree of life only in art carved on stone cylinder
seals or described in writing on clay tablets. How would one find the lati-
tude and longitude of the Garden of Eden? It is a part of every sacred
temple area in the lower Euphrates valley, but Adam's garden is the archetype compacted into wedge-shaped writing on a clay tablet. How
would a laboratory at Hebrew University in Jerusalem find the pollen
grains of the tree of knowledge of good and evil in a sample of earth?

To excavate Adam we begin by reading the dead languages of Sumeria, Babylonia, and Assyria, as well as Hebrew. All of the accumulated learning of these great cultures is locked tightly in the strange wedge-shaped writing on clay tablets. Much of the learning is compacted into symbols that are as simple as the tree of life, yet so profound that the literary excavator never quite reaches bedrock in probing its full meaning. In this world of profound symbols that have fossilized living experience and wisdom, we trace Adam's ancestors and come to know Adam.

More than a century ago, the first giant strides were taken in translating the ancient languages of Mesopotamia. Hard on the heels of the first translation of cuneiform by Henry Rowlinson came the discovery in 1853 of more than 24,000 clay tablets in the library of Ashurbanipal at Nineveh. It had been buried 2,600 years and forgotten. In 1872, a British Museum cataloger named George Smith found among these tablets the Babylonian flood and creation accounts.

The creation account is most significant for us and has been followed up in the last century by the recovery of other fragmentary accounts that deal with origins of "the man." Two characteristics occur repeatedly. "Man's" substance is associated with the earth, and his form and spirit are linked with the gods (see Gen 2:7). The earthy substance of man is minimized in Genesis 1:27, which states matter-of-factly that "God created humankind in his image."

An Old Babylonian tablet (1800–1600 B.C.) expresses a similar idea of the dual ties of humans to the earth and to deity in this translation:

> Create Man that he may bear the yoke:
> That he may bear the yoke (of creation)
> The (yoke) of creation (?) man shall bear.[1]

The tablet is weather-worn and broken, which makes the reading of words in parentheses questionable, but the parallelism of ideas makes possible a reasonably accurate reconstruction of the incomplete words.

One observation should be made here. "Man" is a translation of the Akkadian word *lu-ul-la-a*, which means individualized mankind, the archetype or model of man. In this sense it is the same as "Adam" in Hebrew, a symbolic concept, not a human whose bones we should look for in excavations.

The tablet continues the story of creation with this statement:

> Let them slay a god,
> And let the gods (slay a god?)
> With his flesh and his blood
> Let Ninhursag mix clay.
> God and man
> united (?) in the clay.[2]

Here the ancient tradition that the substance of man is clay, or dust as in Genesis 2:7, is clearly expressed. It must have arisen from the honest observation that the flesh of humankind returns to dust when death comes. The investment of spirit and life makes flesh different from clay, so the impartation of life is the gift of God.

The "forming" of humans from dust or clay is also a common and ancient concept. A characteristic word is taken from the potter's art of making clay pots. In one Babylonian tablet, the "forming" from clay is expressed this way:

> When Anu had created the heavens
> (And) Nudimmud had built the *Apsu*, his dwelling,
> Ea nipped off clay in the *Apsu*;
> He created Kulla for the restoration of the temples.[3]

Apsu is the raw material of the earth, as opposed to Tiamat, the watery waste of oceans and primordial waters outside the creation. Kulla is a craftsman, possibly a brick-god representative of humans whose, function is to maintain the temples. The interesting expression is in the third line: "Ea nipped off clay . . ." with which he created Kulla.

The same expression is found in Job 33:6 where Job says, "See, before God I am as you are; I too was formed from a apiece of clay." The word translated "formed" is not the one used in Genesis 2:7. It is *qaratz*, which means "to pinch off" as the potter pinches off clay to make a vessel on his wheel. A more accurate translation is an echo of the ancient Babylonian expression that seems to have become proverbial. Job says literally, "I too was nipped off from the clay."

Prominent in all of the ancient literature from the region of Abraham's ancestry is the idea that the human spirit and life are associated with deity. There are different ways of expressing the idea, but generally it presupposes the same concept. A favorite tradition in the Near East was that humans were created in part from the blood of a sacrificed god. The Old Babylonian tablet cited above states that man was created from clay mixed with the flesh and blood of a sacrificed god.

The Babylonian creation epic, *Enuma Elish*, brings humans forth in a dramatic but profoundly meaningful episode. After Marduk, the god of Babylon, put down the revolt against law and order in the heavens, he slew the goddess of chaos and watery waste, Ti'amat; and from the carcass he created the heavens and the earth. Then he conceived the plan of creating *lullu*, or "man," who like Adam is a collective individual representing humankind. Having used the raw materials of Ti'amat's carcass for the heavens and the earth, Marduk had a flash of insight. Striding into the midst of the gods assembled around him, he asked:

> Who was it that created the strife,
> And caused Ti'amat to revolt and prepare for battle?
> Let him who created the strife be delivered up;
> I will make him bear his punishment, be ye at rest.[4]

The gods who were to be at rest were those who joined in the revolt with Tiamat and were imprisoned awaiting judgment. The judgment would be a sentence of labor on the earth, newly created. Babylon had to be built, and a temple to Marduk must be constructed and maintained. The stroke of genius that came to Marduk was to slay the ringleader of the rebellion and set free the imprisoned gods, for common labor would be degrading and beneath their status. Confronted with the possibility of pardon, the gods responded to Marduk: "Kingu it was who created the strife and caused Ti'amat to revolt and prepare for battle."[5] Then the creation of humankind took place as follows: "They bound him (Kingu) and held him before Ea."[6] When the gods cast their votes, the following decision was reached:

> In Uzuma, the bond of heaven and earth
> Let us slay (two) Lamga gods.
> With their blood let us create mankind.
> The service of the gods be their portion
> For all times,
> To maintain the boundary ditch,
> Ulligarra and Zalgarra,
> Thou shalt call their names.[7]

Uzuma, the bond between heaven and earth, is the sacred area of the temple, its "Garden of Eden," an appropriate place for the creation of man to occur. The Lamga gods are craftsmen, which implies an inherent gift in humans that equip them for labor, without the inherent sin that the *Enuma Elish* epic implies. Humankind's lot is the same. Persons are born to earn their bread by the sweat of their brow, as Genesis 3:19 expressly says.

Who then is Adam? He is "the man," all humankind poured into one archetype man. His ancestry is found in the intellectual genealogy of ancient Near Eastern thought, where every people from the dawn of historical writing had its collective "man." This is a different kind of genealogy from that of prehistoric man that scientists have found, because we trace the latter's pilgrimage in prehistory through physical remains such as bones, tools, and campsites that are discovered.

Adam's ancestry is traced through a succession of literary symbols that root in historical substance but carry meaning that only symbols can articulate. This is not falsifying Adam. It is finding the essence of historical substance in him, but also ultimate meaning that is more profound than any skeletal remains of one man, surrounded by his tools and weapons, could possibly convey.

Like every symbolic "man" in ancient Near Eastern literature, Adam is made from the substance of dust or clay. Humankind, the historical Adam, thus emerged from the womb of the earth, the head of the earthly creation but related physically to the earth. There is no notion that humans are deposed angelic beings, that their physical ancestry is in heaven, the realm of the gods. Their physical kinship is with their earthly environment, something every biology pupil learns in high school, and something that the ancient sages knew before writing was invented.

If we rob Adam of his symbolic meaning and simply literalize him, then we cut out his soul and give him to the anthropologist, reduced to a cadaver. The anthropologist can measure his skull, calculate his brain capacity, analyze the chemical components of his remains, and possibly obtain a blood count by centrifugating the dust of his dried blood. If this exhausts the meaning for us of humanity's creation from nipped-off clay, then indeed we have abandoned Adam too soon.

Likewise, the intangible of spirit that animates flesh and makes Adam a living being is an abstract concept. Its legitimate genealogy in ancient thought is expressed crudely (to us) in the mixture of the blood of gods in human earthly substance. Adam has divine breath, not divine blood, that animates his body.

Actually, nobody believed that humans had divine blood. Life to them was in the blood, so that blood symbolized life. When a lamb was sacrificed, its blood was caught in a container, and a priest sprinkled some of it on the altar to symbolize the presence of God and some on the people (as in Exod 24:4-8). Through the sacrifice of life, evident in the sprinkled blood, communion was established between the worshiper and God.

Thus in the ancient creation accounts, divine blood mixed with the earthly substance of humans was a euphemism for divine breath or life. Adam is spared this euphemism because his creator is spirit. Whether the divine relationship is expressed by breath or blood, the underlying concept of humanity's uniqueness in creation is similar.

Adam and Prehistoric Humans

If Adam's ancestry is in the thought world of ancient Near Eastern literature and art, where does Adam cross the path of prehistoric persons? The answer to this question is in the biblical teaching that Adam, or humankind, is created in the image of God.

> Then God said, "Let us make humankind in our image, according to our likeness; and let them have dominion over the fish of the sea, and over the birds of the air, and over the cattle, and over all the wild animals of the earth, and over every creeping thing that creeps upon the earth." So God created humankind in his image, in the image of God he created them; male and female he created them. (Gen 1:26-27)

The Hebrew word for "image" means something chiseled out, like a graven image of an idol. It implies that humans in some way are a counterpart image of God. The word for "likeness" means reflection, as in a mirror. Therefore, humankind is in some sense a counterpart of God in appearance, substance, or something else.

It would be a waste of time to thread the maze of speculation about the meaning of "image of God." Extremes from literal physical resemblance to spiritual resemblance in personality, self-consciousness, self-determination, reason, freedom of will, moral capacity, and immortality reflect confusion more than anything else. There is a common notion that "image" implies substance or quality, and the recurring question is this: At what point in the development of prehistoric persons were they made in the image of God?

We must first clarify the primary meaning of "image of God" in Genesis 1:26-27. It should be approached from the perspective of Near Eastern patterns of thinking in biblical times and the place of man in creation in that world.

The characteristic pattern of thinking in biblical times persists to this day among the Muslim Arabs of Palestine. It is evident in the typical response to the American farewell at the end of a day's work on an excavation. "See you tomorrow," the staff members says to their Arab friend as they part to go to their houses. "If Allah wills it!" comes the typical reply, automatically and without exception.

Events move on two levels in this way of thinking. Whatever happens on earth is predetermined in heaven or in the councils of God. In ancient times people actually thought that the action, not just the decision, occurred in heaven preceding counterpart action on earth. A passage in the Babylonian creation account concerning the charge to mankind by Marduk emphasizes counterpart action:

> Throughout the days to come let them,
> without forgetting, make mention of his ways,
> Let him (man) establish great offerings for his fathers;
> Let them provide for their maintenance
> (and) let them take care of their sanctuaries.
> . . . .
> Whatever he (Marduk) does in heaven,
> let him do the same on earth[8]

A similar pattern of thinking is evident in the Model Prayer of Jesus, but there seems to be a counterpart of will instead of action. This represents a theological refinement but no change in the fundamental counterpart ontology or philosophy. Note the familiar words in Matthew 6:10: "Your kingdom come, your will be done, on earth as it is in heaven."

A two-level universe is presupposed: an upper level where deity lives and a lower level where humans live. The upper level is in the heavens; the lower level is the earth. Events on earth are predetermined in the heavens either by action or decision, and counterpart actions follow on earth.

In order that ancient people might learn what was predetermined in the heavens before the action occurred on earth, vast religious institutions were established in centers like Babylon with the purpose of discovering the secrets of the gods. Priests learned of the divine by astrology or mechanical devices such as interpreting the spread of a drop of oil on water in a diving cup. A complicated and secret system was developed for reading the convolutions and shape of a sheep's liver. Clay models of livers with labels inscribed on the various areas have been excavated.

Prophets were specialists in foretelling the future that the gods had ordained. A favorite pre-biblical way of channeling the secret information of the divine decisions was to induce, either naturally or artificially, an ecstatic trance where the prophet "took leave of his senses and was like one possessed." Since a prophet's rational processes were suspended in a trance, it was thought that a hotline was opened through the subconscious to deity, and that the gods delivered their message through the speech or babbling of the ecstatic.

The two-level universe idea lies behind Genesis 1:26-27, which states that humankind was made in the image of God. Reduced to its simplest meaning, it gives humankind a role on earth that is analogous to God's role in heaven. Whatever else we add to this is implicit in the human position at the head of the earthly creation. Speculation about moral capacity, freedom of will, reason, and so forth deal with peripheral meanings that grow out of humanity's unique role as lord of the earth. For instance, certain special qualities could be attributed to the president of the United States, when actually he is a man like other men, except that he has a special role as head of a great nation. The real difference in him and other men is in his unique office, which demands that he act like a president of the United States.

Actually, the primacy of role is stated clearly in Genesis 1:26 in which humankind is given dominion over all creation in the sea, in the air, and on the land. If the writer had envisioned the space age, he would have included the planets of the universe that we know in the command also. Problems between humans and God arise out of the misuse of this earthly role, however.

The human role on earth seems to be a primary concern of most Near Eastern creation accounts. When Marduk created humans in *Enuma Elish*, his motivation for creating them was to provide labor at the temple so the rebel gods could be pardoned:

> Blood I will form and cause bones to be,
> Then will I set up *lullu*, "Man" shall be his name!
> Yes, I will create *lullu*: Man!
> (Upon him) shall the services of the god be imposed
> that they may be at rest[9]

Then, after the creation of humans, Marduk formally decreed human-kind's role: "He (Marduk) imposed the services of the gods (upon them) and set the gods free."[10]

A tablet from the first Babylonian dynasty gives humankind the role of bearing the yoke of creation, especially of laboring like an ox that pulls a plow. The Ashur tablet assigns the human portion as serving the gods in menial tasks such as maintaining the boundary ditches, irrigation canals, and fields.

Genesis 1:26-27 gives humanity a much more important and dignified role than the Babylonian and Sumerian sources do. In the latter, the earth is made in the likeness of the heavens, and humankind is a kind of tragic afterthought created to solve a problem of what to do with rebellious gods. In order to have a future, the human must either become a god and thus be immortal—like Utnapishtim of the Babylonian flood account—or do some mighty deed that will leave a legacy in history such as building a great *ziggurat* tower to the heavens (see Gen 11:4). The image of God in Genesis 1:27 invests a unique dignity in humankind through an earthly role that reflects, or is counterpart to, the role of God in the heavens.

Humankind, not the earth, is in the image of God and is the head of creation, not an afterthought. Thus, the biblical concept of humanity endows one with a future. There is no need to become God, which is the temptation in the Garden (Gen 3:5), or to sacrifice oneself to make a name that endures (Gen 11:4).

Adam is "the man" who is appointed to the office of head of creation. As we noted before, his origin is in the earthly creation symbolized by the "dust of the earth" from which he was formed. Among the earthly creatures his physical kinship and family tree are found. He is no deposed divine being, and the book of Genesis deplores as sin every human effort to escape or even deny the family tree and seek to usurp divinity. The ancient humans whose bones were found on Mount Carmel come somewhere in this family tree of Adam, as do all other identifiable prehistoric people. Even two-million-year-old *Homo habilis* may be our ancestor. We should not be embarrassed, unless we have illusions that we are gods and not people.

One question still tantalizes us: Where in the genealogy of humankind was Adam created in the image of God? The common tendency is to confine this to the point in time when the first person was created. We like to think of a dramatic occasion where God took golden scissors and formally snipped a ribbon that stretched across the human family tree and opened up a genealogical expressway leading to us.

The ancients liked to think in the same way. Our Hebrew Bible, from which present-day English translations derive, traces the genealogy of Adam back to 4004 B.C. Dr. John Lightfoot, vice chancellor of the University of Cambridge at the beginning of the nineteenth century, dated the occasion precisely at 9:00 A.M. on 23 October 4004 B.C.! He made no plus or minus allowance for errors in his calculating method.

The Septuagint, or Greek translation of the Hebrew Bible that non-Palestinian Jews and Christians used, has a genealogy of Adam dating back to 6000 B.C. The Samaritans, who split off from the Hebrews in the time of Ezra about four centuries before Christ, have a Hebrew Bible that dates Adam's creation some 350 years later than 4004 B.C. If we explore the non-biblical traditions, there is a written genealogy of the Sumerians who lived at Ur before the time of Abraham. Their "Adam" was given a kingship 267,997 years, 3 months, and 3½ days before the defeat of Balulu and the fall of Ur some 2,000 years before Christ!

Our quest is not to fix a date for human creation. Neither is this the objective of the book of Genesis. Our concern is with the image of God concept, which is the sole concern of Genesis 1:26-27. So we ask a question that does not send us looking for physical beginnings: At what point did humanity assume the role of ruling over the earth in a way that reflects God's role and rule in the heavens? To answer this question, we must ask every person, of whom Adam is the representative, all humankind poured into an individual. God did not cut the ribbon across the family tree at some point in time and from then on everyone began to use the creation in a way that reflects God's purposes and aspirations. If this were true, there would be no need for a single word of the Bible past Genesis 1:27.

Our answer to this question is found in the genealogical tables of the spirit, not flesh. Each person must find the answer in the family tree of his/her own soul. If we use the language of the Bible, that is the point at which one enters into a covenant with God. The covenant is the external structure, both in the Old and New Testaments, where the aspirations and hopes of humankind are brought into a parallel track with the purposes of God. Within this two-track structure, the human role as the noblest creature of all echoes the role of God in the heavens in a stereophonic hymn of fulfillment.

Our last question brings us back to our original problem. Can Adam live in the same intellectual household with the prehistoric people of Mount Carmel? Why not? Adam, as the representative human, represents them, too. Both were made of dust of the earth. But were those prehistoric humans made also in the image of God? How can we know? This is a quality of spirit, not flesh; of response of the total person to his/her understanding of God, not cultural achievement. Certainly archaeologists cannot capture and analyze the spirit of a prehistoric person, for it has abandoned its house of flesh and only the bones are left. We can only infer spiritual capability from the sanctuary at Jericho.

After we have explored every line of physical evidence, we must still stand outside the inner sanctum of prehistoric humankind's soul, where every Adam meets God in spiritual response. In the private laboratory of the heart the image of God is found, and neither archaeologists nor theologians have learned the techniques of excavating there.

Endnotes

[1] Alexander Heidel, *The Babylonian Genesis* (Chicaco: University of Chicago Press, 1951) 67.

[2] Ibid.

[3] Ibid., 65.

[4] Ibid., 47.

[5] Ibid.

[6] Ibid.

[7] Ibid., 69-70.

[8] Ibid., 50.

[9] Ibid., 46.

[10] Ibid., 47.

Chapter 2

Human Pride and Perversion

Genesis 3:1-24; 4:1-16; 6:1-9; 7; 11:1-9

Genesis 3–11 catalogs the classic ways people fail to realize the promise that is invested in Adam. The option to fail is a part of the birthright of freedom, and failure is one of the disciplines of responsibility. Using here the epic themes of the biblical world, the ways of human failure are written large across the expressway of every person's experience.

Genesis 3:1-24 focuses upon the arrogance of grasping and its devastating consequences; 4:1-16 paints in bold strokes the ugly face of intolerance and its volatile nature; 6:1–9:7 passes quickly before our view, almost unseen in the absorbing story of the Flood, the ungovernable nature of perverted ideals and the extreme difficulty in dealing with them; and 11:1-9 uncovers naked ambition and pride at the roots of confusion among peoples and nations.

The Arrogance of Grasping
Genesis 3:1-24

We are not ready to study the subtle story of humankind in the Garden of Eden until we explore the thought-world of which it is a part. Its penetrating indictment of ultimate human arrogance, the hungry look and open hand grasping for immortality, is as striking in its original setting as it is in ours. The price of the ultimate presumption is failure, failure to succeed in the high enterprise of being human in its noblest dimensions.

The cheap view of humanity in all ancient literature except Genesis provided one of the favorite epic themes. If humans were created to do the menial tasks of the gods, the supreme achievement would be to grasp immortality and become like gods. Perhaps the greatest literary work known in ancient times is the Gilgamesh Epic, a masterpiece built around the theme of the inevitability of death. Gilgamesh, the hero, engages in superhuman exploits that must have been highly entertaining and instructive in the time of Hammurabi, king of Babylon about 1700 B.C. The hero is the offspring of a divine father and human mother, endowing him with two-thirds deity and one-third humanity. His one-third endowment of humanity is his undoing because he is confronted with the inevitability of death, the lot of humanity. His only hope to escape death is to lay hold of immortality.

Among many legendary adventures, Gilgamesh finds his way across the River of Death to the abode of the gods who live in a beautiful land that is off-limits to humans. After many days and nights of traveling through darkness, his first view of the land is of a garden of paradise. The trees are loaded with precious stones for fruit,

> The carnelian bears its fruit
> It is hung with vines good to look at.
> The lapis bears foliage
> It, too, bears fruit lush to behold.

This is the dream land of the gods, where the stones used for rings and necklaces are as abundant as leaves, and where there is no toil nor death. It is a world that embodies the dream of success of the ancient Sumerians and Babylonians. The highest attainment is to acquire much jewelry, wealth, and meat to feast upon every day; to be exempt from work; and to live forever.

One interesting adventure is a visit with Utnapishtim, the hero of the Babylonian flood who has been given immortality because he survived the Flood. Utnapishtim is in no mood to help another mortal reach his exalted place, however, so he puts Gilgamesh to a test that proves his mortality. He challenges him to stay awake seven days and nights. When Gilgamesh is overcome by sleep, he fails to gain an audience with the gods and is sent away with a consolation prize given by Utnapishtim. He is given a prickly plant that will renew his life as a man, but will not confer immortality like that of the gods.

On his way home, Gilgamesh stops by a spring to bathe. While he bathes in the water, a serpent comes up from the water, sniffs the plant, and carries it away. As the serpent slithers away, it sheds its skin, renewing its own life. Gilgamesh sits down and weeps over his failure, and then proceeds back to his city to toil for the gods until death should overtake him.

This ancient epic was very popular in the land of Abraham's ancestry and actually had Sumerian characters who were known in the region of

Ur. It survived into the Assyrian period, during the Hebrew monarchy, and was found in the library of Ashurbanipal at Nineveh, which was discovered in 1853. A fragment of the epic was found in the excavations at Megiddo in Palestine. The theme of the grasping for immortality, with its despair of any future for humanity, was a popular one. The serpent was the epic spoiler of the human dream of becoming like the gods.

The standing serpent was considered the most important symbol of sovereign unapproachableness. Its image is found on Egyptian monuments, statuaries, paintings, and even writing throughout the Old Testament period. In Isaiah's vision of God (6:1-6), the seraphim are none other than standing, winged serpents that are the attendants of God who is invisible on the throne. The standing serpent is in Genesis 3 also, where it has the villain's role in articulating the human desire to grasp immortality.

A cylinder seal from the lower Euphrates valley has an intaglio carving that has been called a "temptation scene." The story behind the scene is not known, but the characters bear marked similarity to those in the Garden of Eden story. A male figure is seated on the right, apparently silent but aware of the presence of a female figure and a standing serpent on the opposite side of a tree. In the center is a tree, either a tree of life or a tree of wisdom. The tree is the focus of the scene and may represent a tree of knowledge of good and evil. Thus, the association of a tree, a serpent, and two persons in a garden provide the setting for the story that is not known but may yet come to light in excavations in the land of Abraham's ancestry.

Another popular story of the human search for immortality is the Adapa epic, found in the library of Ashurbanipal and also in Egypt at Amarna, the capital of Akhenaton in the fourteenth century B.C. The library of Ashurbanipal obviously preserves a much older version than its date of the seventh century B.C. Its characters are actually Sumerian, dating to the time of Abraham; and the text is roughly parallel to the Amarna version, which dates to the period of sojourn in Egypt. The setting of the epic is the lower Euphrates valley, where Adapa, the Sumerian version of Adam, the representative man, is a servant at the sanctuary of Eridu, near Ur. He was created as the "model" of men, and, as the poem puts it, "To him he (Ea) had given wisdom; eternal life he had not given him."

On one of Adapa's fishing trips to obtain food for the sanctuary, the south wind capsizes his coat, causing Adapa to pronounce a curse upon the wind. Naturally, the wind stops blowing from the Persian Gulf, and extremely hot, desert weather oppresses the land. Word is brought to the chief Sumerian deity, Anu, that Adapa has broken the wing of the south wind. Anu cries out a word in Sumerian translated "Mercy!" then rises from his throne and commands that Adapa be brought before him.

In preparations for his appearance before Anu, Adapa is advised by Ea, the god of wisdom, on what to wear, how to act, and what to do with the food that will be put before him. Ea treacherously advises Adapa to refuse bread and water that Anu will set before him because he fears that Anu might confer immortality upon Adapa, a "worthless human." (Adapa had accidentally become "distinguished" by having the invitation to appear before Anu.) Consequently, Adapa refuses to eat the bread of life or drink the water of life when they are offered. He rejects innocently the gift of immortality. As he is carried away from the dream world of the gods, the last words he hears are, "Thou shalt not have (eternal) life! Ah, perverse mankind!"

Adam and the Garden of Eden are at home in this world of literature and symbols. Adam is the model man, living in a garden of paradise in a suburb of the heavens where he can commune with God (3:8ff.). There are symbolic trees in the garden, one of which seems to be the tree of life (vv. 22-24). The serpent also is there (v. 1ff.), and he too is grasping. Because he is standing, he is regarded in Near Eastern thought as belonging to the highest order of creation right next to humankind. So he is grasping for this place by trying to persuade humanity to grasp for the immortality of God. His craftiness has all the subtle and devious intrigue of court life in an Oriental palace. Like an ambitious court plotter, he makes his plan, lays the bait, and then waits for his chance to move. His gamble is bold, but the stakes are high. There really is not much future in remaining a snake! What irony in the thought that a snake should usurp the place of humanity if such should grasp immortality!

Humanity is therefore confronted in the garden with the most alluring temptation of the ancient world, the temptation to grasp immortality and escape the limitations of being human. In essence, the temptation calls up ultimate arrogance, for humanity is of the earth, not the heavens. A scene from another cylinder seal, also Babylonian, illustrates with subtle understatement this human arrogance. The scene is of two gods standing by a sacred tree in a garden. The one on the left has picked a piece of fruit, probably a date, from the sacred tree and is handing it over to a third figure. Obviously, the tree belongs to the gods, and they pick its fruit and hand it to whomever they choose. How arrogant and presumptuous it would be for an earthly being to break into their presence and reach out to snatch fruit from their tree! Even entertaining the idea is a breach of court etiquette.

When Adam, therefore, took the forbidden fruit that was only God's to give, he turned his back on the Old Testament investment in him as man. He disdained his manhood as unworthy, when his humanity was the fruit that had been handed over in the garden to him.

Another dimension in the story should not elude us. The high view of humankind set forth in Genesis 1–2 is confronted with the cheap view that was current in the biblical world. The two views collide in the Garden of Eden and, using the classic symbols of the age, the biblical view is sharpened for our instruction. The tree of knowledge of good and evil represents wisdom, which humankind obtains at considerable hazard. In all of the ancient literature, wisdom causes people to desire immortality and the status of deity.

Wisdom is the endowment that enables humanity to plan and draw blueprints for the world, then to carry through with the plans in a way counterpart to the way God administers the heavens. This quality of God's wisdom is set forth in Proverbs 8:22ff. Possession of wisdom, however, allows a range in thought so far afield that one becomes dissatisfied with the human status and is unable to face mortality, seeing death as the negation of all the good invested in humankind. So humanity turns against the earthly domain and reaches out in the ultimate arrogance for immortality. In the literature, immortality always eludes the human grasp, and humanity turns back in sorrow. Genesis 3:1-24 keeps immortality beyond the human reach and emphasizes the role as keeper of the earthly creation in these words:

> In the sweat of your face you shall eat bread until you return to the ground, for out of it you were taken; you are dust, and to dust you shall return. (v. 19)

The harsh realities of life belong to humanity: the toil, sweat, and dust of earning daily bread; the ever-present awareness that death waits at the end. But wisdom that raises mortals just short of immortality, just out of reach of the tree of life (3:24), is the equipment for dealing with a harsh and brutal world, and that wisdom seems to be pregnant with promise that the tree of life will not always elude the human reach. In fact, the hope of the New Testament is that Christ, the wisdom of God, graciously bestows eternal life upon all who reach out in faith to him.

The Ugly Face of Intolerance
Genesis 4:1-16

I was absorbed with the sight of some "rolling stones" lounging around Trafalgar Square. As I moved forward to focus the camera, someone was at my right elbow. I stepped back to let him pass. My concentration was shattered by his remark that seemed to fall out of nowhere, "Would you have stepped back to let me pass if you had been home?" I saw that he was a young black man. For the first time in my life, I felt the mark of Cain. My white American face was an invitation for retaliation for all of the evils of intolerance deposited in the banks of social injustice in my country.

Intolerance is volatile and unpredictable. Sometimes the intolerant person can be aggressive to the point of making her victim altogether inferior, something less than human. The frail bonds of rationality can snap in violence and leave the victim lying on the ground in his own blood, like Abel. At times noble restraint that can be disarming is called forth from the persecuted person. This reaction is present in a "Cain and Abel motif" story written by the ancient Sumerians around the twentieth century B.C.

The epic dispute chronicled by the Sumerians is between Dumuzi, a shepherd-god, and Enkimdu, a farmer-god. Both are suitors of Inanna, the sister of Utu. The brother advises her to marry Dumuzi, the shepherd, but she flatly refuses and determines to marry Enkimdu instead. Upon learning of her decision, Dumuzi appears and details his superior qualities in an effort to change Inanna's mind. He apparently succeeds, because he appears next on a riverbank rejoicing. There he encounters Enkimdu, with whom he tries to pick a quarrel and start a fight. Unexpectedly, the farmer refuses to quarrel or fight. He offers instead to let Dumuzi's sheep pasture anywhere in his territory. Enkimdu's attitude and generosity surprise Dumuzi, the two are reconciled, and the farmer is invited to the shepherd's wedding. With the tension eased, Enkimdu goes so far as to bring gifts to the wedding. Noble restraint disarms intolerance, and the two part with no blood on the ground.

The aggressor in 4:1-16 is Cain, the rejected one. He is the farmer who is rejected in favor of the shepherd, Abel. The roles are reversed from the Sumerian epic so that one can see a conflict between Canaan, the farmer, and Israel, the shepherd. Or it can be Baalism, the religion of the farmer, against Yahwism, the religion of the shepherd. The identity of the principals is not clear; neither is the reason for the rejection of Cain. It seems to be due to the sovereign choice of God. This is the reason for the rejection of Enkimdu in the Sumerican story. Inanna preferred Dumuzi, although at one time she preferred Enkimdu. We may conjecture that Enkimdu should have pressed his advantage when he had the chance, but he did not, and he lost the girl. Nevertheless, he redeemed himself in the face of Dumuzi's intolerant aggressiveness.

Cain's volatile reaction is important; it mirrors a typical human response to rejection. Apparently Cain has his chance because he brings offerings along with Abel, but he does not win acceptance. He does not fail at the altar of sacrifice, however. He fails in his reaction to Abel's acceptance; he can come again to the altar of sacrifice. He cannot approach his brother again after standing with his feet stained with his brother's blood. Intolerance toward his brother writes failure across his life in blood-red letters, and he cannot flee far enough to escape its mark.

Two significant thoughts emerge from the Cain and Abel story that are of epic importance because of their relevance for all people. First, every person must learn to deal with the unsettling reality of rejection. Second, the one who is rejected will have to live in the same world with the one who is accepted.

Rejection is unsettling because it exposes a side of the soul that may be unknown even to oneself. Rational people do irrational things when they are rejected, and the strangest reasons for irrational action rise to the surface! This is the epic human response to rejection couched in the timeless story of Cain and Abel. We can look back and say that Cain should have gone again to the altar of God before he lost his temper and slew his brother. (Who knows what he and his brother could have done together!) But he did not, and his name was entered on the roll of people who failed. We learn to live with rejection and even win acceptance when we keep the way open to return again to the altar of God.

The Perversion of Ideals
Genesis 6:1–9:17

One would not expect to find a discussion of Noah's flood headlined by this topic, but this topic states the reason the story of the Flood is in the Bible. Its strangeness may reflect how far we have strayed from what is important in the account. The ark and water claim our interest, and we have a vague idea that sin was the cause of it all.

People have always been interested in the Flood, as a continuous stream of literature spread over 4,000 years is the eloquent witness. The interest varies from age to age, however, and the questions people ask differ as the focus of interest changes. We have our special interest, which really is a new one. One question is regularly put to me as an archaeologist, a question that reveals the influence science has had upon the way we study the Bible.

"Did it happen?" everyone wants to know. Most of the time the sentence does not end with a clear question-mark sound. It ends with a sound that begins rising in inflection like a question then abruptly lowers to a sound that pleads more for reassurance than an answer to a question. Intimidated faith sits trembling as though it might learn it is spiritually handicapped if it cannot believe the Flood happened.

I can begin by telling what I have seen in many years of digging up the ancient cities of the Bible. I have seen every layer of earth, every stone, every potsherd, and every object removed from areas that reached from surface to bedrock at Bethel, Shechem, 'Ai, and Jerusalem. Not one layer of silt or earth that could have been deposited by Noah's flood have I seen. I know of none in Palestine. The layers of silt attributed to the Flood by archaeologists have been found in the Euphrates and Tigris River valleys, the land of Abraham's ancestry.

Evidence of the Flood

Sir Leonard Woolley reported a thick layer of water-laid silt at Ur and claimed it was evidence of the Flood. Newspapers quickly picked up the story and spread it around the world. Various books have incorporated the report, even with pictures of the silty layer as physical evidence of the Flood. The whole story was not told, however. First, the Ubaid culture that was apparently destroyed by the flood that deposited the silty layer at Ur reappeared in all of its components on top of the layer. The flood there was only a temporary interruption in the same culture. Furthermore, four miles away from Ur, in another excavation, no silty layer of the flood was found. Woolley's discovery was evidence of a local flood of the Euphrates River, which flowed by the north side of Ur.

The same can be said about flood layers found at other sites along the Euphrates and Tigris valleys. Local floods at Kish, Shurrupak, and Nineveh left deposits of silt; but the floods all occurred at different times, between about 3500 and 2800 B.C. This was the period before the rivers were brought under some measure of flood control by extensive canal and irrigation systems under the rule of the Sumerians. Therefore, the answer of archaeological evidence to the question "Did it happen?" is yes and no. There is evidence of catastrophic floods in the land of Abraham's birth, but no evidence of a universal flood that covered all of the Near East in one great tragedy of destruction.

This explanation, I am aware, is not the kind of straight-forward answer we like. The Flood still has us on the hook. Genesis 6–9 is concerned with a universal flood, and here I am saying there is archaeological evidence of local floods but no evidence of a universal deluge. Where do we go from here?

First, I should point out that archaeologists have dug up more than the physical evidence of layers of silt. At some of the places where layers of silt occur, written stories of the Flood have been found, the oldest one dating to about 2000 B.C. Also, I should note that the biblical story of Noah's flood comes in the tradition of these written accounts, which are not newspaper accounts but epic literature. They capture the violence and tragedy of natural disaster and universalize it as a part of the human experience. These epic accounts of the Flood play upon the instrument of human experience as though it has many strings capable of great subtlety. "Did it happen?" is not one of the strings. The question that absorbs most of our interest is a modern invention for people who want easy answers, answers that come like the punch-line in television comedy in one-eighth of a second.

I believe we should take a more serious approach to the Flood. Our main concern is to know its meaning, the ideas that find their historical genealogy there. Therefore, we go to the ancient written literature where ideas have their history. We can find an honest answer to the question

"Did it happen?" in the process of finding profound understanding of experience that can be ours in the twentieth century.

The oldest known flood account is Sumerian, dating to about 2000 B.C., but reflecting a tradition that was already ancient. It is set in the vicinity of Ur, near the point where the Euphrates and Tigris Rivers come together in a marshy delta and spill into the Persian Gulf. The marsh country, like the Mississippi delta south of New Orleans, was exposed to the constant danger of floods from the mighty rivers that drained a watershed as large as from New Orleans to Chicago and facing the Persian Gulf that was periodically churned by hurricanes that swept inland as they do now in the Gulf of Mexico. Life in the marshes was precarious because it was threatened from the north by floods of the great rivers and from the south by tidal waves blown in from the Persian Gulf by hurricanes.

Evidence of the kind of flood that lies behind the written traditions is found in the Babylonian flood story, dating to about 1700 B.C., and indebted to the earlier Sumerian story. The Sumerian tradition is incomplete, with much of the clay tablet on which it is written broken off and lost. References to the coming of the water reflects the same kind of flood described in the Babylonian story, however. Our imagination takes us to the place.

According to the story, a deadly stillness settles over all the land around Ur when the boat of the Babylonian "Noah" is completed and he is "battened up" in it. The stillness lasts through the night. Then,

> With the first glow of dawn,
> A black cloud rose up from the horizon.
> Inside it Adad (the storm god) thunders,
> While Shullat and Hanish (heralds of the storm) go in front,
> Moving as heralds over hill and plain.

This clearly reflects the approach of a storm, not the overflow of a river. Darkly and ominously, the storm emerges out of the horizon, heralded by lightning and accompanied by thunder. Suddenly it strikes like the clap of a sonic boom, as though the world were coming to an end: "Erragal tears out the posts; forth comes Ninurta and causes the dikes to follow."

Erragal is god of the netherworld, and the posts are the gates at the edge of the earth where heaven and earth meet. Outside the heavens and earth is the watery waste, the body of the rebel goddess who always threatens law and order. The waters of the "deep" are shut out but are always a threat in the form of storms, local floods, or tidal waves. According to this primitive view of the universe, each morning the sun comes through the gates and traverses the sky, going out an exit gate in the west. The gates are guarded until this fateful day when the god of the netherworld tears out the posts, letting in a flood that rushes across the land like water pouring through a hold into a submarine. The story resumes:

> Consternation over Adad (the storm god) reaches to the heavens,
> Turning to blackness all that had been light.
> The wide land was shattered like a (clay) pot!

With destructive instant fury the storm strikes, blotting out the light and shattering reed or mud-brick houses as though a charge of TNT has been set off! A clay pot breaks into a hundred pieces the moment it is struck. Its fury abated in the initial strike, the storm moves on.

> For one day the south-storm blew,
> Gathering speed as it blew, (submerging the mountains)
> Overtaking the (people) like a battle
> No one can see his fellow,
> Nor can the people be recognized from heaven.

Here is the clue to the kind of flood immortalized in the literature of the Babylonians. It was a "south-storm," which blew in from the Persian Gulf. We call such storms hurricanes today, and on at least two different occasions in recent years, similar hurricanes have hit the marsh coastal areas of the Indian Ocean. One storm, reported in the newspapers in 1960, claimed more than 22,000 lives. One survivor said to a reporter, "I thought the end of the world had come."

The same kind of flood probably lies back of the older Sumerian story because it picks up the action, after a gap of forty missing lines, with these words:

All the windstorms, exceedingly powerful attacked as one,
At the same time, the flood sweeps over the cult-centers.
After, for seven days and seven nights,
The flood had swept over the land,
And the huge boat had been tossed about by
the windstorms on the great waters,
Utu (the sun) came forth,
who sheds light on heaven (and) earth.

We are not dealing with a flood of the Tigris or Euphrates in the ancient stories. River floods were commonplace, but a viciously irrational hurricane was something else. It left its mark as an epochal act of God, and the lament of tragedy found its way into the epic literature that played upon the strings of universal human experience. In its literary form, the Flood became the archetype, or representative symbol, of any great natural disaster, which would include local floods of the mighty rivers as well as hurricanes. We can add nuclear explosions, the great contribution of the twentieth century to the roll of viciously irrational disasters symbolized by the Flood.

The Perversion of Ideals and the Flood
Genesis 6:1-8

The flood of Genesis 6–9 comes out of the world of the written traditions of the Sumerians and Babylonians just as surely as Abraham came out of that world. He and his people were not sterilized by all ideas that were common in the land of his birth, as we sterilize spaceships of bacteria before we crash-land them on the moon. Abraham did not crash-land in Canaan. He maintained, as did his posterity, a lively commerce with people of the Euphrates valley region. Then Israel was dragged back to the banks of the same rivers and canals by Nebuchadnezzar in the sixth century B.C., the same place that Abraham's ancestors had left fourteen centuries earlier and the same places immortalized in the ancient flood literature. The ancient epic literature was still in circulation at the time of the Exile in Babylon.

It is not surprising to find some obscurity in the Genesis flood account about the kind of flood it was. In Genesis 7:4, 12, the waters come from forty days of rain. "Forty" is one of the numbers in the Bible that has a more sophisticated vocation than counting. It carries here a meaning of completeness, like forty years of a king's reign, enough days of rain to produce flood waters. Yet, this is still vague because the story has been transplanted from the delta, coastal land of its origin to the hill country of Palestine and thoroughly integrated into Hebrew tradition in content as well as setting. Genesis 7:11, which refers to the "great deep" bursting forth, takes us across both tradition and desert, however, to the original setting. It reflects the ancient thought that the gate-posts at the edge of the deep were torn out and the waters of the great deep imploded the creation and submerged the earth. The specific reflection of a Persian Gulf hurricane has been lost. Numerous other ties with the ancient written traditions are present in the thoroughly biblically-oriented accounts in Genesis 6–9, but exploration of them would require another chapter.

The main point is that the flood story apparently reflects a catastrophic flood in the lower Euphrates valley, probably caused by a disastrous hurricane that swept water in from the sea and inundated the coastal area. It was interpreted to be an act of God, the same interpretation that insurance companies would give to it today. This interpretation led to the development of a flood tradition that became in the literature of all successive peoples in the region the archetype of natural disaster, just as Adam is the archetype, or representative, man in the creation story. So I say yes to the question "Did it happen?"

We have noted that the flood tradition became the peculiar property of every people who produced epic literature of their origins. Creative borrowing adapted the tradition to the particular literary production of which it was a part. In the Gilgamesh epic of the Babylonians, it contributes to the theme of the search for immortality in the face of inevitable death. It is apparently a part of a creation account in the Sumerian version, which is largely missing. In Genesis 6–9, it is a part of the epic introduction of humankind, the main focus of interest. As usual, the story of the Flood gives us a long and interesting excursion into ancient thought, but at the beginning and the end is humanity, whose genius for perverting ideals causes the Flood to be sent.

Genesis 6:1-4 reflects an acquaintance with the ancient stories that we now have, in which trouble is caused by the offspring of women and male deities. Gilgamesh was the son of an earthly mother and a male deity, making him two-thirds divine because a god would double the endowment of any human. Because of his divine endowment, he did not need as much sleep as a normal man would, and he caroused about his hometown of Uruk day and night, constantly stirring up trouble and keeping everyone awake. The nobles of Uruk hit upon a naive solution. They hunted an exact counterpart to Gilgamesh, a hairy giant called Enkidu who, they thought, would occupy the time of Gilgamesh in fighting and thus give the people of Uruk some peace. The fight occurred at the gate of the city and ended in a draw. The two proceeded to team up, since they could not defeat each other, and the nobles of Uruk were in twice as much trouble as they had been at first.

There is a memory of this kind of ancient tradition in the statement that the sons of God took to wife such of the daughters of men as they chose. One of the complaints about Gilgamesh was that he left "not the maid to her mother"; his arrogance was "unbridled." The offspring of the sons of God were the mighty men of renown (Gen 6:4), legendary figures of the past such as Gilgamesh. Genesis 6:5, the verse that describes the failure of humankind that brought on the Flood, implies that these legendary heroes of the past were partly responsible. In any case, they stand in the shadows among the people who were struck down in a great disaster, and their failure is regarded in the biblical tradition as a malignancy that must be traced to its roots and cut out of the human race, even though only one family should be left.

What is this malignancy? I call it the perversion of ideals. The unique gift of humanity in Genesis 1–2 is the mandate to rule over the earth and bring it into a good and fruitful state that reflects the good that has been created in heaven. This requires the exercise of imagination and creative thinking. For instance, the city of 'Ai that was built on a hill ten miles north of Jerusalem about 5,000 years ago was a work of imagination. There was no city in the vicinity except Jericho some ten miles east in the Jordan valley. The builders of the first city of 'Ai selected a strategic site on a bare rocky hill that was worth exactly nothing. They planned a complete city, consisting of an outer wall twenty feet thick that enclosed twenty-seven acres, four times as large as Jericho. Inside the walls, a sanctuary was constructed against the inside of a great tower. A fortified, luxurious ruler's palace was set on the highest point of the city on the west. Villas belonging to the nobles and other citizens covered the spacious, well-fortified hillside east of the acropolis.

The first city of 'Ai was a work of the creative imagination of humans. A bare, worthless hill that had afforded little more than holes where foxes could take refuge was made into a great city in one planned operation. This is the kind of creative work that is called "good" in the creation account (Gen 1:4, 31). "Good" in this sense is the opposite of "evil." It is any work of the hands that furthers the good purposes of creation and implements the ideals that lie behind creation. "Evil" is the perversion of the ideals underlying God's work in creation.

For instance, I believe that the first city of 'Ai was built under Egyptian supervision as one of the first outposts of Egyptian imperialism. This introduces a sinister element into the story of the great city because it seems to have been built as a base from which Egypt could systematically exploit Palestine during the so-called Great Pyramid Age. The creative human imagination evident in building the city was perverted, or evil, because it was not built to further the good purposes of creation. It was built to further the proud dreams of pharaohs who baptized in the sweat and blood of slaves the stones of the great pyramids in Egypt and built lasting monuments to themselves. When we view the towering monuments today, we are apt to forget their cost in human misery. We do not see the blank-faced, open-mouthed horror of mothers in Palestine who watched their sons marched off in bonds as slaves, never to return.

The malignancy of the "evil imagination" in Genesis 6:5 is of this kind. It is an epic malignancy; it is found in every age and from the ruler's palace to the small sidestreet. Like a malignancy, the natural ideals of humans call them to great achievements suddenly gone wild. When this happens, what had been good is perverted into evil, and the groundwork for disaster is laid. The Flood has become the archetype or universal example of irrational natural disaster. It is the appropriate response of the creation to human irrationality because both nature and humanity have taken that which is good and perverted it, creating evil.

As I noted before, a nuclear holocaust would belong in the category of the Flood. It would be the result of modern man's genius, the "imagination" that is capable of planning great factories and marshaling the work of thousands of people to create something new. This is human glory. If modern man should let this creation become an instrument of "evil," working against the good purposes of God's creation, then the work becomes the product of an "evil imagination." In case of nuclear warfare, human irrationality would meet an irrational response from nature, and epic failure would be written in the mushroom clouds of destruction.

The great subtlety of the flood story is its relevance that reaches from the universal scene of international relations to the individual who is carving out a little kingdom in a business or even within the circles of a church or denomination. The "evil imagination," or perverted creativity, can reach to everyone. In Genesis 6:5, we are reminded in a unique way that disaster awaits somewhere down the road. Failure, in this case, is an understatement.

Pride and Its Symbols
Genesis 11:1-9

Obviously, pride always shows off. The very nature of pride demands a symbol that cannot be missed. The supreme symbol of pride in the biblical world was the ziggurat, a multi-story tower of mud-brick on top of which a small temple was usually built. In the flat, delta country of the Euphrates valley, the ziggurat towered above all the city. It was the first thing travelers saw upon approaching the city and the last thing they saw when they left. Consequently, the ziggurat became a symbol of the city and, according to Genesis 11:1-9, a symbol of the culture of the region. The symbol could not be missed, for remains of thirty-three ziggurats have been identified in twenty-nine of the great cities of Mesopotamia.

We may focus the archetype symbol of Genesis 11:1-9 more precisely. There seems to be a thinly disguised reference to the great tower at Babylon in the biblical Tower of Babel. The narrator deliberately connects "Babel," which in the Babylonian *bab-ilu* means "gate of the god," with the Hebrew *balal*, which means "to confound" or "to mix." He is not an ignoramus in doing this. With consummate skill he paints his own graffiti on the Tower of Babylon and makes it a biblical cartoon. His point is that the Tower of Babylon pulls together in one compact symbol all the pride and naked ambition of Babylon that is flogged again in Daniel 4:28-33. To him it is the epic symbol of failure because it is *balal*, or "confusion," and not Babel, "the gate of God."

We have specific information about the Tower of Babylon. It was called "Etemenanki," which means literally "house of the foundation of heaven and earth." Nabopolassar, king of Babylon, began restoration of the great tower during his reign (625–605 B.C.), and it was continued by Nebuchadnezzar during his reign (604–562 B.C.). The original structure probably dated from the time of Hammurabi, around 1700 B.C., and its restoration was a natural component of the renaissance of Babylonian culture and nationalism. If there was a stackpole around which the neo-Babylonian culture and imperialism could be gathered, it was the Tower of Babel.

Nabopolassar records a divine command from Marduk to rebuild Etemenanki and "make its foundations secure in the bosom of the netherworld, and make its summit like the heavens." Then he continues,

> I caused baked brick to be made. As it were the rains from on high which are measureless, . . . I caused streams of bitumen to be brought by the canal Arahtu.

The features of the Tower of Babel in Genesis 11:1-9 are described here. It was located in the land of Shinar (Babylon) (v. 2), bricks and mortar were used in its construction (v. 3), and the top reached up in the heavens (v. 4). Nebuchadnezzar records one further feature present in the biblical story: "All the people of many nations I constrained to work on the building of Etemenanki."

Andre Parrot, the great French archaeologist, reported that a clay tablet now in the Louvre in Paris gives the dimensions of the Tower of Babylon. It is the "Esagil Tablet," named after the *E-sag-il* temple of Marduk on top of Etemenanki, the tower. The text dates itself: "The twenty-sixth day of the ninth month of the eighty-third year of Seleucus king," which can be translated to read 12 December 229 B.C. in the reign of Seleucus II. It was written at Uruk, Erech in Genesis 10:10 and is likely a copy of an older text. Detailed measurements are given in lines 37–42 of the tablet as follows:

First story	Length: 295 ft.; breadth: 295 ft.; height: 108 ft.
Second story	Length: 256 ft.; breadth: 256 ft.; height: 59 ft.
Third story	Length: 197 ft.; breadth: 197 ft.; height: 19 3/4 ft.
Fourth story	Length: 167½ ft.; breadth: 167½ ft.; height: 19¾ ft.
Fifth story	Length: 138 ft.; breadth: 138 ft.; height: 19¾ ft.
Sixth story	Length: 108½ ft.; breadth: 108½ ft.; height: 19¾ ft.
Seventy story	Length: 79 ft.; breadth: 79 ft.; height: 49 ft.

This structure would measure 295 feet long, 295 feet broad, and 295 feet high, a seven-staged tower shaped similar to the five-staged tower found at Nineveh on a seventh-century B.C. bas-relief. The bas-relief carries the artist's interpretation of the tower resting in the bosom of the netherworld, above the waters of "the great deep," inside a sacred garden with trees, including a "tree of life," and reaching into the heavens, right under the waters of "the great deep" that would flood the universe if the windows of heaven were opened. The tall, upper stage is horned, like an altar, for in the heavens the deity abides.

Here, then, is the symbol of human pride in Genesis 11:1-9, a structure for which Hebrew captives may have made brick under the Babylonian taskmaster's whip. Far from being the glory of Babylon, as Nabopolassar and Nebuchadnezzar saw it at short range, it persists in the timeless cartoon of the biblical writer as the symbol of nations or peoples who would "make a name" for themselves (v. 4). It can be a 295-feet-tall *ziggurat*, perhaps nine feet taller than any other tower in the Euphrates valley. Or it can be the largest *succa*, or booth, in Jerusalem during the Feast of Booths, advertised in 1968 by one hotel as seating 250 people. Or it can be the church that claims it has the largest budget, or membership, or building in the convention. Or, perish the thought, it can be the church that moves heaven and earth so it can report more people "saved" than any other church in the land.

In the timeless symbols of pride, there is imperceptible distance between the Tower of Babel and all of these. In the degree to which these distinctions of superiority are aimed at "making a name," they are failures in the same degree.

Chapter 3

Abraham and
the Promise of Faith

Genesis 11:27–25:11

	Mesopotamia	Palestine	Egypt
2050	Neo-Sumerian		XIth Dynasty 2052–1991 B.C.
2000	City of Ur 2060–1950 B.C.	Nomads occupy Palestine	
1950	Migrations to Asia Minor/Palestine		
1900		Age of Abraham	XII Dynasty 1991–1786 B.C.
1850	Old Babylonian Kingdom	Shechem and Jerusalem built	
1800	1830–1530 B.C.		

The father of Israel was a pioneer who left the land of his ancestry, but not the inheritance of culture that ultimately rooted in the great civilization of Ur. He was a part of the general relocation of peoples that occurred after the great city-states of the Near East broke up in the twentieth century B.C. Resolutely, he pioneered a new life in a poor country, the land of Canaan. His approach to life in the new land was tolerant. He worshiped at the local holy places, made friends with the people, and lived by the social customs of the day. Nevertheless, he met the tests of faith that came in the context of his world and passed them.

In a Strange Land
Genesis 12:4-6

If we could move back across nearly forty centuries and meet Abraham, our first reaction would be that he seems very ordinary. A century of research and unflagging interest have rediscovered his world and made it possible for us to enter it. We stop just short of shaking hands with the man. What we see is impressive, although not as impressive as the heritage that he left. We can see, however, some characteristics that underlie his greatness, characteristics that are not out of place in any age.

The land of his heritage is Palestine, so we meet him there. The place is the valley of Moreh, east of Shechem. A long caravan snakes its way into the valley, emerging from the oven-like heat of the Jordan valley. It crossed the Jordan at a ford near what is now the Damiya bridge. For several hours now, since daybreak, the caravan has leaned against the steep slopes as it climbed out of the deep valley, and both animals and men are tired. Cool moist wind blowing from the Mediterranean signals the end of the climb, and the sight of a city looming against the skyline in the distance counsels the need for a rest stop.

We look at the tired donkeys. No camels are in sight. In fact, the beast of burden of the caravan is the little desert donkey, about forty inches high and black. He is a hardy little creature, able to pace about 150 pounds of baggage or supplies and capable of covering twelve miles a day. Desert-bred, he has evolved the ability to store above normal quantities of water in his blood, like the camel, and can travel for several weeks on minimum supplies of water and food. We learn that this little beast is the backbone of the economy in Abraham's world. It packs grain from the field to the threshing floor, pulls the primitive wooden plow with a single awkward handle, and packs the merchandise of caravans that ply the trade routes from Egypt to Mesopotamia.

The people are as tired as the donkeys; most of them walk also. Ten miles of dusty trail, stumbling over stones and donkey droppings and climbing continually, have used up the day's allotment of energy. Men sit cross-legged on their heels on the ground, while women scurry around looking after the baggage and taking inventory of the children. The dust and smell of donkeys penetrate the senses, amid the noise of a hundred people who have not had a chance to talk for six hours.

We see that the people are Semitic, reflecting the tradition in Genesis 11:10-27 that traces the lineage of Abraham back to Shem. Semite, or Shemite, is a very loose term that identifies kindred-language groups that seem to have originated in the Arabian peninsula. The term includes Akkadians, Amorites, Aramaeans, Canaanites, Hebrews, Arabs, and others. The language of these people indicates remote kinship and probable origin from migrations that periodically occurred in the overflow of peoples from the marginal regions of the Arabian desert into the fertile areas of the Near East.

The appearance of men and women varies little. Men wear their hair cropped at the neckline and combed back from the forehead. A small beard runs from the cheek to a point at the chin. There is no moustache. The pointed beard seems to be as common a mark of the mature Semite as the universal moustache is today among the Arabs. Women wear their long, black hair down the back, reaching to the lower side of the shoulder blade. A plain gold band is pressed down, Indian-style, over the hair to the front hairline. Both men and women have a slanting face profile. They have a long, straight or slightly arched nose and a receding forehead, characteristics of the Semitic look.

Variety in dress is also limited. Both men and women wear robe-like garments that are just below knee-length. Some have only one shoulder in the garment, with the other shoulder bare, while others have both shoulders covered. Most garments are sleeveless, something never seen among the village Arabs today in Palestine who cover their arms to the wrists and wear ankle-length robes. The simple garments are both plain and many-colored, like Joseph's coat (Gen 37:3). The long sleeves of Joseph's coat seem to be a mark of favor to him, indicating exemption from work. Colors are woven into the garments in interesting patterns that are mainly geometric in design. Most likely the cloth is wool, woven from the wool of sheep and goats. Shoes are worn by men, women, and children. Men seem to prefer sandals, while women wear an ankle-high shoe made of animal skins.

While the leader of the caravan is paying a courtesy call at Shechem in the distance, between Mount Ebal and Gerizim, which hulk above the mound of the city like a gorilla's shoulders, we have time to inquire about the journey of these people. From whence did they come, and where are they going?

The Ancestry of Abraham
Genesis 11:27–12:7; 24:1-7

Our inquiry begins with the traditions that emphasize two points of origin: Ur and Haran (11:31). Most of the interest, however, is in Haran, a caravan center on the Balikh River in the extreme upper Euphrates valley. The account of the move from Ur to Haran, a distance of some 600 miles, telescopes time by omitting events, so that the people moved 600 miles in one breath, the time it takes to read Genesis 11:31. This is characteristic of traditions that are handed down from generation to generation by word of mouth, not in written form. The important points are preserved, and details that would interest us immensely are dropped in the litter-boxes along the road of history. Using the same technique, I would say my forebears migrated from England, but the actual story of my family that I trace begins in Virginia.

In the twentieth century B.C., Ur was the London of the ancient world. It was the leading commercial center of the Near East, and the influence of its culture penetrated as far as Egypt. For nearly a thousand years, the Sumerian people had developed one of the great civilizations of the world with all of its standard components: writing, education, art and architecture, law, religion, and a city-state political system that prophesied the modern democratic republic. The citizens of Ur were proud of their city. Its origins, in their pre-scientific world, were traced back through the Sumerian people to a creation 241,000 years before the Flood. Five kings are named as rulers for this period. The longest reign was 43,200 years, the shortest 18,600 years. From the time of the Flood down to the time the tradition took up the story of Ur, the life-span of rulers gradually shortened, and we read of reigns of 36 years and 25 years before Ur was destroyed in a battle in the twentieth century B.C.

We would miss the point to try to literalize this tradition of the origins of the people of Ur, because people did not live to be 43,000 years old before the Flood. Neither did they have a different way of reckoning years. The same is true of the long life-spans of people named in Hebrew traditions as living before the Flood in Genesis 5:1-32. This is a method commonly used in the biblical world to trace a people's lineage back to creation and thus legitimatize their claim to a special place in the world. The genealogy of physical lineage was much more important to them than it is to us. Since everyone knew that creation must have occurred in the very remote past, the lengthened life spans were the way of saying it. At the same time, the persons who had long life spans attributed to them became almost superhuman in a legendary sort of way.

No pains were taken to achieve consistency in the dating of creation at the beginning of the long life spans. The Hebrew Massoretic text of the Bible, which is the basis of our modern translations, adds up a total of 1,656 years between Creation and the Flood. The Septuagint, which seems to reflect a text tradition different from the Massoretic text, has life spans adding up to 2,242 years between Creation and the Flood. A third total of 1,307 years is added in the Samaritan traditions of Genesis. No pains were taken to achieve consistency, even among the biblical traditions.

Two focal points were important: Creation and the Flood. They were important because of their prominent place in Near Eastern epic literature that was the property of every people from the dawn of writing. Of major significance was the physical link with Creation, a link that spanned a broad, undetermined expanse of time, and the survival of the physical link in the cosmic catastrophe of the Flood.

To trace one's lineage back to Ur, as Abraham's in Genesis 11:31, is thus very significant. First, it establishes the cultural link behind the biblical traditions with the world of the Euphrates valley, a world different, for instance, from Egypt that had its own unique development. Second, tracing one's lineage to Ur places the world of Abraham in historical and political perspective. It begins the story of Abraham when Near Eastern civilization was at its high point of development, and the story of the chosen people transpires in the declining centuries of that great civilization down to the conquest by Alexander the Great in 331 B.C., which moved the focus of cultural inspiration to the West.

Abraham's ancestry, both physical and intellectual, has its roots in the Ur civilization, and very possibly the breakup of the Sumerian state of Ur in the twentieth century B.C. and the subsequent influx of barbarians led to the emigration of great numbers of people. Among these people would be the "Mayflower" generation of Abraham. According to Genesis 24:4-7, Abraham must have been born at or near Haran in the upper Euphrates valley. The region of Haran was important after the move to Palestine, and close family ties were maintained for three generations before the family of the patriarch acclimated itself to the harsh realities of Palestine.

The word "Haran" means "caravaneer," which probably means that the city was principally a caravan or commercial center. No great cultural reputation is given to Haran. It must have been a kind of nineteenth-century Kansas City of the world of Abraham—a frontier city of merchants, dusty caravans, noise, and money. Traditionally it is in the home territory of the Aramaeans, a Semitic people whose traditions are more hill-country than desert-based, with interests in good agriculture as well as sheep and cattle raising. In the age of Abraham, the population would have been conglomerate, a mixture of Aramaeans, Sumerians (non-Semitic), Babylonians, desert sheiks, and mountain chieftains. Religiously speaking, it would not be classified as "Bible Belt" country.

One set of written records, the Mari Tablets (around 1800 B.C.), reflects the diversity of the people in the upper Euphrates valley in the names given. Our interest is drawn, however, to the names of towns that seem to be equivalent to names of Abraham's relatives given in Genesis 11:27-31. Til-Turakhi is equivalent to Terah (v. 24), Haran is also the name of Abraham's brother (v. 26), Sarugi is the same as Serug (vv. 20-22), and Phaliga is the equivalent of Peleg (vv. 16-18). The coincidence of names is hardly accidental. These are places reflected in the names of Abraham's kinsmen, and the immediate roots of his family may be here.

A tribe of Benjamin is also mentioned. The "Sons of the South" were noted for their military prowess. These people apparently had given up nomadic life and settled in villages along the Khabur, Balikh, and Euphrates Rivers, all in the region south and west of Haran. While most of the peoples mentioned in the Mari records were ruled by kings, the Sons of the South were ruled by chieftains (patriarchs) and elders, a system strikingly similar to that of the biblical patriarchs. When they were not engaged in warfare, they tilled the soil. It remains to be seen whether any of the Sons of the South emigrated to Palestine, taking with them their traditions and becoming known as the tribe of Benjamin. Elements of these people possibly were in the caravan that stopped to rest in the Plain of Moreh east of Shechem.

In the Land of Canaan
Genesis 12:7–14:24; 18:1–19:29

Shechem, the first city of Palestine named in the Bible, had its golden age after Abraham passed through the land. The city that confronted the caravan was actually a small village. Excavations from 1957 to 1968 indicate a new settlement of the site about 1900 B.C., probably due to the breakup of great city-states such as Ur that brought about a general relocation of peoples in the Near East. The people at Shechem were likely immigrants from the Phoenician coastal regions, suggested by similarity in their culture with that found at Byblos and Ugarit. They may be called Canaanites, which means "land of the purple," after the purple dye manufactured from the murex, a snail-like organism that is found along the Mediterranean coast. The Shechem settlers introduced pottery styles and art forms that became typical of classical Canaanite culture for the next 600 years.

The village of Shechem was unfortified then, and its inhabitants seem to have been peaceful. No great danger was posed from within or without the hill country, so free movement of small clans or caravans was possible. Their way of life was both pastoral and agricultural. They were shepherd-farmers, the usual combination of vocations found among new settlers in the land. In the ruins of their houses excavated in 1962 and 1964 were grinders for preparing wheat flour and mortars for preparing food from various kinds of beans. Bones of sheep and goats suggest the source of meat supply, as well as of wool for clothing and rugs for the packed earth floors of houses.

Not all meat was obtained from the flocks and herds. In the excavation deep in Field IX at Shechem, heavy jawbones of dogs were unearthed, suggesting that dogs were kept for hunting as well as for watching the flocks. A story purportedly written by an Egyptian refugee in Canaan about 1900 B.C. tells of hunting gazelles with dogs, as well as hunting other game such as partridges. Thus the meat supply in Abraham's day was adequate, and the sportsman enjoyed the added delicacies of quail and venison.

A rather low-pressure, village way of life prevailed at Shechem, where farmers and shepherds as well as sportsmen kept their hunting dogs in the courtyards of their houses. The climate of the time was peaceful, witnessed by the unfortified, pioneer-like settlements that began to spring up over the hill country. To such a village the caravan leader came, observing the peaceful protocol of ancient custom, harboring no malice nor covetous desires for what the people at Shechem possessed.

What Abraham did at Shechem is an index to his greatness, one reason why he became a father to three of the world's great religions. The scripture is brief, almost abrupt, in its account of Abraham's stop at the village. It reads almost like the visit of a head-of-state in a foreign country, where perfunctory visits are made at the important places and a wreath is laid at the tomb of the nation's unknown soldier. We are told that Abraham stopped at Shechem, built an altar, and moved on to Bethel, where he also built an altar and moved on.

Actually, the stops must have consumed more time than the compressed account indicates in the one verse allocated to Shechem. The Bible, not Abraham, makes the perfunctory, head-of-state-like visit to Shechem and picks up only the partriarch's altar-building as worth recounting. Abraham's caravan spent more time there, because the people at Shechem knew his family later on when Jacob paid a call at the same place (Gen 33:18ff.). Of most importance, however, was Abraham's altar-building at Shechem.

He probably built an altar to El-berith, "God of the covenant," who was worshiped by the people at Shechem. Why do I think so? The account of the destruction of the temple of Baal-Berith in Judges 9:4-49 contains also the alternate name "El-berith" (v. 46), which is the more ancient name of God at Shechem. "El" is a general name for God, used throughout the Near East and indicating a supreme deity who was associated with various local phenomena that identified him with individual places. Thus the temple of Baal-berith in the time of Abimelech, around 1100 B.C., is probably on the site of the house that once was dedicated to El-berith, worshiped at Shechem by the first settlers who moved from the Phoenician coastal region.

The account in Genesis 12:7 states that Abraham built there an altar to Yahweh, who had appeared to him. Yahweh is the covenant name of God in the Old Testament, reportedly, in one tradition, introduced by Moses centuries after Abraham. In the commissioning of Moses, God said to him,

> I am the Lord (Yahweh). I appeared to Abraham, Isaac, and Jacob as God Almighty (El Shaddai), but by my name "The Lord" (Yahweh) I did not make myself known to them. (Exod 6:2-3).

The names Yahweh and El Shaddai are equated here, with Yahweh having the special, personal significance of being the covenant name of God. Therefore, it would not seem out of place to the biblical traditioners to think of the God who appeared to Abraham as Yahweh also. They were the same.

El was a more general name of God, however, used by the Canaanites as well as Aramaeans and Hebrews. One of the Mari texts, referred to above, mentions El Shaddai as an Aramaean deity. It was customary for El to be associated with a second name, usually a local place. Thus El-berith, "God of the covenant," was the special name at Shechem, and the Canaanites worshiped El by that name. El Elyon (God Most High) was the name of God at Jerusalem (Gen 14:17-20), worshiped by the first settlers of the city whose priest was Melchizedek. El Shaddai apparently was the name of God at Hebron (17:1) where God is equated with Yahweh and worshiped by Abraham. In the desert, Yahweh is El Roi, the "God who sees" (16:13), and at Beersheba El Olam, "the eternal God" (21:33). The God who appeared to Jacob at Shechem is called El-Elohe Israel, or "El, the God of Israel," (33:20); and the God who appeared at Bethel is "El of Bethel" (35:7).

El, the transcendent deity of the Canaanites at Ugarit and Byblos, was apparently the deity of the settlers in Canaan when Abraham's caravan arrived there. It is significant that Abraham built altars at the traditional sacred sites of the Canaanites such as Shechem, Bethel, Jerusalem, Mamre, and Beersheba. The scripture indicated that he built altars to the local El, who is equated with Yahweh, the God of the covenant with Israel. Thus, he did not introduce a radical new religion. More likely, Abraham refined his worship within the framework of El worship. For instance, no hint exists anywhere of the sexual connotations usually associated with El worship. Neither are there indications of any images that were a standard component of every variety of extra-biblical religion.

The caravan leader therefore paid his customary respects to the elders at Shechem, worshiped at their sacred place in his own way, enjoyed their hospitality, and left with their friendship. What more should he do? Here is one secret of Abraham's greatness. Never did he leave a place in the land of Canaan without the friendly best wishes of the people, even if his concept of God may have differed from theirs. He was willing to wait for his view of God to prevail.

When Abraham's caravan arrived in Canaan, the central hill country was dotted with a few pioneer villages of new settlers, some from the Phoenician coast whom we call Canaanites, some from northeast Syria who may be called Hittites, and some from the northern reaches of the

Arabian desert who are called Amorites. The land was open, and small groups of various ethnic origins moved in. No outside power, such as Egypt or Babylon, maintained political control over the land, because the great powers had gone through revolutions that had completely changed their political and social structures. Abraham thus arrived in an undeveloped, pioneer land, quite different from the rich, irrigated farmland he had left in the Euphrates valley.

The journey from Shechem to Bethel, a distance of thirty miles, was along trails in the valleys that wound southward among rough hill country. There was no road. Quite likely the trail led along the east side of Mount Gerizim to the valley of Leboneh, north of Shiloh, and then near the site of Shiloh, which was not occupied. It wound southward among a maze of steep hills and deep valleys, possibly along the route of the "Valley of the Robbers," notorious because it is in a wild area of craggy hills with no villages. The valley opens upon more gentle, rolling hills around Bethel where the patriarch built an altar east of the city, paid his respects to the local people and their god, and moved on.

In Genesis 12:10–14:24, two significant events are related that are obscured by legend that diverts the reader's attention from the main points, at least for the western reader. First, we read of the visit to Egypt in time of famine and the game Abraham and the pharaoh played with Abraham's wife. Second, the raid on the cities of Sodom and Gomorrah by kings from the east, which introduces the cities and the story of their destruction, involved Abraham in the role of leader among the hill country fighters who avenged the crime and returned triumphantly to worship at the shrine of El Elyon at Jerusalem.

A painting on the wall of a tomb in Egypt dating about 1900 B.C. depicts the visit of Asiatics to Egypt and thus reflects the freedom of passage across the eastern frontiers of Egypt. They would have traveled the central route across the Sinai desert, avoiding the coastal trail from Gaza to the Nile delta. Probably the patriarchs traveled from Beersheba in the Negeb across the rough sand-dune and craggy mountain wasteland north of Sinai to Egypt, entering at a point about midway of the present Suez canal. Nelson Glueck, who spent twenty years exploring the Negeb and Sinai desert region, found remains of small settlements along this route, indicating that it was well-traveled in the age of the patriarchs. The small settlements would have provided supplies of water and feed for the pack donkeys that transported supplies for travelers.

The visit of Abraham to Egypt is remembered because of the episode with the pharaoh caused by Sarah's beauty. This legendary story enhances the father of the Hebrews by extolling the unusual beauty of Sarah and the cleverness of Abraham in exploiting the pharaoh's sensuousness and returning rich. The pharaoh had an entirely predictable mentality that was as susceptible to clever strategy as the present-day mentality of the Egyptians is susceptible to military exploitation by the Israelis. That Sarah's beauty was legendary is evident in the Genesis Apocryphon, a scroll written on copper, discovered in a cave at Qumran. The fragmentary commentary on Genesis goes into much more lucid detail about Sarah's beauty, almost making an Oriental belly dancer of her in her allurements. The biblical account is more restrained but reflects a popular story that entertained the sons of Abraham across the centuries.

Abraham really went to Egypt on business because of a famine in southern Palestine. Actually, he could have obtained food from the southern coastal region in Palestine that later became known as the Philistine Plain, an exceptionally fertile area. Today it is covered with citrus groves and wheat and cotton fields and is almost as rich as the silt-laden delta of Egypt. The patriarch had business in Egypt that made it desirable for him to go there instead of to Gaza or Ashkelon. The account probably reflects a pattern of trips to Egypt. This point is hidden under the more interesting story of Sarah's beauty and the stupid pharaoh's sensuousness.

The account of a raid on the cities of Transjordan and the plains of the Jordan is also diversionary in that it introduces the story of the cities of Sodom and Gomorrah. It is an authentic tradition that involves people and places that scholars have identified, but its place in the patriarchal accounts is not as normal as, for instance, the visit of Abraham to Egypt. The main point is that Abraham became so much a part of the life of southern Palestine that he led in avenging the capture of Sodom and Gomorrah and was recognized as a notable in the visit to Jerusalem where he offered to El Elyon and paid tithes to the priest Melchizedek.

Actually, the destruction of Sodom and Gomorrah may have occurred during the time of the patriarch. No evidence of the actual cities has been identified, and strong arguments have been made for locating them at the south end of the Dead Sea, as well as at the north end near Jericho. Ambiguous evidence, probably from two traditions, allows location at either place. Some scholars suggest that the cities are buried under the shallow waters of the Dead Sea, south of the Lisan peninsula. North of the peninsula the water reaches a depth of nearly 1,300 feet, while the area south of the Lisan is very shallow, with a broad mud flat extending south of the water's edge.

At the southwest corner of the area is the modern Israeli village of Sodom where salt and minerals are extracted from the water of the sea in huge evaporation vats. Along the west edge of the sea is a high cliff with a 100-feet-thick stratum of fossil salt exposed, presumably a result of the split in the earth's crust that allowed the twelve to twenty-mile-wide Jordan valley to drop straight down 3,000 feet. This occurred in one of the geological disturbances of the region millions of years ago, but it left twin faults running parallel on either side of the Dead Sea that occasion frequent earthquakes, with at least one major quake each century.

Presence of the salt, which appears in the story of the destruction of the cities of the plain where Lot's wife is identified with a pillar of salt, supports the location of the cities at the south end of the sea. Gas and petroleum deposits, as well as sulphur (brimstone), are found there and are now being exploited by Israel. The fire and brimstone associated with "overturning" (Gen 19:25) of the cities suggest an earthquake that ignited the petroleum products and caused the region south of the Lisan to sink enough to be flooded by the waters north of the peninsula. Evidence of a ford across the Dead Sea at the Lisan Peninsula as late as Roman times suggests that all of the south end of the Dead Sea was not flooded in the original disturbance that formed the sea.

The story of the destruction of the cities is introduced in the patriarchal narrative for its human interest and instructive value. The cities were destroyed because of their exceeding sinfulness, a claim by the biblical traditioners that makes God look as capricious as an Oriental king. The story is associated with Abraham because the event happened in Palestine, not in the Euphrates Valley where the setting of Genesis 1–11 occurs. Also it reflects the permanence of Abraham's association with the land of Canaan where he became a recognized leader among his diverse neighbors—a man of substance, authority, and skill. The move from the Euphrates valley region is complete; the patriarch is a permanent part of the land of Canaan.

The Personal Life of Abraham
Genesis 15:1-17; 27; 20:1–25:11

Some of the personal and social customs of the patriarchs are difficult to understand, at the least, and outright embarrassing to the devout Christian, at the most. I refer first to the custom of polygamy, of having more than one wife, and then to the practice of a wife who could not bear a son giving her handmaid as a concubine to the husband to bear a son for her.

According to Genesis, Abraham had at least two wives, Sarah (11:29) and Keturah (25:1); Hagar, an Egyptian handmaid; plus unnamed concubines (25:6). His grandson Jacob had two wives, Leah and Rachel (29:16-30), and two handmaids of the wives, Bilhah and Zilpah (30:1-13), who became concubines. Children were born to both wives and concubines, and the family circle became a center of intrigue and scheming for favors among the women, a standard component of polygamy. We know now that the patriarchs are authentically represented as living according to the accepted customs of the day.

A foremost concern in patriarchal society was to have a male heir who would carry on the clan name and inherit leadership of the group. The desire for a son was so great that almost any device would be used to obtain one. The real focus of interest in the patriarchal narratives from the making of the covenant in Genesis 12:1 to the death of Sarah in Genesis 23:2 is the struggle for an heir. All of the incidents in the life of Abraham revolved around this one ultimate issue, because all of the investments in the covenant would yield nothing if there were not a son to pick up Abraham's name and covenant with God.

Every suspense device enjoyed by easterners is employed to make the narrative interesting. First, the patriarch almost loses his wife who would bear the son of promise to a lecherous pharaoh. One can sense the anxiety of listeners of the story as Sarah steps inside the forbidden confines of the pharaoh's house. Only God can save her now! But God does, and she is returned to her husband undefiled. That a pharaoh could reach out and take any woman who pleased his eye was a fact and remained a practice in Egypt even to our generation when King Farouk took the fiancee of one of his subjects to be his wife, even against her will!

When Sarah bears no son, Abraham appears in Genesis 15:2 with an adopted son, Eliezer, as his heir. This also was a legitimate practice, according to some tablets found at Nuzi in the upper Euphrates valley that contain a provision for the adoption of an heir if a true son is not born. The adopted heir lacks the blood of his father, however, and thus is not an altogether satisfactory bearer of the family name and, in the case of Abraham, the promise. Consequently, it is not surprising to find the next grade of heir being produced. Sarah gives Hagar, the Egyptian handmaid, to Abraham as a concubine (16:1-6) so that the heir will at least have the father's blood. The Nuzi Tablets also bear witness to this custom. One marriage contract obliged a childless wife to give the husband a handmaid who would bear children for him.

This solution of the problem, however, is not ideal, and hope for an heir who will fulfill the ideal requirements dim with Sarah's advancing age. The son is born, however. Isaac becomes the son of his mother's old age, and his colorlessness reflects something of the authenticity of the tradition. He is a legitimate heir, bearing in his veins the right combination of blood. No longer will the patriarch have to struggle for an heir, but there is a final hurdle. Abraham must pass the test of faith by offering his son Isaac as a human sacrifice (Gen 22:1-19). This too was an authentic practice, but in the context of Abraham's anxiety for an heir, it is not a temptation of paganism. Instead, it is the final examination of the patriarch, a test of his worthiness to bear the promise of the covenant. Again the listener edges forward in suspense until the messenger of the Lord stays the copper dagger, and the true heir is preserved to bear the family name.

The story of Abraham in the Bible bears unmistakable marks of the storyteller's art. We should be as grateful for that as we are for an interesting book or sermon. Behind the attractive and absorbing story is authentic life in the frontier land of Canaan, with its eccentricities dictated by the age and land in which it transpired. The man is not reduced in stature by being a part of his world. This is where he finds relevance. I should be quite disturbed if I found the patriarch living an ascetic life, sealed off from the harsh realities of his time, having a kind of spiritual space-capsule existence unrelated to his environment. I think the patriarch has relevance when he is human, when he drinks of the life that he encounters in his world and still passes the tests of faith that all persons must meet in their own circumstances.

Chapter 4

Human Oppression and Freedom

Genesis 26:1–Exodus 16:27

	Mesopotamia	Palestine	Egypt
1750			
	Mari Age		
1700	Hammurabi	Hyksos Period	
	1728–1686 B.C.	1750–1500 B.C.	Hyksos Dynasties
1650		(Age of Jacob)	1720–1570 B.C.
1600	Old Babylonian		(Age of Joseph)
	Kingdom		
	1830–1530 B.C.		
1550			
		Hurrian	XVIIIth Dynasty
1500	Nuzi Tablets	Migrations	1570–1310 B.C.
		1500–1450 B.C. Age of War	
			and Oppression
1450		Egyptian	
		Oppression	
1400	Hittite Empire		Amarna Age
1350		Amarna Revolts	
1300		Egyptian	
	Battle of Oppression		XIXth Dynasty
	Kadesh		1310–1200 B.C.
	1286 B.C.		
1250		Settlements	Anarchy
		of Hivites	
1200	Philistine Migration—›	‹—Exodus of Hebrews	
			Interregnum
1150	Hittite	Hebrew	XXth Dynasty
	City-States	"Conquest"	1180–1065 B.C.

Two revolutionary weapons of war, the composite bow and the horse and chariot, introduced a new age after the death of Abraham. It was an age of war and oppression, with quickly changing fortunes for those persons such as the sons of Abraham who were caught up in the surge of international events. The Hyksos, Semitic chariot-warriors who introduced the new weapons, conquered Syria, Palestine, and Egypt and imposed the first foreign rule upon Egypt.

Canaan or Haran?
Genesis 26:1–36:43

The soldier's life on the eastern frontier of Egypt was monotonous. Lookout towers every few miles marked the border in sand dune country that is now split by the Suez Canal. Traffic of Bedouin or merchant caravans that plied the trade routes was regulated by border patrols at established checkpoints. The boredom and monotony were shattered one day, about 1720 B.C., when the Hyksos chariot-warriors arrived.

They would have been seen first in a rapid-paced cloud of dust among the dunes. A peasant conscript from the Nile stops and looks, then begins ticking off in his mind the possibilities with which he is acquainted. Bedouin? No, too fast. Caravan? Not long enough, and too fast. An army? Not enough people. His curiosity turns to uneasiness as the party stirring the dust seems to glide along, a kind of movement he has not seen before. Then he sees the horses, ten pairs of them. They are horses, but he has never seen horses like them. Two by two they trot as one horse, with plumes bobbing high between their short ears. They are pulling something.

The vehicle has light wheels and is at the heels of the horses. In a small, rounded enclosure between the wheels is a man, standing almost between the flying heels of the horses. Tight lines run from his waist to the bronze bits in the horses' mouths. The man is leaning back, arching the necks of the eager horses with tight lines. He holds in his hands, both of which are free, a bow. A hundred yards from the checkpoint, he reaches into a quiver on the side of the enclosure and smoothly draws out an arrow, signaling his comrades to do the same.

Suddenly he turns his body toward the men at the checkpoint and leans forward, slackening the lines. The horses wheel in the same direction and break into a dead run, right into the open-mouthed faces of the peasant conscripts. In consternation they stand with their arms at their sides. In ten seconds it is over. Slender arrows stick like long pins in the dying soldiers, and bronze arrowheads protrude into the sand. The horses thunder on and leave the first Egyptian witnesses of the war chariot silent on the ground.

Within the year Egypt bowed to the man in the war chariot, and the Asiatic Hyksos ruled the land. Who were the charioteers? Our knowledge of them is scanty. They were a warrior aristocracy who maintained a feudal system supported by the work of peasants and slaves. About 1750 B.C. they swept through Syria and Palestine, penetrating Egypt by 1720 B.C., where a capital was established at Avaris in the Nile delta. The Egyptians called them "Hyksos," a rather derogatory term meaning "foreigner." Little evidence beyond the name is left in Egypt; the humiliation of defeat was so acute that all traces of their occupation of the country were removed. Indicative of the eastern mentality is the thoroughness with which the memory of the Hyksos was erased. The XVIIIth Dynasty, succeeding the Hyksos, reckoned its reign from the last pre-Hyksos dynasty, as though they had not been there!

Information about the Hyksos chariot-warriors comes principally from Syria and Palestine where their cities have been excavated. It seems that the name encompasses diverse ethnic groups. There were Semitic, Egyptian, and Hurrian names among the rulers at various times between the time of their appearance and 1550 B.C., the time of their expulsion from Egypt and Palestine. We can assume that leadership among the rulers changed in the constant struggle of city-states, and that chieftains of various ethnic backgrounds associated with their localities gained the limelight of pre-eminence for brief periods of time. One of the great cities of Palestine during this period was Shechem. It bears mute evidence of the constant struggle for leadership in four major destructions within 200 years.

Nevertheless, the Hyksos period was a golden age materially for Palestine. Open commerce occurred with all parts of the Near East, and the country reached the highest level of cultural achievement in its history. The Hyksos period was known for its artistic achievements in pottery and monumental architecture. Cities such as Shechem and Hazor were fortified and adorned with temples and villas. The city wall at Shechem can be seen today, standing thirty feet high, a 3,500-year-old landmark! The massive triple gate on the east side of Shechem is a marvel of engineering with its cyclopean masonry. Atop an artificial mound on the west of the city stood the massive temple to Baal-berith. No ancient temple in Palestine matched its dimensions of eighty-four feet in length and sixty-eight feet in width. Hazor, fifty miles north of Shechem, was an even larger city, less sophisticated but covering 180 acres within its system of walls.

Jacob, in name and in life, was at home in the Hyksos period. Little is said in the biblical narratives that helps us to localize Jacob in this period, but there is indirect evidence. The ease of travel from Beersheba to Haran is expected. Also the cities of Shechem and Bethel, built into significant centers by the Hyksos, are important in the Jacob narratives. Shechem, the city of the sons of Hamor (33:18ff.), was probably a caravan stopover. "Sons of Hamor" means literally "sons of the donkey," or donkey drovers. Donkeys, we recall, were the beasts of burden in caravans during this time. The invitation to Jacob to live at Shechem "and trade in it" (34:21) suggests also its commercial character.

The biblical narratives dwell at length on Jacob's adventures in the region of Haran. Actually the story is cast in a very interesting and suspense-laden form, once we see the issues involved. The listener, who would be a son of Jacob in Palestine, was aware that the legacy of Abraham rode with Jacob because he, not Esau, claimed the birthright. The hope of Israel was brought repeatedly to the brink of disaster in Jacob's duel of wits with Laban, and every development that rescued the inheritance in the person of Jacob merely preserved it for another game of brinkmanship.

The final peril was that Jacob would stay in Haran, the land Abraham was commanded to leave. This problem was solved in the nick of time, and the inheritance was brought back to the land of promise, even though it was still threatened every step of the way. Of course, the listener of these stories was aware that the birthright and Jacob would always be extricated from every situation, but hearing the story was always a delight. I think the narratives still have magnetic attraction when we approach them in this natural way. To moralize sermons from every verse, I think, kills the story and its message. Here, in summary, is the story.

First, Jacob appears at Haran a penniless refugee who escaped the wrath of Esau with little else than the birthright bestowed by his father. He is drawn to the house of Laban by Rachel, a very attractive relative of Jacob's mother (29:1-14). Jacob innocently bargains with Laban for

Rachel, and the dowry is fixed at seven years of labor (v. 20). Thus far, all is well. At the marriage, however, Leah, an unattractive older daughter, is foisted off on Jacob instead of the woman he wants (vv. 21-26). Laban pleads that he is following local custom, which is probably true. Nevertheless, Jacob finds himself committed to seven more years of labor to meet a second dowry (vv. 27-30). That he had two wives is incidental, as we know from the Nuzi tablets dating about 1500 B.C.

A listener of the story would begin to get concerned about Jacob's long stay in the house of Laban. Canaan was the land of promise, not Haran. Jacob must be extricated from the situation. Yet, he seems to be the heir of the house of Laban because no sons are evident, not until Jacob has begotten quite a family of the two wives and their handmaids, his concubines. Then in 31:1, a new element is introduced. Sons of Laban appear, and they are concerned because Jacob seems to be acquiring Laban's wealth. Probably the sons are younger than Jacob's wives and therefore appear in the picture after Jacob becomes the heir of the house. According to Nuzi laws, their claim is legitimate.

Thus, the extrication of Jacob from Haran becomes possible. He comes into conflict with Laban's sons and, with a bit of trickery that seems to be more legal than moral, acquires most of Laban's wealth anyway and slips out of the country, bound for the land of Canaan (31:1-21). Rachel's theft of the household gods, symbols of the right to inherit clan leadership, adds interest, although the theft is ultimately meaningless since Laban's family remains in the North. Jacob is rescued from Haran and set on the way to the land of Canaan, the land of promise. A threat in the person of Esau brings him again to the brink (32:3-32), but Jacob prevails, first in prayer at Penuel on the Jabbok River (32:24-32), and next with Esau the following day in a meeting of reconciliation (33:1-17). The way is now open for him to enter the land of Canaan, the land of the birthright (33:18-20).

Even yet, his stay in the land is plagued with trouble (34:1-31) until he is purged of the paganism that he acquired in Haran along with his wealth and family. At Shechem, a traditional holy place, Jacob at last becomes the worthy inheritor of the birthright when he puts away the foreign gods and purifies himself (35:1-4). Finally he is extricated from Haran and its paganism in what amounts to a physical and spiritual exodus. Like the migration of Abraham—the first Exodus—little physical inconvenience is caused, although the spiritual struggle seems to be greater. Of more importance is the third Exodus, the harrowing experience of escape from genocide in Egypt that will become the watershed of Israel's religious pilgrimage. The return of Jacob to the land of promise prepares us for it.

In Egypt
Genesis 37:1–Exodus 1:22

Under the Hyksos kings at Avaris, the talented Joseph could have risen to the place of importance given to him in Genesis 37–50. According to an Egyptian record, a Syrian actually "made himself prince" during the chaotic period at the end of the reign of Rameses III, or about 1164 B.C. The Syrian could not have been Joseph, but his career was almost parallel to the rapid rise of Joseph, an Asiatic also. Much is made in the biblical account of Joseph's skill as a seer and a man of wisdom. He could interpret dreams (40:1–41:32) and was reputed to be "discreet and wise" (41:33, 19). The silver cup put in Benjamin's sack of food was a divining cup (44:2, 5), used for interpreting the spread of a drop of oil on water as a technique of divining the future. Thus Joseph is pictured as a counselor and source of wise guidance rather than a hard-nosed political administrator.

Two stories associated with Joseph are particularly at home in Egypt. A tradition of seven lean years (41:1-32) became legendary in Egyptian literature by 2800 B.C., and was popular even in the Ptolemaic period in the second century B.C. Its continued popularity for 2,500 years is probably due to recurrent periods of crop failure, which the proverbial story communicated best for the people. Also, the story of Joseph's temptation in Potiphar's house (39:1-23) has its parallel in a story of two brothers, Anubis and Bata, which is known in a colloquial version dating to about 1225 B.C. The story is probably much older, perhaps belonging with the entertainment literature that began to develop during the XIIth Dynasty near the patriarchal period.

Joseph enhanced the position of the Hebrews in Egypt, but the real test of their worthiness to be the people of the covenant came when the Hyksos were driven out. "A new king arose over Egypt who did not know Joseph" (1:8). Actually, the resurgence of nationalism with the rise of the XVIIIth Dynasty trapped Asiatics who had enjoyed privileges under the Hyksos, and they were put in the labor gangs that built the incredible monuments that we see today at Karnak, Luxor, Thebes, and other places along the length of the Nile.

Egypt entered the age of the war chariot with vigor. The country had lagged behind in a dangerous provincialism before the Hyksos conquest and suffered 200 years of servitude and humiliation. Its deep determination to avenge the loss of power, reminiscent of sounds heard in Cairo today, was evident in a little speech made in Thebes about 1570 B.C. A man of noble blood named Ka-mose spoke in a local council:

> (One) prince is in Avaris (Hyksos), another is in Ethiopia (presumably at Elephantine), and here I sit between an Asiatic and a Nubian. Each man has his slice of Egypt, . . . no man can settle down, being despoiled by the imposts of the Asiatics. I will grapple with him (the Hyksos), that I may cut open his belly.

And he did. The Hyksos were driven out of Egypt soon after 1570 B.C., and from Palestine by 1550 B.C. Egypt became intoxicated with its power and soon marshaled all of its national resources for building weapons of war. The chariot and the composite bow put Egypt in the "nuclear club"; and Egyptian craftsmen, the world's best until the time of Alexander the Great, concentrated upon building superior weapons.

The world's best war chariot was developed. Lightweight enough that one or two men could carry it, the Egyptian chariot rode on two strongly made six-spoke wheels, improvements over the Asiatic eight-spoke wheels. The platform rode on the breast-pole of the horses, with the axle under the rear edge. Asiatic chariots had the axle under the center of the platform, limiting considerably their capacity to turn sharply. On the side of the platform hung the warrior's equipment: spare bows and arrows.

We cannot quite imagine the significance of the composite bow. Simple bows had been used since the Stone Age, but a simple bow was not in the same class with a composite bow. To achieve power in a simple bow, the body of wood had to be quite large and unwieldy, and it would be too long for use in a chariot. The composite bow provided incredible power and toughness in a size that could be handled from the swiftly moving platform of a chariot. Basically, the composite bow was made up of four components: (1) a skeleton of fine wood for the body; (2) sections of animal horn on the inside of the bow for power; (3) dressed sinew of animals for the back; and (4) glue to weld the parts into one tough, powerful, veneer-type unit. The double-convex form of the body gave maximum power. A well-crafted bow of this kind had a zero range of 50 yards, an effective striking range of 100 yards, and an absolute range of up to 300 yards.

Egypt did not lack in able field generals during the War Chariot Age. The most famous engagement of the time in Canaan was the battle of Megiddo in 1468 B.C. It was the first of many great battles of Megiddo, down to the fateful day in 609 B.C. when King Josiah of Judah was slain in a battle with Pharaoh Necho of Egypt at the same place (2 Kgs 23:29-30). Battles at Megiddo were decisive for the control of Palestine because the city sat astride the natural commercial route between Syria and Egypt. Its strategic significance lay in its location at the mouth of a deep, narrow pass on the south edge of the Plain of Esdraelon through which the route passed. The decisiveness of battles for Megiddo became legendary, to the extent that the great final apocalyptic battle in Revelation 16:16 is called the battle of Armageddon, specifically, a final battle at Megiddo.

Thutmose III of Egypt marched north along the coastal road, reaching Gaza on 25 April 1468 B.C. His army required about twelve days for the eighty-mile march to the pass at Megiddo. On 7 May he camped at Ye-hem, south of the pass, and held a war council with the generals. A few miles straight through the pass sat Megiddo, secure behind its stone walls and reinforced by soldiers and chariot contingents sent by cities in Galilee. The fate of the cities of Galilee and the broad fertile plain of Esdraelon hung on the defense of Megiddo. On the other hand, the Egyptian thrust northward would be blunted into ineffectiveness if Megiddo were allowed to stand. Thutmose III called for advice from his generals at the war council meeting.

We pick up the council debate: "What is it like to go (on) this (road) which becomes (so) narrow?" One general says, . . . "Will not horse (have to) go after (horse, and the army) similarly? Will the vanguard of us be fighting while the (rear guard) is waiting here, . . . unable to fight?" We can picture a general producing a map or drawing it with his baton on the ground. He points at the map. "Now two (other) roads are here. One of the roads—behold it is (to the east of) us, so that it comes out at Taanach."

The city of Taanach, less formidable, did in fact sit astride the entrance of another pass east of Megiddo. To divert the army to that pass, however, would require a detour through hilly country where the prized

Egyptian chariots could not be used. Such a tactic would be the equivalent of grounding the air force of a modern army in enemy territory. Another option is proposed: "The other (road)—behold, it is to the north side of Djefti, and we will come out to the north of Megiddo. Let our victorious lord proceed on one of them (of the two options proposed), . . . (but) do not make us go on that difficult road!"

The council debate ceased momentarily when new intelligence about enemy reinforcements at Megiddo was brought in. Then the pharaoh announced his decision: he would take the road through the pass to Megiddo. The generals were charged to "hold fast to the stride" of their leader on the road that became so narrow. Thutmose III would ride at the point of the army, and his elite troops would follow, horse following horse.

Three days after the council meeting, the army moved out. Through the pass they went, without meeting an enemy troop. The strategists at Megiddo, for some inexplicable reason, had dispersed forces to guard the passes at Taanach and north of Djefti and left the approach to Megiddo open, like an arrow pointing at the heart of the city. The Egyptians poured onto the plain and, by the time "the shadow turned" (noon), the chariot legions covered the plain of Megiddo. Surprised and panic-stricken, the defenders of Megiddo fled headlong toward the city. They abandoned their horses and chariots and ran to the walls of the city where the gates were not shut. Comrades on the walls hoisted some of them up to safety, while others fell before the merciless onslaught of the Egyptians.

On that day, 12 May 1468 B.C., Megiddo was doomed. Its bleak future was symbolic of Canaan. The whole land, from Sinai to the Euphrates, became a prey for Egypt to loot and destroy and enslave in almost annual military campaigns. Then the people were taken back to Egypt to build great monuments to these campaigns of looting and destroying. Tourists make annual pilgrimages to Egypt to gaze at the monuments at Karnak, for instance, where Thutmose III inscribed the story of the battle of Megiddo. They do not realize that the forest of gigantic stone columns with capitals more than twenty feet across were built by slaves whose story of destruction the columns were built to tell.

For 100 years the grim statistics of human misery were recorded:

From Megiddo: 340 living prisoners and 83 hands; 2,041 horses, 191 foals, 6 stallions, 1 chariot worked with gold; 892 chariots of the wretched enemy; 502 bows; 1,929 cows; 2,000 goats; 20,500 sheep; .

. . From villages near Megiddo: 38 maryanu (chariot-warriors); 1,796 male and female slaves; 103 pardoned persons; numerous unique objects of silver and gold, and 207,300 sacks of wheat!

All of this, mind you, is listed from Megiddo and its vicinity! The "83 hands" indicates a primitive body count method used by the military. "Pardoned persons" were those who surrendered during a siege of a city and thus escaped the orgy of destruction that came with the fall of the city. "Pardoned persons," however, could expect little more reward than their lives because they were led off with other captives into slavery.

The statistics got monotonous during the War Chariot Age:

From Tunip in north Syria, in the fifth campaign of Thutmose III: 1 prince of the town; 329 tether (chariot) warriors; 100 deben of silver (about 25 pounds Troy); 100 deben of gold; . . .

And on the way south from Tunip, the army came upon a village in the midst of harvest. Fruit was on the trees, wine was in the vats, and grain was on the threshing floors. The army looted it all and was "as drunk and anointed with oil every day as if at feasts in Egypt."

From another campaign are numerous lists of Asiatics taken prisoner and inventories of loot. Thutmose III penetrated the upper Euphrates and was credited with hunting 120 elephants. One of his great warriors detailed in his own diary two notable exploits for which he was rewarded. On one occasion he came to the rescue of the pharaoh when a large elephant was on the verge of killing him. The warrior claimed he stood "in the water between two rocks" and cut off the trunk of the elephant. On another occasion, when the Egyptian chariots were attacking Kadesh, the prince of Kadesh set free in the midst of the chariot horses a mare that was intended to disrupt the attention of the horses. It apparently did; the warrior noted in his diary that he ran after the mare on foot and ripped open her belly with his dagger, an action for which the pharaoh gave praise to God!

The list of cities plundered and captives taken is endless. Perhaps we should note one last inventory that was written by Amenhotep II, successor to Thutmose III. When the victorious king reached Memphis on his return from Syria and Palestine, his scribes counted the captives as follows: princes of Retenu (Asiatics): 127; brother of princes: 179; Apiru: 3,600; living Shasu: 15,200; Kharu: 36,300; living Neges: 15,070; the adherents (ar allies) thereof: 30,652; total, 89,600 men. The figures given total 101,128, which suggests that two of the readings are questionable. There follows a list of loot that includes 60 silver and gold decorated chariots; 1,032 regular chariots; and 13,050 weapons of war.

Of special interest here are the 3,600 Apiru, which is the Egyptian name of the Habiru, equivalent in name to Hebrew. Much has been written about the Habiru, but no evidence actually equates the Habiru with Abraham's sons known in the Bible as Hebrews. Habiru seems to denote a landless people whose fortunes varied in different periods. They appeared as merchants, mercenary warriors, slaves, or wanderers. The term seems to have descriptive rather than ethnic significance in its usage. As a result, it seems that the Hebrews could have been called Habiru because they shared some of the descriptive characteristics, although the Hebrews did not compose all Habiru. The 3,600 Habiru carried captive into Egypt by Amenhotep II about 1440 B.C. may or may not have included kindred of the Hebrews.

In any case, Canaan lay prostrate under the thin, sharp chariot-wheel of Egypt. The land was systematically plundered and looted by barbarian pharaohs who built the great monuments from Memphis in the delta to Abu Simbel south of the Aswan Dam. Human life was cheap, and populations of whole cities, along with their surrounding villages, were marched off into slavery or slaughtered. One indicator of the magnitude of slave labor was the cost of relocating the temple at Abu Simbel on top of the cliff on which it was built. The cost was $36,000,000 in a land where labor is still cheap. Imagine the cost of building the original structure!

A brief respite came to Canaan during the Amarna Age, 1412–1366 B.C., when Amenhotep III turned attention from wars of conquest to the pursuit of sports and building more temples along the Nile. He reportedly killed 102 lions during the first ten years of his reign and engaged in one minor military campaign into Nubia. During the last years of his reign, he apparently suffered from arthritis, so his son, Amenhotep IV (Akhenaton), became co-regent. By the time Akhenaton became sole ruler about 1375 B.C., he had inaugurated far-reaching religious reforms in the land that claimed all of his interest. The capital was moved from Thebes to Amarna, hence the name "Amarna Age" for the period.

In Canaan, Egyptian control exercised through vassal, or puppet, rulers began to break up. A collection of letters written from rulers of cities in Syria and Canaan reflects the chaotic, revolutionary situation. Biridiya, petty ruler of Megiddo, complained that the troublemaker from Shechem named Labayu had shut up the people in the city and they were not able to shear the sheep. Furthermore, the city was stricken with pestilence and could not last without archers from Egypt. Another letter from Biridiya of Megiddo reveals the source of his trouble. He said,

> Behold I am working in the town of Shunama, and I bring men of the corvee (slave labor) but behold, the governors who are with me do not do as I do.

The vassals were required to conscript slave labor in Canaan to work on royal projects, probably road building, for the king of Egypt. Thus, the lot of people in Canaan was not better than that of the slaves in Egypt. The Amarna Letters reflect a growing revolt against the vassal rulers, however, and in this case, only the prince of Megiddo still conscripted slave gangs. The misery of Egyptian oppression is reflected in a copy of a letter from the king to the prince of Gezer that requested forty concubines who would be taken from the families in the city. Still another letter, from the vassal at Pella to the king, complained that Yanhamu, the local Egyptian commissioner, was trying to blackmail him of 2,000 shekels of silver, an extracurricular activity that probably was profitable in the chaotic political situation.

Letters from Jerusalem, Shechem, Hebron, and other places reflect revolution against Egyptian rule, while Akhenaton was preoccupied with problems in Egypt. Order was not restored until the XIXth Dynasty came to power in 1310 B.C. Seti I was the iron-fisted ruler who brought Syria and Canaan back under Egyptian rule, using the war chariot as his ultimate weapon. His forceful military style earned the proverbial saying that he was like a flame when it goes forth and no water is brought. His son, Rameses II, expanded the empire to the Euphrates again until he battled the Hittites in 1286 B.C. at Kadesh on the Orontes. The battle ended indecisively, and Rameses II began concentrating upon expansion into Nubia, to the south of Egypt, and monumental building projects. The temple at Abu Simbel is but one of many incredible structures built by Rameses II that amaze rational people to this day.

Exodus 1:11-14, which states that the Hebrew slaves in Egypt labored at Pithom and Rameses, takes us to the time of Rameses II. He was the first Rameses to do significant building, his grandfather, Rameses I, having ruled only two years. The XIXth Dynasty, to which the Rameses family belonged, built its capital in the Nile delta on the site of Avaris, the Hyksos capital of 400 years earlier. It was renamed Rameses. The mention of brickmaking (1:14) reflects labor in the delta, although structures were built of bricks in upper Egypt.

A tomb painting that dates about 1470–1445 B.C., or during the period of Hebrew slavery in Egypt, pictures Semites and Nubians working together. In the upper panel, two Nubians take water from a pool on the lift to moisten the clay, which is being kneaded by another Nubian at the lower right. His tool is a short-handled hoe. The man above him, a Semite, is molding bricks, as is the Nubian at the upper right of the lower panel. A Semite in the lower panel tightens his hoe, while the Nubian on the extreme lower right carries a bundle of bricks to a mason. The Semites are fair-skinned and bearded, while the Nubians are darker. Sitting on a brick in the upper right of the lower panel is the Egyptian taskmaster, armed with a stick to urge on the workmen. This picture echoes verses 11 and 12 of Exodus 12, which tell of Moses becoming angry at seeing "an Egyptian beating a Hebrew" and his slaying the cruel taskmaster.

The Hebrews were not, therefore, the only slaves in Egypt. In fact, the whole economy of Egypt to the end of the XIXth Dynasty was based upon looting Syria and Canaan, as well as Nubia, in frequent military campaigns and employing slave labor on a massive scale in Egypt itself. The exodus of the Hebrews would occur in a time of general unrest and instability in Egypt that would allow slaves of other ethnic origins to escape also. The Exodus, for instance, would not take the Semites from work such as the brickmaking operation and leave the Nubians still working with the taskmaster. The biblical account focuses, as we would expect, upon the lot of the Hebrews, but a historical perspective must see also the other unfortunates such as the Nubians bent under the load of bricks, who would be thinking of their own "exodus."

The Exodus from Egypt
Exodus 2:1–16:27

The biblical account of the lot of Hebrew slaves (1:14) and their undercover resistance to Egyptian oppression (1:15-22) is at home in the slow disintegration of the XIXth Dynasty. Rameses II was succeeded by

Merneptah (1224–1216 B.C.) who campaigned in Canaan and Syria to bring them back under tight imperialistic control. One such campaign occurred in the Esdraelon plain, where Bethshan was brought back under vassalage; and cities in the region, one of which is called Yanoam, were pillaged. The spirit of conquest was dead in Egypt due to the deterioration of the XIXth Dynasty. We must see this dimension of life in Egypt to see the Exodus in the perspective of life.

Rameses II was indeed a strong ruler, and he began his reign vigorously with expeditions into Syria. The records indicate an exceedingly long reign of sixty-six years for him: 1290–1224 B.C. He was not a child-king when he began to reign because his major expeditions into Syria occurred within the first decade of his rule. The simple fact is that he lived to be quite old, and during the last twenty years of his reign, he was too old to carry the responsibility of government. Therefore, the empire began to come apart and, in Egypt, the spirit languished. Merneptah, the thirteenth son and successor of Rameses II, was also an old man when he began his rule. His chronicles reflect this. Two old men ruled Egypt for at least thirty years at the end of the thirteenth century B.C., in a time when empires were held together by the continued presence of military power and the throne at home was occupied by reason of widespread support among the nobles and a strong army.

When Merneptah died, all of the intrigues and conspiracies that had fermented under the surface at the royal court came into the open. Armed conflict for the throne ensued between Amenmeses and Siptah. Amenmeses, a usurper, seized the throne but was immediately ousted by Siptah. Meanwhile, rebellion broke out in Nubia, far to the south of Thebes, across the cataracts of the Nile from Egypt proper. Apparently Siptah spent most of the six years of his reign, from 1216 to 1210 B.C., regaining control of Nubia, because he established a viceroy there.

Siptah may have fallen a victim to the intrigues of the viceroy, Seti II, because Seti appeared as pharaoh about 1210 B.C. Powerful undercurrents of conspiracy were at work, and the struggle for power in Egypt became the preoccupation of many aspirants. Seti II could not master the situation, and the whole land was thrown into a state of anarchy. "Every man was thrown out of his right," a record states matter-of-factly. "They (Egypt) had no chief for many years." Actually the period of struggle may have lasted twenty years, an interregnum when nobles ruled over their districts and jockeyed for the prize of the throne. In a time like this, deals of all kinds were made among aspirants, and utter chaos in government occurred.

The Exodus occurred sometime during the waning years of the XIXth Dynasty, when Egypt was ruled by old men, and the ensuing period of anarchy. The Bible is not specific in identifying the pharoah. I am inclined to place the Exodus in the period of anarchy, at the end of the XIXth Dynasty, for several reasons.

(1) The biblical account of Moses' negotiations with the pharoah (5:1–11:10) was in a time when the pharoah was negotiating with many factions to consolidate his power. It is unlikely that a slave-labor representative would have obtained repeated audiences with Rameses II or Merneptah, who ruled in the proud and arrogant tradition of their predecessors.

(2) The entry into Palestine, as I shall detail later, probably occurred in Iron Age I, or in the twelfth century B.C. This is the opportune time, and both biblical and archaeological evidence support it.

(3) The tradition of a period of wandering in the wilderness of Sinai, the Negev, and Transjordan fits into the evidence of the twelfth, not thirteenth, century B.C. Nelson Glueck's theory of an occupational gap in these regions between 1900 and 1200 B.C. is related to this discussion, though Glueck's position is not as firm as was once thought. Beginning in Iron Age I, cities were built in the Negev, Edom, and Moab, the places where the Israelites are said to have encountered cities (Num 20–21).

The biblical account of Moses' confrontation with the pharaoh is probably historical, although the present form of the narrative is the result of a thousand years of handing down the tradition and interpreting it as an almost cosmic struggle between Yahweh and the gods of Egypt, who appear in the role of Rahab, the great rebel monster of chaos. Therefore, a ritual form shapes the narrative, and it is practically impossible to rehistoricize the events in the complexity and sequence of the actual occurrence. We should not fret when we find ritual form preserving in its stereotyped structure the substance of living history. The Last Supper, for instance, is such an event that Christians preserve in the same manner. A variety of rigid ritual forms catch an event in living history in stop-action, and one would be hard-put to translate the actual event from the variety of rituals practiced by Protestants alone.

Actually, the ritual form makes the event in living history important. This is true of the Exodus from Egypt or the Last Supper. Through ritual we can participate in the event and appropriate its significance in the living present. If we had only a straightforward historical account such as the account of the capture of Megiddo in 1468 B.C., we would remain interested spectators, but the victory of Thutmose III would remain in 1468 B.C. The Exodus from Egypt is a victory preserved in a form in which every Jew and Christian can participate and find relevance.

A vital part of the Exodus was the crossing of the sea of water-plants, or marshy sea (15:4), translated "Red Sea" in the Septuagint and taken from there into the English versions. The geography of Exodus 14 places the crossing north of the Gulf of Suez in the marshy, lake area that is now a part of the Suez Canal. The lakes are still there, as some readers will remember from newscasts that told of some fifteen ships that were trapped in the canal by the Six-Day War.

The miracle of the crossing was the deliverance from a detachment of chariots that pursued the fleeing slaves. Some details are embedded in the layers of tradition of the account that accumulated over the centuries. We are told, for instance, that the group turned back at "Etham, in the edge of the wilderness" (13:20), probably a border fortress protected by a platoon of soldiers. They encamped "before Pi-hahiroth, between Migdol and the sea" (14:1-2). "Pi-hahiroth" means "house of marshes," suggesting the marshy area, and "Migdol" means fortress. The camp was between the fortress and the sea in a marshy area. Obviously, it was not the normal place to cross the border. Therefore, the miracle of the crossing was the unexpected occurrence of a "strong east wind" that blew all night (14:21) and caused the marshy area to become solid enough to cross on foot, but still too muddy for the horses and chariots to follow. Exodus 14:25 contains the memory that the chariot wheels clogged with mud and drove heavily, disabling the pursuing forces.

The intervention of the strong east wind was an act of God and was interpreted as such by the bedraggled followers of Moses. Exodus 15:1-18 is the victory song that was probably sung at the Passover ritual. Later traditioners naturally embellished the event of the crossing, making the sea stand as though congealed on either side of the triumphant Israelites (14:29) and the ground dry like a highway. We are inclined to do the same thing; we think that we demonstrate more faith if we make the sea deeper and the way of the crossing drier. This can become a kind of blasphemy, like handling live rattlesnakes to prove how much faith we have. It is not more necessary to make the sea deeper than it is to handle rattlesnakes to prove we have faith! The miracle of the crossing need not bog down in the mud of exhibitionism; it is the prelude to the commitment in covenant at Sinai.

The age of the war-chariot came to an end in a sense when the Hebrews crossed the eastern frontier of Egypt. Slaves with their clothes still caked in the clay of brick-making breathed the free air of the Sinai desert and turned toward a new age. It was an age in which promise, invested in man at creation and to a lesser degree in Abraham, would come to pass. Underlying the bold adventure of realizing accumulated promises in building a people of God was a peculiar sense of destiny, couched in the form of covenant law. It has its own history, which can be explored in the interlude at Sinai.

Chapter 5

Law and Order
for the People of God

Exodus 15:22–25:9; 34:10-28
Leviticus 19:1-18; Deuteronomy 5:6-33

Ancient Near Eastern Law Codes

2050 B.C.	Ur-Nammu Law Code—Sumarian
1900 B.C.	Eshnunna Law Code—Amorite
1850 B.C.	Lipit-Ishtar Law Code—Sumero-Akkadian
1700 B.C.	Code of Hammurabi—Babylonian
1450 B.C.	Hittite Laws
1350 B.C.	Assyrian Laws
1200 B.C.	Hebrew Covenant Code

A motley band of slaves followed Moses out of Egypt and into the wilderness of Sinai. The ethnic origins of this group were likely as diverse as the slave lists of the Pharaohs indicate. Lacking the common bond of blood, they found unity in the historical experience of the Exodus. The bond of common experience became the basis of a covenant code at Sinai that bound the people to a system of law and order.

The People Who Followed Moses
Exodus 15:22–18:27

We cannot go to some place along the Suez Canal and say with absolute certainty, "Moses led his people out of Egypt here." Neither can we identify the specific route through the desert. Many specific places are mentioned, but they defy absolute identification with actual sites. Specific places and routes cannot be pointed out with certainty for two major reasons.

First, archaeological exploration of the eastern frontier of Egypt and the Sinai desert has not kept pace with work in more accessible localities. This one fact, along with the natural difficulties of carrying on sustained research in a desert and rugged region, has limited the confidence of archaeologists in locating specific places associated with the Exodus and journey into the desert.

Second, more than one tradition of the Sojourn and Exodus is preserved in the biblical narrative. Some scholars see in Exodus 15:22 and Judges 11:16 a tradition of a journey straight from Egypt to Kadesh-barnea, south of Beer-sheba. This was a regularly traveled route to Egypt and possibly the one taken by Abraham from Beersheba. Others see in the incident of the quails in Exodus 16:13 and Numbers 11:31ff. a journey along the coastal road next to the the Mediterranean. Quails abound here and are still caught in nets by Bedouin near El Arish and north toward Khan Yunis and Gaza, and are exported to Europe as a Sinai delicacy. Quails are not plentiful in the interior of the Sinai region, on the route to Kadesh-barnea, however.

The dominant tradition of the journey into the wilderness takes the Israelites to Jebel Musa southeast of the ancient Egyptian copper mines at Serabit el-Khadim. Attesting the traditional identification of Jebel Musa with Mount Sinai is the early Christian monastery of Saint Catherine, where Codex Sinaiticus, one of the oldest Greek manuscripts of the Bible, was found by Tischendorf. Moses' association with the Kenites, a tribe of Bedouin metalsmiths, fits well in the region of the copper mines.

We need not be surprised to find several traditions of journeys from Egypt. They do not call into question either the Exodus or the covenant-commitment at Sinai. Egyptian border records indicate the passage of Asiatics through border posts for a century before the Exodus took place. Accumulating evidence suggests that additional slaves were carried into Egypt for a long period prior to the end of the XIXth Dynasty, and small groups also either escaped or obtained permission to leave. The multiple traditions therefore give the biblical account historical credibility that a single, contrived account would not have. Nevertheless, the major exit from Egypt was the Exodus led by Moses, an account that became normative for interpreting the other traditions.

Two further observations should be made about the people who escaped slavery in Egypt. First, Moses led a motley band of slaves out of Egypt, many of whom had reasons for following him that were not necessarily religious. Many of the followers, I am sure, simply wanted to get out of Egypt. The lists of people from all parts of the Near East and Nubia indicate that slaves were brought *en masse* and put to work in interracial groups. The Bible does not suggest that the Hebrews received special treatment. In fact, the opposite is evident in Exodus 1:8-14 and 2:11-15, passages that describe the people of Israel working at building the delta capital, Raamses (1:11).

The biblical traditions also reflect the mixture of races in the followers of Moses. Moses himself was mistaken for an Egyptian by the daughters of Reuel in Exodus 1:19, probably because his skin was dark like that of Egyptians. Also he had an Egyptian name, "Moses," which may very well have originally been compounded with the name of an Egyptian deity such as Thutmose, or Amenmose, or Kamose, or even Rameses. Exodus 12:38 states that a "mixed crowd" went out from Egypt with the departing Hebrews, and "the rabble" is identified in Numbers 11:4. Among the "mixed crowd" could have been Egyptians, one of whom was married to an Israelite woman (Lev 24:10), and Cushites, one of whom Moses married (Num 12:1). The group was enlarged by the addition of Midianites (Num 10:29-32), Amalekites (1 Sam 15:6), Kenizzites (Josh 14:13f.), and Kenites (Judg 1:16).

Therefore, the blood of Jacob did not unite the people of Israel in their venture into the desert. The bond was one of common experience in the Exodus and common commitment at Sinai. The faith of Jacob and Abraham, more than their blood, united the new people of Israel gathered around Moses.

The second observation is that an unusually large number of people followed Moses out of Egypt. When we add the normal complement of families to the 600,000 men (Exod 12:37), a total of more than 2,000,000 is required. This number represents as many people as the present-day population of Israel and probably as many as Israel ever numbered during biblical times. Some scholars think the number is taken from later census figures obtained by David (see 2 Sam 24:2). Others point out that the word *'eleph*, translated "thousand," is also translated "family" or clan, as in "the heads of the divisions (*clans*) of Israel" (Num 1:16), "my *clan* is the weakest in Manasseh" (Judg 6:15), or "I will search him out among all the thousands (or clans) of Judah" (1 Sam 23:23).

It is difficult to avoid translating *'eleph* in Exodus 12:37, however, as "thousands," and repeated references in the book of Numbers bear out the deliberateness of the figures. Numbers 1:46 and 2:32 and Exodus 38:26 give a number of 603,550 fighting men. The 550, which causes difficulty in translating the number as "603 clans," indicates that "thousands" is meant. The biblical traditions persistently reflect a small number of the refugees from Egypt, however. Two midwives, Shiphrah and Puah, are said to have assisted at the birth of Israelite children in Egypt (Exod 1:15), and for a time Moses was able to listen to all of the disputes among the Israelites between Egypt and Sinai. A much smaller group of people is implied by these two traditions. We could examine much more evidence.

I should say first that I have no way of knowing exactly how many people followed Moses out of Egypt. I do not think 2,000,000 people went into the wilderness of Sinai, a desert that normally supports less than 30,000 Bedouin who are acclimated to its harsh climate and wise in the ways of survival. The presence of persistent records implying a small number along with the deliberately stated high numbers leads me to suggest the following approach to the problem.

I am aware that numbers in ancient Near Eastern literature, as well as in our own day, can communicate information other than mathematical counting. For instance, has anyone ever added up the published "body counts" of enemy dead claimed by the military? The numbers are exaggerated for the purpose of communicating a climate of opinion that though we lose soldiers, the battles are won. I suggest that the theologians who handed down the biblical traditions chose to include some traditions of large numbers, probably taken from a census list, for theological purposes.

The overriding purpose would be to show that "all Israel" *did* indeed experience the Exodus. We have noted that the people at Sinai were of various ethnic origins, and we shall see the addition of still other peoples who were always in the land of Canaan. The Exodus was so much of a cornerstone experience in building the people of Israel that all Israel went back symbolically, in the numbers and in the Passover ritual, in spiritual pilgrimage.

A second reason for the large numbers would be to emphasize the lack of faith of the people in the wilderness. With such an army of people, it seems a little grotesque that they should turn back in the Exodus at Etham on the edge of the wilderness, where there was probably a border post, and get trapped between the wilderness and the marshy sea

(Exod 13:20–14:3). Also the decision to avoid the well-traveled coastal highway or the desert road and take a roundabout, hide-and-seek route by Sinai seems to reflect a lack of faith if there were 600,000 fighting men. Also, the lack of courage to invade the land of Canaan from the south (Num 13–14) and the failure at Arad (Num 21) are understood as failures of faith, with the army so commandingly large.

The high numbers, therefore, communicate a part of the biblical message, but we can miss it if we woodenly literalize the figures and see nothing more than the total from a Hebrew adding machine.

Law and Order
Exodus 19:1–25:9; 34:10-28
Leviticus 19:1-18; Deuteronomy 5:6-33

Three days after the Exodus, Moses was confronted with the need for law and order among the fleeing refugees. When there was a water shortage for three days, the first case of murmuring against his leadership occurred (Exod 15:24). We should remember, however, that Egyptian soldiers died in Sinai from thirst and dehydration after four days of wandering without water in June 1967. The journey to Sinai of the fledgling people of Israel was therefore a miserable one, and the constant threat of rebellion or riot must have made it a nightmare experience for Moses. Commitment to a system of law was the first item of business if the refugees expected to get beyond the initial step toward becoming a people of God.

The particular system adopted was novel and unique. It was novel in that it used a familiar treaty or covenant form within which the law was operative. It was unique because the covenant bound the people to Yahweh, their God, in a personal relationship that had parallels only in the sovereign-subject relationship of kings and their subject-rulers in subordinate kingdoms. The best example of this parallel is a covenant mediated between the Hittite king, Mursilis, and his subject, Duppi-tessub, in the century preceding the Exodus from Egypt.

The covenant begins: "These are the words of Mursilis." Authority is implied in calling the covenant "the words"; the written word had a finality about it that spoken words did not have. The authority is that of the sovereign who offers the covenant to his subject. His authority rests on a two-fold premise: (1) Mursilis, the sovereign who appoints Duppi-tessub as ruler of the subject kingdom and (2) Mursilis, who is mediating the covenant that establishes Duppi-tessub in a personal relationship that gives him status and insures his well-being. The titles appended to the name of Mursilis qualify him graciously to make the covenant and indicate the scope of his authority. He is the "king of Hatti-land," particularly of all the Hittite empire that is made up of numerous subject-kingdoms; and he is "the favorite of the Storm-god," the deity of the Hittites.

The "words" of the covenant begin with a historical review of the relations between the sovereign and the subject. This review orients the covenant and places the subject in debt to the grace of Mursilis, which obligates him to observe the covenant. Covered in the review is a history of dealings between the families of the two men over the previous generation.

"Aziras the grandfather of you, Duppi-tessub," Mursilis continues, "rebelled against my father, but submitted again." Apparently a general rebellion among the subject-kingdoms took place, and Aziras joined the revolt. He submitted again, however, and fought with the Hittite king against the rebellious subjects. "He (Aziras) remained bound" by his covenant and "loyal to my father," Mursilis says.

The covenant required loyalty to the sovereign. Transgression, or willful rebellion, against the king violated the spirit and letter of the covenant and was the most serious breach that could occur in the personal relationship of the two parties. Loyalty to the king required faithfulness and annual tribute that was fixed according to the means of the subject. "Three hundred (shekels of) refined and first-class gold, the tribute which my father imposed upon your father; he brought for years; he never refused it." Duppi-tessub's forebears had, therefore, brought regularly the assessed tribute as evidence of their subordinate status and also to support the institutions of government law and order that allowed them to function.

At the death of Duppi-tessub's father, Mursilis, who had succeeded his father, was requested to appoint Duppi-tessub as ruler of the subject kingdom of Amurru. "In accordance with your father's word," Mursilis states, "I did not drop you. To be sure you were sick and ailing, but I put you in the place of your father and took your brothers and sisters and the Amurru land in oath to you." Here is the indebtedness of Duppi-tessub. He was chosen by his father and approved by Mursilis before he became the subject-ruler, and he is subject-ruler only by the grace of the sovereign. Therefore, he stands under a historical obligation to honor the covenant and be loyal to his sovereign.

The "commandments" of the covenant follow. "But you, Duppi-tessub," Mursilis says, after he had pledged loyalty to their covenant, "remain loyal toward the king of the Hatti (Hittite) land." Then, reminding the subject of the 300 shekels of "good, refined first-class gold weighed with standard weights" that his father had brought as tribute, Mursilis says, "You shall present them likewise." Finally, the ultimate commitment is demanded. "Do not turn your eyes to anyone else!" Duppi-tessub is warned.

In the context of the personal covenant and commandments, a body of specific case-law regulations follows. The subject's relations with other subjects are spelled out, as are his relations with foreigners, refugees from other countries, and the military of the Hatti land. "With my friend you shall be friend," Duppi-tessub is reminded by Mursilis, "and with my enemy you shall be enemy." The covenant is concluded with an invocation to the gods who are witnesses, a series of curses that lie in reserve for Duppi-tessub "should (he) not honor" the covenant, and a list of blessings "if (he) honors these words" of the covenant that "are inscribed on this tablet."

Law and order for the subject-rulers in the Hittite empire rested upon this kind of covenant. It was more than a system of law to be observed; it was a personal relationship to be maintained within the legal structure of regulations. Deviation from the covenant threatened the relationship, and willful rebellion was the most serious breach a subject could initiate.

The covenant-law detailed in Exodus 19–24 ordering the relationship between Yahweh and his people is similar in form and almost contemporary in time with the Hittite covenant between Mursilis and Duppi-tessub. Yahweh, the God of Israel, is sovereign, and the people of Israel are the subjects of Yahweh. "I am the Lord (Yahweh) your God," the covenant begins (Exod 20:2), identifying God as the sovereign party who authorizes the words that follow. A long list of titles is not needed because the power of God has been experienced by Israel in the Exodus. The words, "Who brought you out of the land of Egypt, out of the house of bondage," review the relationship that preceded the act of mediating a formal commitment.

In Joshua 24:2-13, a more lengthy review precedes the stipulations of the covenant that is being renewed at Shechem. All of the pivotal events in Israel's history are recalled. God's dealing with Abraham, Isaac, Jacob, and Moses is remembered as prologue to the call to faithfulness in the present covenant. Israel is put in debt by the gracious acts of God that are sovereign, and the people are given historical reasons why they should subscribe to the commandments that follow.

That the commandments begin with the words "You shall have no other gods before me" (Exod 20:3) is not unexpected. This is the first thought of a sovereign toward his subject. It always comes first in one form or another. "Now therefore revere (honor and respect) the Lord" is the way the commandment is expressed in Joshua 24:14. On this command turns all the law that follows; any compromise of it jeopardizes the personal relationship that undergirds the entire covenant.

The commandments spell out additional regulations that cannot be compromised without endangering the personal sovereign-subject relationship. Where Duppi-tessub is forbidden to turn his eyes to anyone else, the Israelite is forbidden to turn to any other god or to make any representation of God to which he/she might bow down. The tribute God requires is obedience and loyalty (Exod 20:4-11) and high standards of ethics in dealing with fellow subjects (20:12-17). Here, in the commandments, rests the authority of the entire covenant. Case-laws regulating day-to-day life in the application of the great principles of the commandments may be flexible, but the principles are inflexible because they are the ultimate words of authority. Beyond them we can go only in spirit, but even then the words are not nullified. They are simply mediated on a different level of communication.

Case-laws, enunciated in Exodus 21:1–23:19, spell out the application of the covenant in specific circumstances. There are regulations concerning slaves, marriage and domestic problems, civil disputes, specific crimes, and so on in the case-law system. We should not think, however, that all of these laws were created on the spot at Sinai. They are in the tradition of the case-law systems that have been known in the Near East since 2000 B.C., in the same way that laws in the United States come in the tradition of the English law system. The laws at Sinai reflect adaptation to the covenant with Yahweh, however, so that they serve the covenant between Israel and their God in both spirit and letter.

We can see the thoroughness of adaptation of case-laws to the covenant in two examples. The "law of retaliation," for instance, ranks with the hardest and most inflexible punitive systems known in the ancient law codes. "Whoever strikes a person mortally shall be put to death," reads Exodus 21:12. These words are part of a paragraph that leaves no ambiguity about the severity of retaliation. It ends with these words:

If any harm follows, then you shall give life for life, eye for eye, tooth for tooth, hand for hand, foot for foot, burn for burn, wound for wound, stripe for stripe. (vv. 23-25)

The same degree of retaliation is required in the laws of the Amorites, dating to the time of Abraham, where these stipulations occur:

If a seignior (citizen) has destroyed the eye of a member of the aristocracy, they shall destroy his eye. If a seignior has knocked out the tooth of a seignior of his own rank, they shall knock out his tooth.

The Hittite laws, however, seem to be less harsh, and retribution seems to require something less than an eye for an eye and a tooth for a tooth. The idea of compensation seems to be more prominent than strict retribution. For instance,

If anyone kills a man or a woman in a quarrel, he has to make amends for him/her. He shall give four persons, man or woman, and pledge his estate as security. If anyone blinds a free man or knocks out his teeth, he shall give twenty shekels of silver and pledge his estate as security.

There are succeeding versions of the Hittite laws, but the changes are in compensation to be paid for whatever violation. No strict retribution of life for life, eye for eye, tooth for tooth occurs. Probably the Amorite and Hebrew laws of retaliation grew out of a Semitic background where the blood-revenge code governed tribal associations. The non-Semitic Hittites apparently did not have the harsh revenge element in their culture, which makes it appear more humanitarian than the Semitic cultures. This harsh and retributive component of the Semitic culture was a part of the Sinai law and remained a part of it throughout the Old Testament period. In fact, it penetrates the theology of the Old Testament in which Yahweh is a jealous and avenging God, exacting strict retribution for wrong-doing even to "the third and fourth generation" (Deut 5:9).

A second example of the thorough integration of standard case-law into the Sinai covenant is the social system reflected. It is thoroughly

Israelite and seems to be more humane than the rigid caste systems of the Amorites and Hittites. This system would be expected in the circumstances of the Israelites because they enjoyed a kind of classless society throughout the period of the Judges. In fact, feudalism with its rigid class stratification was never a generic part of the Israelite social structure, although slaves were kept from the time of Solomon and laws provided for their rights. Slavery, however, seems to be out of place in the covenant-law system.

On the other hand, the Amorite laws discriminate in meting out justice, depending upon the status of the person in the social system. We have noted that the law of exact retribution—eye for eye, tooth for tooth —applied where people who were free citizens were involved. In a case where a free citizen destroyed the eye of a commoner, or a tenant who did not enjoy equal standing with the aristocracy, a fine of one mina of silver (about 500 grams) was paid by the citizen. If the citizen destroyed the eye of a slave, he paid one-half of the value of the slave to the slave's owner, presumably. The penalty seemed to be compensation for damage to the property of another citizen, not because the slave himself had any rights as a person.

Three levels of justice are evident then in the Amorite laws, and these levels can be found in Hittite, Assyrian, and other law systems of the biblical world. Strict retribution applied in cases where free citizens of equal rank was involved. A serf-tenant who found himself living a life bordering on slavery because of debts, which could be inherited from one's father, or for other economic or personal reasons was regarded as less than a person in the courts. Any injury done to him could be compensated with a fine, and we may assume that such a person found real justice an illusive thing. The slave, however, was the property of a free citizen; so compensation was made to the owner, making the slave a "nobody" in the purview of the law.

We are surprised to find regulations concerning Hebrew slaves in Exodus 21:2-6, right at the head of the covenant-law system. The law is rather impersonal and legalistic, stating simply that "when you buy a Hebrew slave, he shall serve six years, but in the seventh he shall go out a free person, without debt." Deuteronomy 15:12-18 interprets the same law, reminding us that the Hebrew slave was a brother, and that all Hebrews had a background in Egyptian slavery. Thus the Hebrew slave did not lose his standing as a Hebrew or a brother. He was not reduced to a "nobody" in the law.

Leviticus 25:35-46 repeats the same thing concerning a Hebrew slave. He was not to be regarded as any less a person because of his unfortunate status, and the owner was encouraged to treat his brothers as "hired or bound laborers" (v. 40). On the other hand, slaves could be purchased from "the nations that are around about you" or from the strangers "residing with you" (vv. 44-45), and they were to be treated simply as slaves. I take this to mean that they were "nobodies" in the eyes of the Hebrew and the law.

These laws concerning slaves look back to the Exodus and to Sinai, implicitly from a time when the Hebrews had become established in Canaan and a feudalistic society with its aristocratic class had arisen. We know that Micah had much to say about the injustices of this kind of society in the eighth century B.C. (2:1-2; 3:1-3). Most likely, slaves were not owned by slaves during the desert sojourn at Sinai. Therefore, we should expect a system of law that regulated the affairs of the people as though they were equals in the sight of the law and God. A major difference in the Sinai covenant law, therefore, and the existing law codes of the Near East was its view of a democratic, classless society where at least all males had status before the law and equal claim for justice.

This is a fundamental implication of the covenant concept. The covenant establishes a personal relationship between God, the sovereign, and the Israelite. On the analogy of the Hittite covenant, the subject is a free males with authority and a kingdom in his own right. His kingdom is subject to the covenant with the sovereign, and his life is governed by stipulations that are a part of the covenant. The subject is not a "nobody," however, not even the poorest and most wretched Israelite. We find therefore a broad equality of approach to God as Lord, which was a major attraction of the Israelite system when the Israelites arrived in the land of Canaan. Slavery in all probability was introduced into the social order and legal system when Israel became established in Canaan and eased into a feudalistic type of society. At Sinai, slavery was not at home in the unique system of law and order of the people of God and never was at home in the spirit of the covenant.

Chapter 6

Israel and the
Liberation of Canaan

by John C. H. Laughlin

Numbers 13–36; Deuteronomy; Joshua 1–14; Judges 1

Of all the problems facing archaeologists and historians of the Bible, none has been more difficult and vexing, controversial and debated, than that of the so-called "conquest of Canaan" by the "Israelites." The questions and problems facing the serious student of these traditions can perhaps best be focused by examining the most dramatic of all the biblical conquest stories, the destruction of Jericho (Josh 6).

We are told in this story that after crossing the Jordan River from Moab, the Israelites marched around Jericho once a day for six days. On the seventh day they went around seven times while seven priests blew on seven rams' horns. At the end of the marching, the priests blew a long trumpet blast that was followed by a shout from the people. Then, we are told, "The wall fell down flat" (6:20).

The site of ancient Jericho (Tell es-Sultan) is just off the highway that runs through the modern town with the same name. It rises some 65–70 feet above the floor of the valley, and from its summit one can see for miles in all directions. To the north stretches the Jordan valley, which continues for over 150 miles to the Sea of Galilee. To the east lies the River Jordan and the modern state of Jordan. About 6–7 miles to the south is the desolate region of the Sea of Salt, the "Dead Sea." To the west are the Judean hills and about 18–20 miles, as the crow flies, the city of Jerusalem.

The site of Jericho was inhabited as early as the Neolithic period some 10,000 years ago and is still referred to as the "oldest city in the world." It is the perennial spring, the Ain es-Sultan, that no doubt attracted those first settlers. In the ruins of this mound lie what is left of the human struggle for survival over ten millennia. In some ways it is thus unfortunate that the site is known in the popular mind only because of its connection with the biblical story, for we can learn much from this place apart from its biblical reference.

The "biblical connection" brought the first archaeologists, the German excavators E. Sellin and C. Watzinger, to this site in the early part of this century. At that time, the "conquest" was usually dated around 1400 B.C., based upon the biblical tradition in 1 Kings 6 that Solomon built the temple in Jerusalem 480 years after the Exodus from Egypt. Even so, these excavators reported nothing on the site earlier than the sixteenth century B.C. and concluded that there was no city there during the time of Joshua.

Their effort was followed by John Garstang of England who dug at the site in the 1930s. Unlike his predecessors, Garstang claimed to have found the collapsed walls mentioned in the Bible. Based on the same biblical tradition (1 Kgs 6), he dated these walls, or what was left of them, to about 1400 B.C. He concluded that he had confirmed the historicity of the biblical account, and his conclusions made all the major newspapers. Garstang conducted his work, however, as indeed did those who came before him, without the modern methods that are now essential for careful, archaeological analysis. Among these methods is the "stratigraphical analysis." Simply put, this term refers to the controlled removal of the layers of earth or soil as they have accumulated or built up through the years.

Beginning in 1952, another archaeologist from England, Dame Kathleen Kenyon, began her own work at Jericho using the above method and totally disproved Garstang's earlier conclusions. She was able to show, among other things, that the collapsed walls Garstang had dated to the end of the fifteenth century B.C. had actually been destroyed some 900 years earlier during the Early Bronze Age, and had subsequently been buried beneath a hugh Middle Bronze Age rampart wall. Elsewhere, Kenyon reported that the top-most soil of the site had been badly eroded, and from the time now accepted for the "conquest" (1250–1200 B.C.) by most scholars, she found virtually nothing.

Kenyon did claim to find some evidence (a small oven and a juglet) that the site had been occupied between 1400 and 1325 B.C. In an attempt to salvage some historical value for the biblical story, she then suggested that maybe during this time, the fourteenth century B.C., Joshua and the Israelites showed up. One of the major problems with this theory can be seen if we examine the next story in the biblical version of things, the destruction of 'Ai (Josh 7:1–8:29).

As with the story of Jericho, the same archaeological fate awaited 'Ai, located a few miles north of Jerusalem, about one mile east of another important biblical site, Bethel. Garstang also excavated here and claimed to have found evidence of a 1400 B.C. destruction. Later excavations by Judith Krause in the 1930s and by my own teacher, Joseph Callaway (to whose memory this chapter is dedicated), in the 1960s and early 1970s, have clearly shown that no Late Bronze Age city at 'Ai existed. In fact, they concluded that the site had lain in ruins (hence its name: 'Ai="ruins" or "heap") from about 2400 B.C. to around 1200 B.C. or later. If Joshua lived during the thirteenth century, as most scholars today believe, there was simply no 'Ai for him to destroy despite the dramatic biblical story. Certainly if Kenyon was correct, there is an even greater problem: Joshua would have had to be at Jericho in the fourteenth century and at 'Ai in the twelfth century.

The archaeological/historical problems raised by the excavations of Jericho and 'Ai with regard to the nature of the Israelite conquest are but symptomatic of the problems in general when archaeological data are compared with the biblical stories. This will become clearer if we look now at the way the Bible presents its own account.

The traditions in the book of Numbers recount that the Israelites were terrified after spies came back from a reconnoiter of Canaan and reported that giants were in the land (Num 13–14). Rebelling against Moses and Aaron, the people made plans to return to Egypt, only to agree to an abortive attempt to invade Canaan from the south that led to their immediate defeat by the Amalekites and Canaanites (Num 14:45).

Condemned to wander around the desert for "forty years," they encountered various groups of people with whom they have armed conflict. Among these were the king of Arad, the Amorites, and the king of Bashan (Num 21). By the end of the book of Numbers, the Israelites were said to be massed in the Transjordan opposite Jericho. Following the death of Moses and under the leadership of Joshua, they invaded the land of Canaan (Josh 1–12), organizing their attack into three phases: (1) the central hill country, including Jericho and 'Ai (6–10); (2) a southern campaign, defeating Libnah, Eglon, Hebron and Debir (10:29-43); and (3) a northern assault that resulted in the destruction of Hazor (11:1-15). Thus we are told that within a space of five years (14:7, 10)

> Joshua defeated the whole land, the hill country and the Negev and the lowland and the slopes, and all their kings; he left no one remaining, but utterly destroyed all that breathed, as the LORD God of Israel commanded. (10:40)

The impression one gets from the above readings is that the "conquest" of Canaan by Israel was sudden, swift, and complete. Something is very wrong with this picture, however, not only from the point of view of archaeology, but even from within the Bible itself. Judges 1, for example, opens with the announcement of Joshua's death, with the Israelites having taken *none* of the Land of Canaan. Furthermore, what is described here is neither a unified effort by "all" Israel, nor is the land taken solely by military action. Rather, scattered military battles by individual tribes or groups of people are reported, and in at least one instance, the peaceful migration of one group is noted (v. 16). In fact, this version of the story ends with a long list of some twenty cities whose inhabitants the Israelites could not drive out and that were among the most important cities in the land, such as Megiddo (v. 27), Gezer (v. 29), and Jerusalem (v. 21).

To make matters worse, the literary discrepancies in the Bible are not just between the traditions in Numbers–Joshua and those in Judges 1. A careful reading of Numbers–Joshua also reveals tensions within the text that are hard to reconcile with one another. For example, after the sweeping claims of Joshua 10:40 and 11:16-20, we are told in 13:1ff. that Joshua "was old" and much land still remained "to be possessed." Then follows a long list of unconquered territories. Joshua 10:29-43 states that Joshua destroyed all of the cities of the hill country, including Hebron and Debir, but in 15:13-19, we are told that Hebron was destroyed by Caleb and Debir by Othniel.

Many other examples of the inconsistencies in these traditions could be cited, but enough has been said to enable a careful reader to realize that the stories of the taking of the land of Canaan by the Israelites are highly idealized and overly simplified. While a detailed discussion of the scholarly suggestions for dealing with these problems lies beyond the scope of this brief chapter, a summary of these attempts in their main outline follows.

Attempts at Historical Reconstruction of the "Conquest" of Israel

The biblical and archaeological data available for the interested student of this problem are extremely varied and complex. Thus, any attempt to evaluate these sources with the goal of reconstructing the actual process by which "Israel" came to occupy the land of Canaan involves a significant amount of subjective judgment, regardless of the final interpretation one embraces.

The Traditional Pan-Israelite Model

Some persons still basically interpret the Numbers–Joshua account as historically accurate. To do this, ways of harmonizing the apparent inconsistencies within the text have had to be created. For example, between verses 2 and 3 of Numbers 21, a long period of time may have occurred during which Joshua died and Israel conquered the Canaanites as described in Judges 1. Such harmonizing efforts present many problems, but I will mention only two.

First, in order for it to work, one is asked to accept as "historical" a scenario that is not mentioned in any biblical text. In other words, no biblical story states that Joshua died during the period between verses 2 and 3. Second, such efforts simply cannot explain the archaeological evidence now available. No amount of harmonizing can reconcile the biblical story with the data now known from excavations and surveys. This pre-critical way of looking at these traditions simply fails to appreciate either the literary critical work that has gone on in biblical studies for the past 100 years or the archaeological picture that is now emerging.

Albright's Military Model

One of the most influential theories developed to deal with this problem was put forth by W. F. Albright back in the 1920s and 1930s. A professor for many years at the Johns Hopkins University, Albright knew there were inconsistencies and other problems with these stories, but he believed that essentially they were historical. He used what was known archaeologically at the time to support his views, including the evidence, as it was then known, from such sites as Lachish (Josh 10:31-32), Bethel (Judg 1:22-26), and Tell Beit Mirsim, which Albright identified with Debir (Josh 10:38-39; this identity is disputed today). All of these sites were destroyed at the end of the Late Bronze Age or, in the case of Lachish, maybe at the beginning of Iron Age I. If, of course, Tell Beit Mirsim is not ancient Debir, then it is an unknown site that suffered destruction.

Albright's reconstruction has had wide-ranging influence, especially in America, because at first it seemed as if archeology could be used to support his claims. Today few archaeologists would do so. Albright dated his interpretation of the conquest to the end of the Late Bronze Age based precisely on the excavation results of such sites as those mentioned above. Unfortunately for his theory, the evidence from other sites such as Jericho and 'Ai cannot be made to fit his model. In fact, Albright's reasoning was very circular in the extreme. He used the biblical stories to interpret the archaeological evidence and then cited the archaeological evidence to support his interpretation of the biblical stories.

Of the sixteen sites in the Bible that are said to have been destroyed by the Israelites, only three—Lachish, Bethel, and Hazor—are known to have destruction levels dating to the end of the Late Bronze Age or the beginning of Iron Age I. On the other hand, at least a dozen other sites that are not mentioned in the Bible at all show evidence of having been destroyed at this time. Some of this destruction must be attributed to the Philistines. Other sites may have been destroyed by the Egyptians. Some of the destruction may have been due to natural causes. The point is, that while Albright and his students demonstrated that *some* of the available archaeological evidence from the end of the Late Bronze Age *could* be interpreted in terms of a thirteenth century B.C. Israelite invasion, none of the evidence requires such an interpretation.

Furthermore, even if the archeological evidence could be used to support the basic historicity of the stories in Joshua, such evidence could never validate the biblical writers' interpretation of this "history" as "acts of God." Regardless of the historical questions involved, archaeological results can never be used validly to support a preconceived theological agenda.

Alt's Migration Model

While Albright and his students were formulating the military conquest model in America, an entirely different approach to the problem was advocated in Germany by Albrecht Alt and his students, chief among whom was Martin Noth. These scholars were not archaeologists but skilled literary critics. Using the scholarly disciplines known as "form" and "traditio-historical" criticisms, they concluded that the stories of the conquest in Joshua were for the most part legends with little historical value. They said that "Israel" emerged in the land of Canaan through the peaceful infiltration of pastoral groups or nomads over a long period of time. One of the major strengths of this theory is its recognition that the Israelite settlement was a long, complicated, and multi-faceted process.

As attractive as this point of view is in some respects, however, it too has earned no few critics. One of the most common criticisms leveled against it is that the notion of "nomadism," which is central to its claims, has all but been disproven by more recent studies. For example, the sharp dichotomy thought to have existed between "nomad" and "farmer" in antiquity has been shown to have been overdrawn. Perhaps most telling are the studies that have concluded that full-blown nomadism, which depended in part on the development of the domestication of the camel and camel saddle, did not occur until *after* the emergence of early Israel. For these and other reasons, few scholars today would embrace this "nomad infiltration" model as proposed by Alt and his students.

The Internal Revolt Model of George Mendenhall

In 1962, George Mendenhall of the University of Michigan wrote an article entitled "The Hebrew Conquest of Palestine" in which he argued that the so-called conquest of Palestine by Israel was actually a "peasant's revolt against the network of interlocking Canaanite city-states."[1] According to Mendenhall, this revolt was triggered by a small group of slaves who had escaped from Egypt to Canaan bringing with them the worship of a deity named YHWH (LORD in English Bibles). This small religious group was then able to polarize the indigenous populations of Canaan, namely the peasants, who in the main joined forces with this group, and the city-state kings, who opposed them. In the end, the peasants won, and the kings and their supporters were either driven out of the land or killed.

This seminal essay has been followed up both by Mendenhall and others who rely heavily upon sociological paradigms to support their point of view. This way of assessing the emergence of Israel in Canaan has been found attractive to them because it avoids many of the problems created by the two models already discussed.

This reconstruction has also attracted its share of critics, including those who support the theory in some aspects. Many complex issues are involved that can only be summarized here. For example, some scholars think that Mendenhall put too much emphasis upon religious ideology as the explanatory factor resulting in Israel's emergence while not placing enough emphasis upon geographic factors as well as socio-political concerns such as the acquisition and use of power.

Others have rejected outright this model, arguing that the archaeological evidence will not support it. Again the questions and issues are very complex, but some of the main points may be described as follows.

(1) Some scholars have argued that the destruction of various Canaanite cities at the end of the Late Bronze Age and the appearance of new, architecturally impoverished villages, mostly in the central highlands of Canaan, fit better the model of intruders than that of an indigenous revolt.

(2) These critics argue that many Canaanite cities that are located in the coastal region were not destroyed at this time but should have been if there was this universal revolt of the masses.

(3) Some of the coastal cities that were destroyed were done so by other groups such as the Philistines. Thus at the end of the Late Bronze Age, different groups of people were present in Canaan who were causing the destructions recorded in the archaeological record, none of which needs to be assigned to a revolt of peasants.

(4) Some critics are quick to point out that the model of a peasant's revolt finds no support in the biblical traditions. They maintain that if an internal revolution was the process by which Israel came into existence, one would expect to find evidence of it in the biblical stories, particularly in the book of Judges.

All of these objections have been answered by those who advocate one form or another of Mendenhall's suggestions, albeit not to everyone's satisfaction. To be certain, the complexity of the data involved, both written and archaeological, makes absolute conclusions difficult if not impossible. The questions are many and complex. The following is a summary of where some of the lines of argument seem to be headed at the moment. As always, one should realize that these suggestions are tentative, incomplete, and open to revision as more evidence becomes available.

Towards an Emerging Consensus

The Nature of the Biblical Traditions. Except for the most conservative of biblical students who still refuse to accept as valid the modern critical study of the Bible, generally scholars accept that the "conquest" story in the book of Joshua is a late "official" version of Israel's beginnings. As such it represents a complex rewriting of older traditions no longer available in their original form. To compound matters even more, this "official" version was written to serve the theological agenda of its author(s). That is, the writers of the Bible wanted to show in dramatic fashion how the God of Israel had fulfilled all divine promises to the ancestors (Deut 30:20). In other words, the Bible does not present the history of Israel's origins but a highly idealized interpretation of Israel's origins.

The historical situation that necessitated such a biased version of things is believed to be the Exile (587–539 B.C.E.). During this period the Jewish people faced a dilemma of catastrophic proportions. Having lost land, home, and temple, they were faced with many perplexing questions about their destiny, their God, their identity, their very future. In this context, the story now contained in the book of Joshua offered hope. Because its central message seems to be that since "Israel" began its journey only by the grace of God, hope remained if Israel would obey God in covenant fidelity (Josh 24).

If, in fact, the present form of the book of Joshua was written hundreds of years after the settlement of Israel took place primarily for theological, not historical purposes, then the story as we have it is really a barrier to any attempt to try to penetrate behind it to the actual events underlying the formation of Israel. This is precisely why all attempts to reconstruct the history of early Israel from the Bible have failed. The written sources simply will not bear up under such historical scrutiny. Perhaps it is time to stop trying to use these late reworked traditions as though they were historical sources. As Callaway himself came to realize, we must give up our attempt to maintain what he termed the "essential historicity of the conquest traditions."[2]

All of this means that the Bible is not the primary source at our disposal for trying to reconstruct the early beginnings of Israel. This claim must go to archaeology, which alone can provide us with contemporary evidence from the time periods that concern us the most: the end of the Late Bronze Age and the beginning of Iron Age I.

Along this line of thought, we should remember that the word "history" does not occur in the Hebrew Bible. Many scholars now concede that the Bible is a "minority report" expressing the views of an ultra right-wing priestly party following the destruction of Judah and Jerusalem by the Babylonians in 587–586 B.C. As one archaeologist put it: "The biblical writers are not telling it the way it was, but the way it would have been had they been in charge."[3]

The Emerging Archaeological Picture. Since the 1970s, an enormous amount of archaological data that was not available to earlier archaeologists and biblical historians interested in the question of Israel's origins has been recovered from excavations and surveys in Israel. Some of the most important of this new information has originated in regional surveys. Not all archaeologists agree on the meaning of this new evidence, however. While there may be just one totally correct interpretation of what is found, we can never be absolutely sure that we have it. This uncertainty and disagreement drives research forward and moves us closer to the truth. Regardless of this caveat, any discussion today concerning the emergence of ancient Israel must take this evidence seriously.

Furthermore, archaeologically speaking, we have practically no evidence for the origins of Israelite religion, particularly the worship of the God YHWH. The Late Bronze Age/Iron Age I inhabitants of the central highlands of Canaan probably had religious beliefs and engaged in cultic practices, but at the moment there is little unambiguous archaeological evidence of the nature of such activity.

Within the past fifteen to twenty years, regional surveys have identified over 300 Iron Age I sites that were established in the central highlands of Canaan. These small, unwalled villages were either built on previously uninhabited sites or, like 'Ai, on sites that once had been inhabited but abandoned, in most cases for centuries. The evidence seems to indicate that at the beginning of this process, most of these villages were located between Jerusalem and the Jezreel Valley. In biblical terms this area comprises the tribal allotments of Ephraim and Manasseh. The sites located in this region represent 90 percent of all known Iron Age I villages in the central hill country.

Surprisingly, very few villages from this same period have been found in Judah in the south. The usual explanation given for this is geographical and ecological. Much of Judah is extremely rocky and covered with thick shrubs, making agricultural activity in antiquity very difficult. Judah did not become significantly populated until the time of the united monarchy (tenth century B.C.). This archaeological fact raises serious questions regarding the biblical traditions of the penetration into this area from the south (see Judg 1 and the above discussion).

If such activity did occur, it left little archaeological evidence. On the other hand, Judges 1 may be a post-exilic document written for purely propaganda purposes as has recently been suggested by one scholar. Should this be the case, then Judges 1 would be no more relevant to understanding Israel's origins than the book of Joshua. In any case, there is at present little archaeological evidence from Judah to help us in understanding the processes that resulted in "early Israel." While the archaeological evidence is always complex and incomplete, any discussion of the material remains must include at least the following.

Pillared Courtyard Houses. At a site called Khirbet Raddana, located about ten miles north of Jerusalem, Joseph Callaway discovered an Iron Age I village with well preserved examples of what are generally referred to as "pillared courtyard houses." The pillars in these houses are believed to have supported upper stories where the inhabitants lived and slept, while the ground floor may have served as a retaining area for animals. In the courtyard of this house, which was open to the sky, cooking pits were found. Additional housing remains were found around the main house, indicating an extended family arrangement. Remains of similar houses have been found in many excavated sites. They may represent what the Bible refers to as "the house of the father" (Judg 6:27; 9:1, 5, 18). Other such houses have been found at Shiloh, 'Ai, and 'Izbet Sartah as well as at other sites.

Rock-cut Cisterns. Associated with these houses are rock-cut, bell-shaped cisterns usually dug under the floors of the houses and in the courtyards. This technique allowed for the habitation of sites in the central hill country of Canaan located away from perennial water sources such as wells and springs. While the newcomers to this region during the Iron I period did not "invent" such cisterns (they have been found as early as the Middle Bronze Age), they did use them to their fullest advantage in this new environment.

Agricultural Terracing. Intensive terracing of the steep hillsides, which is essential to any type of farming activity, was also significant. Since the terraced walls were built of fieldstone, terracing also provided a practical way to clear the ground of rocks. This terracing process also helped to conserve water run-off from rainfall.

Ceramic Remains. One of the most important types of archaeological evidence is the ubiquitous pottery remains found on all sites in Israel. Not only do the pottery shapes, manufacturing techniques, and other factors indicate when the pottery was made, these characteristics can also suggest the ethnic identity of its manufacturers, lines of cultural contacts, and even migration and trade routes. The Philistine culture is an outstanding example where pottery remains clearly indicate ethnic associations.

While learning to "read pottery" is a long and difficult task, archaeologists have developed a sophisticated pottery typological profile for most of the archaeological periods since the first appearance of pottery during the Neolithic Period.

The question here concerns what the pottery found at these Iron I central hill country sites tells us about the origin and identity of the peoples who settled there. After studying this pottery carefully and comparing it with the preceding Late Bronze Age Canaanite pottery forms, William Dever, of the University of Arizona and one of the leading archaeologists of our time, drew the following conclusion:

> The common early Israelite pottery turns out to be nearly identical to that of the late thirteenth century B.C.E.; it comes right out of the Late Bronze Age urban Canaanite repertoire.[4]

Conclusions

When all of the above archaeological evidence is taken into account, the most unbiased assessment seems to be that the people who settled in the central highlands of Canaan during Iron Age I came not from the desert as the biblical version claims, but from the Canaanite culture of the coastal plains. In other words, the early "Israelites" who built and inhabited these small villages were displaced Canaanites. Callaway himself had moved to this position before his untimely death.[5]

Many difficult questions still remain, particularly regarding the origin of the worship of the God, YHWH; the relationship of the term "Hebrew" to "Israelite"; and what role, if any, a group of slaves coming out of Egypt might have had to do with any of this. Yet, the older models for reconstructing Israel's origins are now considered to be erroneous or in need of serious modification. (The sociological model advocated by Gottwald and others many prove to be the most promising.)

That the Bible seems to know little of the view now advanced by scholars need not surprise us nor upset us. How much the biblical writers actually knew of Israel's historical origins is questionable and in the end really irrelevant. From their perspective, Israel only existed because of God's grace and guidance. In the end, Israel was God's "miracle." No amount of archaeological discoveries can prove or disprove such a belief. In this regard, like ancient Israel we too must live by faith and not by sight.

Endnotes

[1]"The Hebrew Conquest of Palestine," in *The Biblical Archaeologist Reader 3*, ed. E. F. Campell, Jr., and D. N. Freedman (Garden City NY: Anchor Books, Doubleday & Co., 1970) 107.

[2]" 'Ai (Et-Tell): Problem Site For Biblical Archaeologists," in *Archaeology and Biblical Interpretation,* ed. L. G. Perdue, L. E. Toombs, and G. Lance (Atlanta: John Knox Press, 1987) 92.

[3]Herschel Shanks, William Dever, et al., *The Rise of Ancient Israel* (Washington DC: Biblical Archaeology Society, 1992) 28.

[4]Ibid., 40.

[5]" 'Ai (Et-Tell)", 87-99.

For Further Reading

Callaway, Joseph A. "A New Perspective on the Hill Country Settlement of Canaan in Iron Age I." J. N. Tubb, ed. *Palestine in the Bronze and Iron Ages, Papers in Honour of Olga Tufnell.* London: Institute of Archaeology, 1985.

Dever, William. *Recent Archaeological Discoveries and Biblical Research.* Seattle: University of Washington Press, 1990.

Finkelstein, Israel. *The Archaeology of the Israelite Settlement.* Jerusalem: Israel Exploration Society, 1988.

Gottwald, N. *The Tribes of Yahweh.* Maryknoll NY: Orbis Books, 1979.

Chapter 7

The Rise of David's Kingdom

1 Samuel 4:1– 2 Samuel 9:13

1100	Midianite oppression ended by Gideon
1075	Philistine oppression of Israel
1050	Fall of Shiloh to the Philistines (1050–1050 B.C.)
	Samuel, the leader of Israel (1050–1000 B.C.)
1025	Saul, king over Israel (1020–1000 B.C.)
	Wars with the Philistines
1000	David, king over Israel (1000–961 B.C.)
975	Revolt led by Absalom
	Accession of Solomon (961 B.C.)
950	The kingdom secured under Solomon

David is the central figure in Israel around which we must see the Philistines, Samuel, Saul, and Jerusalem in perspective. The Philistines, a collective name for refugee tribes of sea peoples who migrated from the Aegean Sea area, occupied the fertile coastal regions about the same time Israel entered Canaan from the east. By the time of Samuel, they had penetrated the hill country, destroyed the sanctuary at Shiloh, and cornered Israel in small, inaccessible pockets of the hill country. Samuel began the war of liberation from Philistine oppression and anointed Saul to carry on the struggle. David, the son of Jesse, actually broke the Philistine yoke and secured Jerusalem.

The Philistine Threat
1 Samuel 4:1–7:14; 13:2–14:52; 17:1–18:30

Azekah sits high on a hill beside the valley of Elah, looking west over the foothills of Judah but guarding the strategic valley that is nature's highway into the mountains leading to Bethlehem. It has witnessed

historic battles from the "gate" to the mountains of Judah. The most
famous battle took place on an unnamed day in the last quarter of the
eleventh century B.C.

A Philistine army that probably numbered fewer than a hundred men
camped on one side of the rather broad valley, and Saul's soldiers sat on
the other side. They sat facing each other for some time, apparently preferring to negotiate in the traditional Near Eastern way before they
crossed swords. The negotiation, of course, was an exchange of threats,
taunts, and bluster. The strategy was to break the will of the opposing
side and throw the enemy into a panic. People whose minds operate in
this fashion panic easily when they are confronted with a situation they
do not understand.

Saul's band of warriors was intimidated; the Philistines had rolled out
their secret weapon, a human tank called Goliath. Clad in armor of
bronze from head to toe like an Aegean warrior and accompanied by an
assistant who carried his shield, he was a fearsome sight to Saul's provincial mountaineers. When the rays of the morning sun picked up the gleam
of polished bronze from a crested helmet to greaves that protected the
shins, Goliath must have looked nine feet tall! With him standing out
front and threatening Israel, the Philistine warrior band looked larger too.
So he stood and threatened with challenge and invective: "Today I defy
the ranks of Israel! Give me a man, that we may fight together" (17:10).
When Saul heard these words, he was dismayed and afraid. The war of
words was getting to him. It was high noon in the valley of Elah.

Enter David. When Saul's band has been polled and no man will face
Goliath, the real champion appears. At first he is only a rumor. Someone
says he will face the Philistine if the price is right. "What shall be done
for the man who kills this Philistine?" the rumor went (17:26). The rumor
comes to Saul, and the price is confirmed. A bounty will be paid, the
king's daughter will be given in marriage, and the clan will be exempt
from taxes (17:25). Then the man who leaked the rumor appears. He is
a shepherd, lightly clothed, young, and deceptively small-looking in the
presence of bearded men. But he is bold and confident, and he has a plan.
The plan is not to fight the Philistine in Saul's armor (17:38-39), but with
the weapon he has used from his boyhood up to protect his flock. He will
fight with the mountaineer's sling.

The confrontation is dramatic and legendary. There is the seasoned
Philistine, bronze-coated in his armor, a heavy javelin with throw-string

at his side, a formidable shield in front, a proud crested plume bobbing over the shield. Incredulous and scornful he faces the deceptively brash youth who moves easily over the rocky ground and appears to be unarmed except for his staff. "Am I a dog, that you come to me with sticks?" the Philistine shouts (17:43). Then he goes into a predictable ritual of pronouncing curses on David and all Israel. The curses have to be pronounced before the duel begins. (How far along he got in cursing Israel, we do not know.)

David never stops moving. When possibly twenty paces separate the two, he draws out of his shepherd's pouch a rounded stone the size of an egg. Goliath is busy with his ritual of cursing. In one fluid movement, the stone is placed in the leather pocket of a sling, which is held straight out in front of the body with the left hand, while the right hand tightens the attached leather thongs in a move straight backward. The pocket holding the stone is pulled backward in an upward arc, and the right hand comes down and forward in one powerful underhand movement. It is a move similar to pitching a softball with one move of the arm, and as fast. The missile of flintstone swings down and forward with the gathering speed of a golf club head. Ankle high above the ground, the missile is released, speeding upward as though shot out of the rocky ground. At twenty paces, the human reflex cannot react in time to dodge the missile. Right out of the ground it speeds and over the shield to its mark. The entire move of hurling the round stone into the face of Goliath takes one second of time. He has time to curse David's family possibly back to Jesse, his father.

David's victory over the Philistine is legendary, as it was in biblical times. The confrontation is dramatically staged in the story, in a highly entertaining pattern that is known at least from 1900 B.C. Sinuhe, an Egyptian refugee in southern Palestine about 1900 B.C., fights a great duel with a boastful champion of the Retenu to decide the outcome of a war. As Sinuhe confronts the dread champion of Retenu, the whole camp groans for him. He artfully dodges the arrows and javelins of the enemy until he has a chance to shoot his own bow. His arrow finds its mark in the neck of the enemy, who cries out and falls "on his nose." Sinuhe, like David, then slays the enemy with the victim's own weapon and raises a shout of triumph over the body. "What he had planned to do to me, I did to him," he says, in the age-old golden rule of the warrior.

The tradition of David's victory over the Philistine is persistent, regardless of its legendary embellishments, and we may assume that the battle associated with the duel marked the beginning of the end of Philistine penetration of central Canaan. It signaled also the emergence of David as a rival of Saul. We may ask, who were the Philistines, and how did they reach the point of threatening the very existence of Israel?

Egyptian records list sea people called the Luka and Shardina among the mercenaries of Rameses II at Kadesh in 1286 B.C. They were among a variety of peoples that migrated from the Aegean world to the Levant in the thirteenth century B.C. The chaos that followed in the Aegean area is evident in the disparate refugee groups that seem to have appeared like debris washed up by the sea all around the eastern Mediterranean coast.

Merneptah names other tribes of sea people: 'Aqiwasha, Turushu, and Shakarushu whom he fought in Canaan around 1220 B.C. Rameses III lists other tribes in the twelfth century B.C. who were driven back in an attempt to invade Egypt itself. Among the tribes he mentions are the Pelasata, the biblical Philistines. This name seems to encompass in the Bible all of the various tribes from different points of origin who threatened to take over the hill country during the latter part of the period of the Judges.

The entry of the sea peoples, or Philistines, into Canaan therefore is almost counterpart to the Israelite entry from the east. Pictures on Egyptian monuments show families traveling in two-wheel carts drawn by oxen. The men are clean-shaven, fair-skinned, and usually wearing a little cap with feathers standing up around the sides, shaped like a G.I. cap. One panel at Medinet Habu shows a naval battle between the Philistines and Egyptians, the first representation known of a naval engagement. The various tribes came by ship and over land, fleeing the chaos of the Aegean sea area and pioneering a new life around the sea coast from north Syria to Egypt. Their migration around the coast of Asia Minor broke the power of the Hittites, and the sea people picked up the secrets of iron metallurgy, which they managed to monopolize for a century (see 13:19-23).

Driven back from the Egyptian delta by Rameses III, the sea people established settlements at Gaza, Ashkelon, and Ashdod on the coast and at Gath and Ekron farther inland at the edge of the Judean foothills. The fertile coastal plain became the stronghold of this "pentapolis" of cities and a base for penetration into the hill country of Judah. Farther north, other tribes of sea people settled at Dor in the narrow coastal plain between Mount Carmel and Joppa. This area also was fertile, and the people of Dor seem to have engaged in sea trade. The Esdraelon plain also became a Philistine base, with evidence of their occupation reaching to Beth-shan. Plans of temples found at Beth-shan reflect the kind of structure described in Judges 16:23-30. The Beth-shan structures are as large as any that have been found in Palestine.

By 1050 B.C., the sea peoples, known collectively as the Philistines, had squeezed Israel into little pockets in the hill country or made certain areas subject to them. Along the western hills of Judah, the Philistines held all of the coastal plain and lower foothills inland to the edge of the mountains. The Esdraelon plain was theirs to the Jordan River, and the Jordan valley seems to have been penetrated southward from Beth-shan to the mouth of the Wadi Far'ah. Shechem, bordered on the north by Philistine cities, was cut off from the land of Benjamin by the campaign that defeated Israel at Aphek (1 Sam 4:1-22). Shiloh apparently was sacked also, because Jeremiah refers to the destruction of the sanctuary (Jer 7:12-15). A base also was gained at Michmash, and an army was poised to take the valley of Elah to Bethlehem when David entered the war by slaying the champion, Goliath.

Israel had entered the hill country from the east at about the same time the Philistines entered the coastal areas from the north. Israel settled in the hills, a relatively poor area, while the Philistines occupied the entire coastal plain and all of the fertile valleys that led inland. Israel was united in a loose federation of tribes that had no centralized control nor national army. On the other hand, the Philistines had a strong city-state system and well-organized armies. Consequently, in time the hill country would fall under Philistine control unless Israel took measures to meet the threat. This threat was understood by Samuel, a prophet from Ramah in the land of Benjamin, and he led Israel into a new way of life in meeting Philistine aggression.

Samuel and Saul
1 Samuel 1:1–3:21; 7:15–12:25; 15:1–16:23

Shiloh stood on a high hill in the midst of a fertile valley in Ephraim about twenty miles north of Jerusalem. It was "on the east of the highway that goes up from Bethel to Shechem, and south of Lebonah" (Judg

21:19). The ancient mountain road followed the watershed ridge north-south, running south of Bethel by Jerusalem to Bethlehem, Hebron, and Beersheba. Shiloh was the only city of consequence between Bethel and Shechem. It was excavated by a Danish expedition between 1926 and 1932 that discovered the site was settled anew on the abandoned ruins of an older city about the time the Israelites entered Canaan. A destruction about 1050 B.C. terminated this settlement, and it is attributed to the Philistine war related in 1 Samuel 4:1-22.

Shiloh was the recognized religious center of Israel during the period of the Judges and represents the old order of Israel when the federation of tribes was structured loosely around the stackpole of the covenant. Therefore, the destruction of Shiloh and the capture of the Ark struck at the heart of the confederacy, and occupation of the region by Philistines essentially terminated the old order.

Samuel and Saul belong to the interim between the old order of the confederacy symbolized by Shiloh and a new order represented by the kingdom of David. Samuel was the last of the Judges, attached in his heart to the way of life of the confederacy, but reaching out with his reason for a new political system. Strong, impulsive, and slightly paranoid, Saul was caught up in the conflict of reaching for a new system and became a victim of the circumstances of his age. In a more settled time he could have been a success; but caught in the cross-currents of transition between the strong personalities of Samuel and David, his life was a tragedy.

Apparently Samuel was brought up at the sanctuary at Shiloh as a protégé of Eli (1:1-3:21). As an apprentice to the old priest, he learned the traditions of Israel and the covenant-law that were the responsibility of the priestly family. When the family of Eli failed in measuring up to the standards set by the young novice, he came to be recognized as the leader at Shiloh. If the city had not fallen to the Philistines, presumably he would have continued the tradition of service to the house of Eli. His career at Shiloh was aborted, however, when the city was destroyed and its region placed under the military government of the Philistines.

When we find Samuel after the disaster at Shiloh, he is back at his ancestral home at Ramah (7:17) and engaged in an itinerant ministry that takes him on a circuit to Bethel, Gilgal, and Mizpah (v. 16). He has grown old, his life apparently having been spent in a faithful ministry to hold the tribes together in their covenant with Yahweh their God. He seems to have organized a school of prophets in his effort to keep the old traditions alive (10:5-13), because we have not seen them before.

These prophets were actually ecstatics who went into frenzies with the aid of monotonous, repetitive, trance-inducing music from "the harp, tambourine, flute, and lyre" (v. 5). When the prophets went into a trance, people thought that the spirit of the Lord possessed them and that they were "turned into a different person" (v. 6). Whatever one said while he/she was in the ecstatic trance was thought to be from the Lord, because the trance bypassed the rational faculties of reason with a hot-line to heaven.

The ecstatic element was always present in Old Testament religion, but it was not the uncontrollable, primitive type that we encounter here. Nevertheless, this is the beginning of prophetism in Israel, and the classical prophets always bear the mark of their heritage among the ecstatics. The idea of a hot-line that bypassed rational processes gave way to an inspiration that heightened the rational faculties in prophetism.

Possibly in Samuel's band of ecstatics we have an essentially protest phenomenon. Ways of protesting new developments and old clichés are especially prominent in ages of transition. Ecclesiastics in our generation protest excessive institutionalism of the church, I think, by reverting to ecstaticism, which bypasses institutions and education. Possibly the ecstatics of Samuel were also basically a protest phenomenon in an age of radical transition.

Saul makes his appearance in the midst of a serious military threat by the Philistines and the probing for a new order evident in the ecstatic phenomenon. The people were asking for a leader, a king (8:6), and Samuel had the responsibility of finding one.

Two factions in Israel seem to be evident in the narratives concerning the election of a king. One faction appears to be hostile to the idea of setting up a monarchy (8:1-22; 10:17-27; 12:1-25). In these passages, Samuel is pictured as opposed to the idea of a monarchy himself, but yielding under pressure of popular demand. Another faction seems evident in 9:1–10:16 where Samuel is favorable to the establishment of a monarchy and anoints Saul in private before he presents him to the people in a public investiture.

Saul does not come off well in either account. In the first, he is a replacement for the sons of Samuel, who are rejected by the people in a meeting that displeased Samuel (8:4-6). His selection is by lot at Mizpah

(10:17-27), and when he is selected, behold he has to be dragged out of hiding for presentation to the people (10:20-24). He appears as a bashful country bumpkin who is pushed onto the stage of prominence by accident.

The second account also pictures Saul as an unwitting party to an election that began in a secret anointing by Samuel (10:1). The prophetic appointment of Saul ends a strange search for some asses that have strayed. He begins the trip looking for his father's animals and concludes it as the anointed king of Israel! A hint of some behind-the-scene politics is suggested by the inquiry of Saul's uncle when Saul returns home: "Tell me what Samuel said to you" (10:15). The uncle seems to intrude mysteriously into the narrative.

Saul became a charismatic leader of Israel in the war against the Ammonites (11:1-15), following the ancient tradition of the Judges. He proved to be a successful warrior in subsequent battles with the Philistines that renewed hope in Israel and pulled the people together in supporting him. The most significant victory apparently occurred near Michmash where a raid on a Philistine garrison (13:2-4) precipitated a decisive battle.

Jonathan seems to have led a daring commando raid on the Philistine camp at the pass of Michmash (14:4-5) that threw the army into a panic (v. 15). The rout of the enemy was apparently unexpected even by Israel, but Saul seized the initiative (vv. 16ff.) and drove the Philistines out of the land of Benjamin. Hebrews who had gone over to the Philistines deserted them and rallied around Saul (v. 21), making the victory complete and securing the region for Israel.

With hope renewed and a spirit of nationalism kindled, Saul reportedly spent the years of his reign fighting the Philistines (14:52). Sometime during this period, he had reason to turn on the Gibeonites in an action that is referred to later in 2 Samuel 21f. but not reported. The Gibeonites, we recall, made a treaty with Joshua, probably breaking one with the Amorites, which in turn led to the war with the Amorites (Josh 1). In fact, they are called Amorites in 2 Samuel 21:2, reflecting the old alliance; whereas in Joshua 9:7, they are referred to as Hivites. In any case, the Gibeonites probably played politics when Israel's fortunes ebbed during the Philistine aggression, and Saul punished them harshly after the battle of Michmash returned Israel to a position of strength.

The tragic decline of Saul began with his break with Samuel. Seemingly he made no effort to establish a kingdom in the traditional sense, with a capital and bureaucracy that would have centralized power. In fact, he appeared as a widely recognized leader in the tradition of the charismatic Judges. His fortress-palace at Gibeah, excavated by W. F. Albright, reflects a very simple and austere way of life. Nevertheless, he did not fulfill the expectations of Samuel. We do not know whether Samuel was actually for the election of Saul or against it. He is reported to have taken both positions. The reason, moreover, given for the rejection of Saul by Samuel in 1 Samuel 13:8-15 borders on pettiness.

Samuel told Saul he would come to Gilgal in seven days to offer sacrifices, but he delayed his coming, implicitly to test Saul. Meanwhile, Saul was losing his army of volunteers (13:8) in the face of a massive Philistine threat, so he proceeded to offer sacrifices himself to hold the people together. Samuel immediately appeared, as though he had been hiding until Saul began the priestly function, and proceeded to upbraid Saul in a public display of temper that did him little credit. Samuel, I think, exhibited petty vindictiveness that was unworthy of his office. He seemed to fear that Saul was grasping for control of the priesthood, but the account actually is sympathetic with Saul.

In any case, the break with Samuel brought out Saul's personal weaknesses. He became subject to spells of depression called "the evil spirit from God" (16:23). He sought refuge in the music that had once led him into ecstatic trances under the power of the spirit of God (10:10). The demise of Samuel and the rise of David were attended by the sad spectacle of Saul's disintegration, which caused him to strike out blindly at David and destroy the place in history that he undoubtedly deserved.

Saul and David
1 Samuel 19:1–2 Samuel 4:12

There is some ambiguity about David's victory over Goliath. 2 Samuel 21:19 reports "Elhanan, the Bethlehemite, killed Goliath the Gittite, the shaft of whose spear was like a weaver's beam." The tradition in 1 Chronicles 20:5, perhaps in an effort to harmonize 1 Samuel 17 and 2 Samuel 21:19, states that "Elhanan son of Jair killed Lahmi the brother of Goliath the Gittite, the shaft of whose spear was like a weaver's beam." One interpretation is that Elhanan and David were the same person, with

David being his throne name. In any case, we cannot deny that David made an overwhelming impression on the nation in some spectacular feat that suddenly made him a candidate for the kingship.

From the beginning David seemed to have had ambitions for Saul's position. He became the fast friend of Saul's son Jonathan (1 Sam 18:1) and married Michal, the daughter of Saul (18:27). Acclaimed a hero, he led further small expeditions against the Philistines (18:30) that increased his reputation. Saul was driven to insanity by the reports of David's exploits and tried to kill him. Perhaps the event that alienated David and closed the door to reconciliation was Saul's massacre of the priestly family at Nob (21:1-9; 22:9-19).

The family of Ahitub was the surviving remnant of the family of Eli, priest at Shiloh (1 Sam 14:3). When Shiloh fell to the Philistines, the priestly family moved to Nob in Benjamin when Samuel moved to Ramah. A report by Doeg, the Edomite, that David had received assistance from the priests at Nob in his flight from Saul (22:9-10) convinced Saul that they were a party to a conspiracy against him (22:13). He ordered the execution of the priests on the spot, but his guards refused to "raise their hand to attack the priests of the Lord" (22:17), whereupon Doeg, the Edomite, fell upon the priests and slew them. The survivor of the massacre, Abiathar, fled to David (22:20) and threw all of the influence of the legitimate priesthood of Israel behind David.

David's civil war with Saul made David an outlaw in southern Judah, where he became the leader of a band composed of kinsmen and political refugees from Israel. His skill as an astute politician and ruthless military leader was evident in numerous skirmishes with Saul (1 Sam 23:19–24:22; 26:1-25) that were turned to political propaganda and the exaction of "protection" tribute from well-to-do citizens such as Nabal (25:2-22). A formidable guerrilla band was organized, and David married Abigail, the widow of Nabal (25:42), and Ahinoam of Jezreel, apparently to secure the support of strong families in the north. This chapter of his life steadily became blacker as he despaired of prevailing against Saul (27:1), probably because his activities turned the populace against him. His final decision was to become a vassal of Achish, the king of Gath (27:2-4).

The strategy was to play both sides against the middle until Saul died. Pretending to be loyal to Achish, David claimed that he made raids against southern Judah (1 Sam 27:10), when actually his raids were directed against the Bedouin tribes of the desert. He became stronger among the peoples of the Negev, while biding his time as the "trusted" friend of the Philistine king (27:12). The end came for Saul in renewed war with the Philistines in the North. David's defection weakened Israel and strengthened the Philistines, creating the situation that would cause the death of Saul and Jonathan and open the way for him to become king of Israel. Saul died at Mount Gilboa when his army was caught by the Philistines on the plain and cut to pieces in a poor execution of strategy (31:1-5). David, who could have turned the tide for Saul possibly, sat out the battle as an ally of the Philistines, although his participation was rejected by them because his loyalty was suspected (29:3-11).

In the tragedy that befell Saul and Jonathan, David appeared as a ruthless politician in his rise to power in Israel. When a messenger from Israel came to him with tidings of Saul's death, the messenger reported that he slew Saul, currying favor with David (2 Sam 1:9-10). Feigning sorrow at the death of Saul, for which David could be made indirectly responsible in his treacherous alliance with the Philistines, he put on a show of mourning and slew the messenger for taking the life of "the Lord's anointed" (vv. 14-16). Then he sent messengers to the men of Jabesh-gilead and complimented them for their "loyalty to Saul" in giving him a decent burial (2:5). These acts were intended to make political propaganda for David in Saul's kingdom and create an image of David that was compatible with the young man of legend who slew Goliath instead of the man who was an outlaw and an ally of the Philistines.

Meanwhile, David became king of Judah at Hebron, apparently as a vassal of the Philistines who controlled the area that Saul had ruled in the North. Ishbosheth, or Eshbaal, the heir of Saul, was a refugee along with Abner, Saul's general, in Transjordan (2 Sam 2:8-10). This was a convenient arrangement for the Philistines and the people of Judah who supported David. His kingdom was based at Hebron and probably claimed the loyalty of the tribes living south of Benjamin and Jerusalem into the Negev south of Arad to Beersheba. David thus became a rival king to Eshbaal, and "Israel" and "Judah" began to assume identities that would influence them throughout the period of the monarchy.

A minor incident that had serious consequences occurred at Gibeon. Abner, the *de facto* ruler of Israel, met Joab, David's commander, at the pool of Gibeon on the border between Israel and Judah. A battle ensued. Abner's band was put to flight, but he succeeded in slaying Asahel, a brother of Joab (2 Sam 2:12-23). This initiated a blood feud between Joab and Abner and civil war between Israel and Judah. When Abner quarreled with Eshbaal (3:6-11), Abner determined to switch his allegiance to David (vv. 12-13), whereupon David requested the return of Michal, Saul's daughter who had been taken from David and given to Palti, the son of Laish (I Sam 25:44) after the break with Saul. Michal reestablished David's ties with the dynasty of Saul; he already had the support of Abiathar, the surviving member of the priesthood at Shiloh.

Joab found his chance to avenge the death of his brother, Asahel, when Abner came to Hebron to turn over Israel to David. A feast was prepared for Abner, the transaction was completed (2 Sam 3:17-21), and Abner was sent on his way. Word was brought to Joab that Abner had been in town, whereupon he sent messengers to fetch him back to Hebron. When Joab greeted Abner, probably with the traditional embrace, he slipped his dagger with his left hand into the belly of Abner and avenged the death of Asahel (v. 27). David disavowed any complicity in the murder of Abner and pronounced a curse upon Joab (vv. 28-29), but did nothing. His public lamentation for Abner was accepted by the elders of Israel.

The final event that brought Israel over to David was the assassination of Eshbaal by two officers who thought David would reward them for eliminating the heir of Saul. As proof of their deed, they brought the head of Eshbaal to Hebron (2 Sam 4:8) and proclaimed their allegiance to the king. David reminded them he had put to death the messenger who brought the news of Saul's death and that they were more wicked than he (v. 10). Anxious to clear himself of a conspiracy to eliminate the house of Saul, David had the two officers executed, humiliated by cutting off their hands and feet and hanging them in public display in Hebron (v. 12). His public show of remorse at the death of Saul's heir apparently was believed, because Israel petitioned him straightway to become king over the northern tribes (5:1ff.).

David
2 Samuel 5:1–9:13

Two obstacles lay before David at Hebron when the northern tribes asked him to become their king. First and foremost was the Philistine threat. Israel north of Jerusalem was occupied by the Philistines or in vassalage. David's own little kingdom was probably in vassalage also, and he was the ally of the Philistines. To build a kingdom, he had to turn against his masters and at the same time inspire Israel to fight a war of liberation. The battle that turned the tide for him occurred near Jerusalem in the valley of Rephidim (5:17-25).

The Philistine strategy was to cut off Judah from the north at Jerusalem and close off the route along which recruits and supplies could be sent to Hebron. How David won the battle is not clear. Probably the Philistines camped out as they did in the valley of Elah (1 Sam 17) and prepared for battle rather formally and predictably. The capture of idols referred to in 2 Samuel 5:21 suggests unhurried preparation by the Philistines that included due homage to the gods to insure success. On the other hand, David must have used guerrilla methods, striking suddenly and unexpectedly, reflected in the breaking through of his forces "like a bursting flood" (2 Sam 5:20). Anyway, the enemy was routed from the hill country, and likely a series of aggressive raids followed up the victory and secured the hill country (2 Sam 8). 1 Chronicles 18:1 indicates that David took Gath. The Cherethites and Pelethites (2 Sam 8:18) of his mercenary army probably were professional soldiers hired among the Philistines.

Establishment of a capital around which the North and South could be united was the second problem. Jerusalem, city of the Jebusites, was chosen by David because it lay at the southern border of Benjamin and therefore was a neutral location. The Jebusites had apparently lived in peace among the tribes of Israel and Judah. Actually, Jerusalem was not worth taking until David decided to locate the capital there. Excavations show that the city, actually a village, covered not more than eight acres on a steep-sided ridge that had about four acres on its fairly level top. Houses were set into the forty-degree slope on the east side almost down to the Gihon spring, which flowed out at the base of the hill. A stone city wall was set into the side of the hill above the spring.

To insure a water supply in time of siege, the Jebusites excavated a tunnel into the stone of the hillside from an opening inside the fortification. The tunnel, called Warren's Shaft after its discoverer, connected with the spring underground, deep under the city wall. David's strategy for capturing Jerusalem, which was too difficult to take by storming the city wall on the forty-degree slope, involved entry through the watershaft. He had a plan, therefore, when he faced the taunting Jebusites who said

"You will not come in here, even the blind and the lame will turn you back" (2 Sam 5:6).

The plan was already laid. David said, "Whoever would strike down the Jebusites, let him get up the watershaft to attack the lame and the blind" (v. 8). We are told in 1 Chronicles 11:6 that "Joab son of Zeruiah went up first" and was rewarded by being appointed commander of the national army. The watershaft actually was difficult to climb in some places because people drew water from the spring as though it were a well. Certainly a large band of soldiers could not have entered the city secretly. It is not unlikely that David had some friends inside Jerusalem who assisted Joab in gaining entrance; one strong man with a club could have guarded the entrance to the shaft.

After Jerusalem was captured, many of the inhabitants no doubt simply pledged allegiance to David. Nothing is said about destruction of the city or deportation of the inhabitants. In fact, David took Jerusalem with his personal bodyguard, not with an army raised from the tribes; and Jerusalem became *his* city, not the property of either the North or the South. Jebusites who remained, among whom is mentioned Araunah (2 Sam 24:18-25) who sold the temple site to David, would have added to the neutrality of the capital.

To consolidate the tribes into a nation, David made Jerusalem the religious center to which all Israel would come on feast days. His first act was to bring the Ark of the Covenant that had been parked at Kiriath-jearim, a Hivite city, for a generation. The Ark was the most holy object from the ruined sanctuary at Shiloh, and its transfer to Jerusalem linked the kingdom with the old confederacy of the Judges. Abiathar, the only survivor of the priestly family of Eli that was massacred by Saul at Nob, was made the high priest alongside Zadok, whose origin is unknown, unless he was a member of a Jebusite priestly family as one scholar has suggested.

David's rescue of the Ark of the Covenant was a shrewd political move. Its presence in Jerusalem with Abiathar as high priest symbolized the prominent place given to the people of Ephraim and Benjamin in the new kingdom, although the presence of Zadok suggests that David maintained checks on the influence of Abiathar and his northern supporters. The way was prepared for building the nation around Jerusalem as its capital city and the religion of Israel around the temple, which was built by Solomon.

The first order of the day was to make Jerusalem the capital. Repairs of the eight-acre Jebusite city were undertaken at once. The walls were repaired "all around from the Millo in complete circuit" (1 Chron 11:8), and the Millo, or "filling," itself was probably strengthened. No definite location of the Millo can be claimed, but the best candidate seems to be a deep fill of terraced stones at the crest of the hill above Gihon spring. The fill is some forty feet deep, strongly terraced and bound by lateral walls of stone. Its purpose seems to be to fill in a bay in bedrock and widen the narrow top of the ridge above the steep incline of the east slope. A public building, possibly the palace of David (2 Sam 5:11), was constructed on the terrace. Jerusalem was David's eight-acre city.

In the perspective of Israel's history, the interval of time between that morning when David slew the Philistine in the valley of Elah and the day he moved into the new Phoenician-built palace at Jerusalem was short. Like the one second of time that it took to topple Goliath, however, this short period of David's rise to power was historic. It was a formative period for a new age, and the new age was shaped by the person of David. We may look a second time at some of the political maneuvers of David, but to his people, the age that he shaped far outweighed the way that he shaped it. Consequently, he stands high at this moment on the rebuilt Millo at Jerusalem, above the shadows below that obscure the paths he took in getting there, silhouetted against the dawn of a new day that was full of promise. This promise is articulated in the covenant of 2 Samuel 7:16, "Your house and your kingdom shall be made sure forever before me; your throne shall be established forever."

Chapter 8

The Fall of David's Kingdom

2 Samuel 10:1–1 Kings 14:31

United Monarchy		
1000	David, king over Israel (1000–961 B.C.)	
	Wars with Philistines and other nations	
975	Revolt led by Absalom	
	Accession of Solomon (961 B.C.)	
950	The kingdom secured under Solomon	
	Visit of the Queen of Sheba	
925	Exiled rebels await Solomon's death	
	Death of Solomon (922 B.C.)	
	Judah	**Israel**
	Rehoboam (922–915)	Jereboam I (922–901)
	Invasion by Shishak I	
	of Egypt (918)	
915	Abijah (915–913)	
	Asa (913–873)	
900		Nadab (901–900)

The scandalous affair of David and Bathsheba was an ominous sign of failure that began to show up everywhere in David's kingdom. David failed as a person when he succumbed to the allure of Bathsheba. He failed as a father and king when Absalom, his son, found cause to lead a revolt to overthrow the government. His kingdom failed when Sheba managed to recruit enough rebels among the northern tribes to stage a secessionist movement. Finally, the kingdom was shaken to its roots in the conflict between Adonijah and Solomon for the throne.

David's Kingdom
2 Samuel 10:1–24:25

Jerusalem is beautiful in the spring of the year. Bathed in fresh mountain air breathed in from the sea, and decorated with spontaneous spring flowers that search out every niche in the rocks of its slopes, the city basks in the sun and warms to new life. A haze settles over the hills each afternoon, sometimes barely covering the landscape with a delicate veil of beauty, sometimes clothing it in the soft mystery of semi-visibility that stretches into nothingness on the horizon. On one such afternoon, David awoke from his siesta and walked upon the roof of his house to enjoy the view (11:1-2). Below him, the houses of his subjects stuck into the steep hillside like steps on a stairway. He could see every roof down the slope to the city wall, as though he had a box-seat in a theater. On one of the roofs was Bathsheba, the wife of Uriah, the Hittite. It was probably no accident that she happened to be there just when the king took a stroll on the roof of his house.

The king's indiscreet affair with Bathsheba (11:3-25) strikes a jarring note in the story of his success. Without this blemish on his record, the expansion of the little kingdom into a formidable Near Eastern power would appear nothing less than phenomenal. As it is, the conquest of Transjordan, Syria, and the Negev to the Gulf of Aqaba gets only passing notice in 2 Samuel 10, while the details of the Bathsheba affair get extensive coverage in chapters 11 and 12. The reason is that David's abuse of his power as king in causing the death of Uriah, something that would not be noticed in any other oriental kingdom, is viewed as the cause of troubles that immediately beset the royal family.

Having reached the pinnacle of success, the king cannot enjoy the years that lie before him because of the constant intrigue, palace revolutions, and downright wrong-doing among the members of his family and court. Consequently, we take leave of what should have been the golden years of his reign and embark upon the sad story of struggle for the throne among his sons. In fairness to the sons, however, it should be noted that they simply lived up to the example of their father to his rise to power. We also might blame David for spoiling his sons. For instance, 1 Kings 1:6 states that "his father had never at any time displeased him by asking, 'Why have you done thus and so?' "

A rebellion was instigated by the handsome Absalom, and an attempted coup that almost succeeded shook the kingdom to its foundations. Absalom was born of an Aramaean wife to David (2 Sam 3:3) and, as was the custom in polygamous families, was brought up by his mother. He had the ways of a man of the desert and the attractiveness of his father, David. Therefore, when his sister was raped by an older half-brother (13:1-22), Absalom bided his time to get blood revenge. At the end of two years, when most people had forgotten the incident, Absalom treacherously slew Amnon at Baal-hazor, north of Bethel (13:23-29). He acted in the classic tradition of the desert code. David was plunged into sorrow over the tragedy, while Absalom fled across the Jordan and found refuge among his mother's kindred (13:34-39).

When time healed the grief of the king over Amnon's death, a return for Absalom was negotiated by Joab, the faithful servant of David (ch. 14). Absalom, however, returned with ambitions to seize the kingdom. He outfitted himself in princely style with a chariot and horses, attended by an honor guard of fifty men (15:1), and began to solicit the secret support of disgruntled citizens (15:2ff.). As David found in his own struggle to supplant Saul, many people had grievances. Absalom needed four years to marshal enough support to stage a coup, but the day finally came at a celebration at Hebron (15:7-10). The conspiracy reached zero hour without David learning of it, presumably. Furthermore, the kind of support Absalom had was not revealed until the revolt began. At Hebron, however, the real mastermind of the conspiracy was unmasked. He was none other than Ahithophel, David's trusted counselor. The fact that he was the father of Eliam (23:34), the father of Bathsheba (11:3), may be significant. I suspect that he had a personal debt to settle with David because of the scandal with Bathsheba.

Absalom must have been poorly advised about the support he could count on in the revolt. David, reluctant to battle his son, fled Jerusalem toward Transjordan where he had loyal allies (17:24-29). The priestly families followed David, but he sent Zadok and Abiathar back into the city (15:24-29). He may have known that Absalom did not have a chance of succeeding, or he may have sent them back to lay a subtle trap for his rebellious son. Hushai, a loyal counselor, was sent back to counter the strategy of Ahithophel (15:32-37), and the return of Zadok and Abiather made Hushai's false defection to Absalom look genuine. Absalom naively misinterpreted the withdrawal of David. He stopped in Jerusalem to take possession of the king's harem and failed to follow up his initial success in putting to flight the king's court and bodyguard (16:15–17:23). Consequently, the king escaped across the Jordan and had time to organize his troops to meet Absalom's rather unprofessional band that pursued.

When the battle was joined with Joab's regrouped forces in "the forest of Ephraim" (18:6), Absalom's men were divided and defeated in the unfavorable terrain, and Absalom himself was put to death by Joab. David had counseled leniency in dealing with his son, and only Joab would have risked the king's wrath in executing his son. Nevertheless, the crafty, self-appointed protector of the king's interests did not dally when he saw the chance to eliminate the young rebel. "I will not waste time like this with you," Joab said (18:14) to an unnamed man who remonstrated with him to spare Absalom. Taking three darts, or javelins that probably were equipped with throw-strings to rifle them toward their target, he hurled them into the semi-conscious body of Absalom and ended his brief career on the spot. The revolt, deprived of Absalom and of Ahithophel who had committed suicide (17:23), ended immediately. Rebel clans negotiated peace, and David was reclaimed by Judah, his own kinsmen who had followed Absalom (19:9-15).

Before the king could return to Jerusalem, a second revolt broke out in Benjamin (2 Sam 20:1-2), led by Sheba who was possibly a kinsman of Saul. He was called the son of Bichri, which may be the same family name as "Becorath," in the genealogy of Saul (1 Sam 9:1). In any case, the rebel cry indicates a secession movement to withdraw the North from David's kingdom. Its stereotyped form indicates that it had become a familiar cry: "We have no portion in David, no share in the son of Jesse: everyone to your tents, Israel" (20:1).

Amasa, Absalom's rebel general who was restored to favor with David, was dispatched to put down the revolt. He commanded what we might call a national army, made up of conscripts and volunteers from the people. When Amasa did not move as quickly as David thought he should (20:5-6), Joab was dispatched with the mercenary force of Cherethites and Pelethites to pursue Sheba. Joab's meeting with Amasa at Gibeon (20:8-10) was reminiscent of his meeting with Abner at Hebron (3:27). Feigning friendship, he grasped Amasa's beard with his right hand to embrace him while with the left hand he stabbed Amasa in the belly. The picture of Amasa "wallowing in his blood in the highway" (20:12) seems to have impressed itself graphically upon the traditions of Israel.

It reminds us that the dagger was the decisive weapon in this "primitive" age before the invention of gunpowder.

David's mercenary army decided the conflict with Sheba (Sam 20:15), and the secession was aborted. Nevertheless, the deep unrest of the northern tribes was unmasked. It would lie dormant under the repressive rule of David's successor before the war cry for secession would be heard again. Meanwhile, the final struggle for the throne of David began in Jerusalem. David is reported to have promised Bathsheba that Solomon would succeed him (1 Kgs 1:17), but he did not follow through on the promise. Consequently, the peace of his old age was rocked by palace intrigue and, eventually, open conflict between Solomon and Adonijah for the throne.

The Struggle for David's Kingdom
1 Kings 1:1–2:46

David's failure to designate clearly the heir to his throne brought about a palace struggle that once more rocked the nation. The struggle had far-reaching significance because the future of the nation would be shaped by its outcome. Leaders of the factions involved were Solomon, son of Bathsheba (2 Sam 12:24), and Adonijah, son of Haggith (2 Sam 3:4). The key to what was involved in the struggle is evident in the persons and factions supporting each man.

Solomon seemingly had an indefinite designation as the successor to David. He was begotten in the scandalous union with Bathsheba and named Jedidiah, "beloved of Yahweh." Where he got the name Solomon we are not told. It may have been a throne name. Nevertheless, it suggests a dilution of strict Yahweh worship because the name Solomon may have been a derivative of Shalom, who was likely a Jebusite deity at Jerusalem. The change of name from Jedidiah to Solomon suggests accommodation to a flexible kind of Yahwism that could bring the native religion of the Jebusites into its cult.

On the other hand, Adonijah, whose name means "My Lord is Yahweh," seemed to represent a more strict and orthodox Yahwism. He was born at Hebron, the original capital city of David, and his family ties probably rooted deeply in the strict Yahwistic traditions out of which David came. Adonijah therefore represented the ancestral traditions of

David, and in person he must have had much of the attraction that his father had as a youth.

Adonijah began the struggle as the underdog. He recruited popular support in the same way that Absalom began his conspiracy: by parading through the country in his chariot with the bodyguard of fifty men running before him (1 Kgs 1:5). His significant support came, however, from Joab and Abiathar. Joab had been the faithful friend of David from the day Jerusalem was captured in a commando raid until the entire kingdom was brought under David's rule. Nevertheless, Joab had incurred the king's displeasure in murdering Abner first, then the king's son Absalom. The final break came when Joab treacherously killed Amasa, Absalom's general. He represented in Adonijah's camp the leadership of the national army, probably loyal kinsmen from the Hebron area.

Abiathar, we recall, was the surviving priest of the family of Eli at Shiloh. He was placed at the head of the priestly hierarchy with Zadok when the Ark of the Covenant, which had been at Shiloh, was transferred to Jerusalem. Abiathar represented the ancestral priestly order of the northern tribes, the ancient orthodoxy we might say. Since there was no significant military leadership from the North after the death of Amasa, Abiathar was probably the major leader of the northern tribes. Therefore, Adonijah seemingly had wide popular support in both the North and South. Joab and Abiathar were leaders of the people, the working man and the village elders. They essentially represented the old order that was pre-kingdom in tradition and anti-kingdom in sentiment.

Solomon, on the other hand, stood at the head of factions that represented a new order, one patterned after the city-state kingdoms of Canaan. Zadok, the priest who appeared after David made Jerusalem his capital, was in Solomon's camp (1 Kgs 1:8). Possibly Zadok's heritage was rooted at Jerusalem, although a tradition in 1 Chronicles 6:4-8 traces Zadok's lineage to Aaron. Zedek was the name of a deity worshiped in Jerusalem, evident in the name of Melchizedek (Gen 14:18), and Zadok's name may be God-bearing. In any event, Zadok represented in Solomon's camp a faction of priests not identified with the old-time religious traditions of the North or South.

Benaiah likewise represented no popular segment of the people. He was the commander of David's army of foreign mercenaries, Cherethites and Pelethites (2 Sam 7:8) and probably Gittites (2 Sam 15:18). All of these were professional soldiers recruited from the Philistine tribes. They formed a hard core of loyal troops who kept the kingdom intact during the revolt of Absalom and of Sheba. Benaiah and the palace guard of mercenaries therefore represented the personal support of David in Solomon's camp, but not popular support. Nathan, the prophet (1 Kgs 1:8), was of unknown origin also. He was a courageous personal chaplain to the king who did not hesitate to condemn the Bathsheba affair (2 Sam 12:1-15), but his loyalty to the new order in Jerusalem was unquestioned. Undoubtedly he had a part in planning the construction of the temple that Solomon built (2 Sam 7:1-17). His prophetic oracle in 2 Samuel 7 was invested with the theology of Davidic kingship, which was forward-looking at the time of Solomon. Fragments of an Aramaic monument from Tel Dan refer to the "house of David," indicating that this king—with all of his flaws—left a legacy for later generations.

The struggle for the throne of David was therefore a struggle between two orders. Adonijah represented the popular sentiment, which had grown weary of supporting the royal establishment in Jerusalem. Solomon represented a small inside clique that wanted a professional, efficient, and absolute monarchy. Actually, Adonijah had little chance of overcoming Solomon because the national forces led by Joab were disorganized and no match for the disciplined, professional army of mercenaries led by Benaiah. Consequently the popular acclamation of Adonijah as king at En-rogel, down the Kidron valley from Gihon spring, was meaningless. Solomon's seizure of power broke up Adonijah's party and scattered the people out of fear of retaliation.

Adonijah was spared until his request for Abishag (1 Kgs 2:13-24), the king's concubine, was interpreted as covert treachery. Benaiah executed him at the express order of Solomon (v. 25). Abiathar was restricted to Anathoth, a two-acre village just north of Jerusalem, and Joab was executed by Benaiah as he clung to the altar of God seeking a place of refuge. The struggle ended quickly. Merciless and efficient, Solomon and his professionals soon brought Jerusalem and the kingdom to heel, and the voice of the people was not heard for another generation.

Solomon
1 Kings 3:1–11:43

The story before us now is one of David's kingdom in the hands of Solomon, the astute ruler. He was an enigmatic person. Lacking the charisma of David, he more than compensated by demonstrating a cool, ruthless efficiency that was intimidating. I suppose we would call him a computerized personality if he lived today. There were no loose ends in Solomon's administration. All rivals were eliminated, and proper measures were taken to secure the throne. With the kingdom extended in all directions by David, Solomon had only to organize and exploit it. A better person for the task could not have been produced.

Security for the kingdom was sought in peaceful negotiations rather than military strength. Alliances were made with the major powers around Israel's borders and sealed in the exchange of royal princesses for the harems of the rulers. This custom connected the royal families by blood, giving substance in the eastern mind to the covenant of words. Therefore, Solomon "made a marriage alliance with Pharaoh, king of Egypt; he took Pharaoh's daughter and brought her into the city of David" (1 Kgs 3:1). The Pharaoh would have been a XXIst Dynasty ruler of a new powerless Egypt. That Solomon could obtain a daughter of Pharaoh indicates the deterioration of Egypt because of internal factional wars and the rise in power of Israel under the inspired leadership of David. The Egyptian princess was placed at the head of the harem in a special position of prominence befitting her rank (7:8). The vulnerable southwest flank of Israel was secured in this clever, non-violent transaction with Pharaoh.

A second major alliance brought Tyre, ruled by the Phoenician king Hiram, into a significant relationship with Israel (5:1ff.). The Phoenician state was in a great period of maritime expansion in the Mediterranean and at the center of commercial activity. The Phoenician ships sailed to Italy, North Africa, and even to Spain, tying the states round the sea into a kind of common market that brought unparalleled prosperity to all of them.

Solomon's alliance with Hiram I of Tyre (969–936 B.C.) was equivalent to joining the common market. This is reflected in artifacts discovered in excavations because, prior to the reign of Solomon, evidence of imports was almost non-existent. Beginning in the tenth century B.C., however, imported pottery and wares began to appear everywhere, indicating the commercial outlet for Israel's trade at Tyre (5:7-18). The northern border of Israel was secured in the alliance that put Israel into the Mediterranean common market.

Security in the kingdom and on the eastern borders was achieved in two ways. First, there was the non-violent way of marriage alliances, which Solomon apparently pursued vigorously. He is reported to have taken 700 wives and 300 concubines (11:3), figures that sound like a generous estimate. Nevertheless, they are significant because they reflect the Oriental way of securing the kingdom with its own people.

King Saud of Saudia Arabia reportedly used the same system in the present century. His practice was to have four wives, the maximum allowed by Moslem law, but three of them were more or less permanent, and the fourth one changed every month. The fourth wife was taken from the leading clans of the kingdom, kept one month and impregnated if possible, then passed on to a relative in the court. This system established a political base cemented by family ties with the leading families of the kingdom.

Solomon, uninhibited by Moslem law, had many more-or-less permanent wives such as the daughter of Pharaoh. He also had a rotation system that brought in daughters from the clans of Israel and troublesome foreign tribes east of the Jordan (11:1ff.). Therefore, Solomon's celebrated harem was the symbol of his foreign policy and a kind of welfare program in the state, because each family that contributed to the harem got a hand in the royal treasury. It had its liabilities, however (11:2).

The second security measure in the kingdom was a military one. At strategic places where trouble was apt to break out, Solomon built military bases armed with war chariots, the first extensive use of them in Israel. One report (10:26) puts this police force at 1,400 chariots and 12,000 men who were stationed at Jerusalem, Ezion-geber on the Gulf of Aqaba, Gezer, Megiddo, and Hazor. 2 Chronicles 9:25 reports 4,000 stalls for the chariot horses (40,000 stalls of 1 Kgs 4:26 are too many), which were probably like those found in excavations at Megiddo. An estimated 450 stalls were found there. This formidable striking force was the mailed fist of Solomon that kept order in the kingdom, moreso the people of Israel than at the borders to secure them against foreign encroachment.

With a bulging and increasingly expensive royal establishment, the tax burden became oppressive. The daily requirement of "thirty cors of fine flour (337½ bu.), and sixty cors of meal (675 bu.), ten fat oxen, and twenty pasture-fed cattle, 100 sheep, besides deer, gazelles, roebucks, and fatted fowl" (1 Kgs 4:22-23) was met by assessing taxes in kind of the various districts. Solomon shrewdly reapportioned the kingdom and organized administrative districts whose boundaries did not coincide with the old tribal boundaries (4:7ff.). The realignment of boundaries diminished the possibility of any district organizing a rebellion and made exploitation of the district easier. Consequently, the populace was harnessed to the burden of the royal establishment by heavy taxes, and the northern tribes seem to have borne most of the burden.

The opulent court of Solomon probably required more income than even oppressive taxation could yield. In fact, the added income of Solomon's royal business enterprises made possible the legendary wealth credited to him. Several sources of this added revenue are mentioned. We have mentioned the trade channeled through Hiram of Tyre with the Mediterranean world. This, of course, was not a private enterprise of the king. The construction of a fleet of merchant ships based at Ezion-geber, on the Gulf of Aqaba seems to have been a royal enterprise, however (9:26). Solomon saw possibilities of building a maritime trade in the Red Sea area that would be patterned after the Phoenician system in the Mediterranean. Exotic merchandise from Arabia, East Africa, and India was the attraction, and quick wealth awaited Solomon if he could operate the seagoing vessels.

Hiram of Tyre was enlisted to build the fleet, and he sent seamen to operate the ships (9:27), because the Hebrews had no skill in operating ships. The ships began plying the long Red Sea corridor to Arabia and Africa (9:28), and wealth began pouring into the coffers of the kingdom. Details of the Red Sea trade are scarce. We read of gold and silver, ivory, and apes and baboons (not peacocks, as in 10:22) for entertainment at the court and possibly for trade. Not specifically mentioned are probably the most important items that attracted Solomon to the Red Sea enterprise. Frankincense and myrrh, resinous secretions of trees in the balsam family, were the most expensive and exclusive products of the area. In fact, they were produced only in South Arabia along the southern coast that is now Aden and across the straits of the Red Sea in East Africa, which is now Somaliland.

Frankincense and myrrh were burned as incense, giving off an evergreen odor that could be sweetened with the addition of perfumes. Extravagant use of incense in religious ritual created a constant demand, and use of the resin in perfumes and medicines simply increased the price. The supply was limited by exclusive production in the Aden region and overland transport once a year by camel caravan over the 1,200 mile-trade route to Palestine, Egypt, and Syria. Caravans were taxed by every sheikdom along the trade route. By the time the produce reached the market, it was prohibitively expensive.

Pliny told of the precautions taken at Alexandria to prevent theft of the incense by workers who prepared it for sale:

> A seal is put upon the workmen's aprons; they have to wear a mask or a net with a close mesh on their heads, and before they are allowed to leave the premises they have to take off all their clothes.

The cost per camel load of frankincense, about 300 pounds, amounted to 688 denarii, according to Pliny. Translated in terms of the average Roman's wages and cost of living, a pound of incense would cost around 5 percent of a wage-earner's annual income. In present-day values, a pound of incense would be worth more than $175.00, depending on the grade! Solomon's merchant fleet in the Red Sea was a bolder and more shrewd venture than it appears on the surface in reading the brief biblical accounts. He actually moved to corner the frankincense market, and camel caravans certainly could not compete with a fleet of ships in economical transport!

The visit of the Queen of Sheba (10:1) to Solomon's court is, I think, to be understood in the context of the frankincense business. Sheba was in South Arabia where frankincense was produced. The queen came by camel caravan, bearing gifts of spices, gold, and jewels (10:2, 10). Her mission to Jerusalem, according to the scribes, was to confirm the reports she had heard of Solomon's wisdom (10:1). This may have been a part of the mission, but I doubt that she rode a camel 1,200 miles—as far as from Houston, Texas, to Indianapolis, Indiana—just to see if Solomon was as clever as he was rumored to be. Most likely, a major purpose of her mission was to negotiate some agreements for the frankincense trade. The expensive gifts that she brought imply that she bought off Solomon so that she could retain a monopoly of and control the frankincense market. He was free, however, to concentrate on trade in spices from India and rare woods and ivory from East Africa.

One export of Solomon's seems to have been copper, mined in the desert region south of the Dead Sea. The mines, scattered over the desert from the Dead Sea to Sinai, had been worked since about 3500 B.C., when a community of metalsmiths living at Beersheba began copper work using nuggets mined south of their village. Egypt's Middle Kingdom systematically mined copper and turquoise at Serabit el-Khadem, near Mount Sinai. Likely, Solomon organized the most effective exploitation of the copper resources, and his returns must have been handsome. Solomon's fleet of "Tarshish ships" (10:22) was probably modeled after the Phoenician "Tarshish" vessels that plied the Mediterranean, transporting smeltery products. Copper, which was used extensively by Solomon at home (7:13-22), was probably exported and traded for the gold and silver that was brought back by the fleet in the Red Sea area.

Two other sources of revenue should also be mentioned. Following the custom of the desert tribes, Solomon exacted taxes from the caravans that crossed his territory in the south and engaged in a profitable trade in horses and chariots, armaments that were in much demand. Horses were imported from Que (10:28), the ancient name of Cilicia in Asia Minor where the apostle Paul grew up. Chariots were purchased from Egypt, home of the world's best craftsmen. The purchase price of a chariot was 600 shekels of silver (about 240 ounces, at .4 ounce per shekel), and a horse cost 150 shekels. These were exported to kings of the Hittite and Syrian city-states (10:29) for a tidy profit, we would assume.

With the wealth brought in by his business enterprises, Solomon built a luxurious royal complex at Jerusalem. Thirteen years of work were required in building the palace (7:1) and seven years for the temple (6:38). We have been accustomed to thinking that the temple plan—with its free-standing pillars (7:15-22), vestibule (6:3), holy place or sanctuary, and holy of holies (6:14-17)—was Phoenician in design. Similar plans of small sanctuaries have been excavated at Ramat Rahel, near Bethlehem, and at Arad, dating from the time of Solomon. These sanctuaries indicate that the temple plan was indigenous to Judah, and that the elaborate decoration was probably the only genuine pagan element in its symbolism.

The temple was essentially Solomon's royal chapel, because other sanctuaries were located at holy places over the land. As a royal chapel, its opulence was evidence of the king's wealth. Therefore, it was a status symbol, like the 700 wives and 300 concubines. The temple also was the first temple of the land, and its priestly hierarchy was first in importance because it kept the national shrine. An ostracon from Arad indicates that the Jerusalem sanctuary was recognized by the provincial shrines as the first among equals. We may conclude that Solomon's temple was designed to pull the people together in a kind of federated religious loyalty, but hard and fast centralized control from Jerusalem did not come until the reforms of Hezekiah and Josiah.

Finally, we should note the ominous implication of Solomon's marriage to Pharaoh's daughter. Israel had traveled a long road from the land of Goshen to Solomon's court. The Egyptians had done some bending to marry off a royal princess to a Hebrew. The ominous suggestion is that Solomon had adopted the ways of the Egyptians, evident in the organization of his kingdom and in the widespread use of forced labor on kingdom enterprises. The corvée, or forced labor for the king, was one reason for the revolt in Canaan during the Amarna period prior to the entry of Joshua into the land. No doubt it was practiced by the Amorite and Canaanite kings in the oppression that led to Joshua's wars of liberation. Solomon became the oppressor, following the reintroduction of slavery by David (2 Sam 12:31).

Solomon reportedly forced many minority groups such as Amorites and Hittites into forced labor gangs (1 Kgs 9:20-21) creating a Hebrew aristocracy of soldiers, officials, commanders, and captains (9:22). This plan was reminiscent of the chariot-warrior aristocracy of the Hyksos that was based on a feudal system. Even though it elevated many Hebrews, the system tended to eliminate the Hebrew working class and thus created a class stratification. Eventually, Hebrews would get worked into the stratification, and there would be Hebrew serfs and aristocrats, a social system inconsistent with the covenant, as we noted previously.

A new order was imposed upon Israel by Solomon. The old order of the tribal federation was suppressed by the inexorable pressures of building an oriental dynasty and court. Heavy taxation was required, and strict means of collecting taxes were introduced. The land was re-districted, and provincial administrators were set over the new districts. The final indignity imposed upon the people was the corvée, or forced labor, system. It inevitably stirred much unrest, because the rural citizen had come from a heritage of a variety of popular democracy and fierce individualism. When religion was made one of the instruments of binding the people together for more efficient exploitation, the spirit of the old order that recognized Yahweh, the God of the covenant, as king was battered to the point of breaking.

We recall that David's last days were turbulent with struggle among his sons for the throne. We read of no stirrings led by impatient sons of Solomon, although there must have been seething discontent among the people. Hints of this situation are evident in the exile of Hadad, the Edomite, who had enough desert blood in his veins to rebel against Solomonic oppression (11:14-23). He was nurtured by Pharaoh, who craftily awaited his opportunity to help break up the kingdom of Israel and diminish its threat to him.

Another implacable adversary was Rezon, the son Eliada, who found refuge in Damascus (11:23-25). Rezon organized a guerrilla band that raided the border settlements along the Syrian frontier, a tradition that has persisted in historical hostility between Israel and Syria. Jeroboam, a corvée labor taskmaster, conspired against Solomon (11:26-31) under the encouragement of Ahijah of Shiloh.

Ahijah represented the suppressed people of the north. Establishing a tradition that would persist until the time of Amos, the prophet Ahijah led in a conspiracy to overthrow the government. The rebellion never got out of the plotting rooms, because Jeroboam was driven into exile in Egypt also (11:40). Pharaoh gave him political asylum and encouragement and waited out the death of Solomon. Ominous signs of revolt appeared in Edom, Syria, and among the northern tribes. The iron grip of Solomon was such that no move could be made until he died. His celebrated wisdom did not perceive the causes of discontent, or if it did, he had not the quality of compassion that could be moved by people in despair. By the time he died, the northern tribes were ready to sacrifice everything for freedom.

The Disintegration of the Kingdom
1 Kings 12:1–14:31

The sad story of Israel's disintegration followed hard on the heels of Solomon's death. We are not given any details about Rehoboam's selection as king or any struggle that took place in Jerusalem. Strangely, he sought ratification of his appointment by the northern tribes at Shechem after apparent acceptance in Jerusalem by the southern tribes (12:1). Meanwhile, the elders at Shechem had sent for Jeroboam to lead in the bargaining for improved conditions under the new ruler (12:2ff.). Rehoboam seems to have inherited little of the cool level-headedness of his father; he laid down a hard line for the men following Jeroboam. Reportedly, he said, "Now, whereas my father laid on you a heavy yoke, I will add to your yoke," (12:11).

The inflexibility and arrogance of Rehoboam apparently frightened the elders at Shechem. When they came together with Jeroboam to give their answer to his demand for allegiance (12:12ff.), the counsel of the prophet Ahijah prevailed (12:15), and the secession cry heard once before in Sheba's abortive rebellion was heard again: "What portion have we in David? We have no inheritance in the son of Jesse. To your tents, O Israel! Look now to your house, David" (I Kings 12:16).

A riot occurred when Adoram, a hated corvée taskmaster, was sent to put down the budding revolt at Shechem, and he was stoned to death (12:18). The northern tribes defiantly refused to submit to Jerusalem and declared their independence. Jeroboam was elected king over the north, henceforth known as Israel, and built a capital at Shechem. Civil war threatened but never materialized. Rehoboam had not the forces necessary to bring Israel back under his control, and the prophets Ahijah of Shiloh (12:15) and Shemiah (12:21-24) marshaled overwhelming support for the secession among the people of the northern tribes. The cost of suppressing the revolt was too high for Rehoboam, so he returned to Jerusalem.

Two events followed the revolt that essentially brought to an end the age of David and Solomon. First, the Egyptian Pharaoh, Shishak, who had given political asylum to Jeroboam, struck Judah and Israel a devastating blow in the fifth year of Rehoboam's reign (14:25-28). Shishak was a Libyan who had seized the throne in Egypt and founded the XXIInd Dynasty. He seems to have had ambitions of bringing Palestine and Syria back under Egyptian control The invasion of Judah and Israel was therefore the first step in Shishak's plan of rebuilding the empire. He was not able to follow up with more campaigns, apparently, because of internal conflict and weakness in Egypt.

The invasion of Shishak ended whatever aspirations Rehoboam had of uniting the kingdom, and it probably hit Jeroboam harder than the biblical traditions indicate. An inscription at Karnak in Egypt names 156 cities that Shishak claimed he captured. The list includes cities in Transjordan and as far north as the Esdraelon plain. Megiddo is named, and a fragment of a triumphal monument to Shishak found in excavations there seems to support the claim. Shechem seems to have been burned to the ground. One field of excavations had a layer of pinkish-gray ash over one foot deep from a conflagration that is dated to the time of Shishak. Consequently, the Egyptian destruction raged like a fire of retribution over the entire kingdom of David and Solomon and left the land devastated.

A second event occurred that was as destructive of the spirit of Israel as the Egyptian invasion was to its cities. Jeroboam yielded to probable counsel from the prophetic leadership and set up sanctuaries at Bethel and Dan (12:26-33). This move was both political and religious.

Jeroboam said,

> If this people continues to go up to offer sacrifices in the house of the Lord at Jerusalem, then the heart of this people will turn again to their master, King Rehoboam of Judah. (12:27)

So the king took counsel and made two calves of gold (v. 28). We are not told who counseled him, but the counselors obviously wanted religious independence from Jerusalem. Their plan to set up sanctuaries with the golden calf symbol and staff them with a priestly hierarchy was not hatched on the spur of the moment. In fact, the whole revolt against Jerusalem was a move back to the old-time ways of government and worship. Quite likely, the old tribal boundaries were restored that broke up the oppressive administrative system of Solomon. A granary found at Shechem, the probable center of one of Solomon's districts (4:8), went out of use at this time.

The golden calf sanctuaries likewise were a return to old-time religion. We know little about them because the biblical traditions that we have were preserved by priests in Jerusalem. These priests saw only an idol in the golden calf (14:9) and an illegitimate priesthood at the sanctuaries (13:33-34). The northern priests probably were of legitimate lineage, however, because Jonathan, the priest at Dan who set up a "graven image," claimed Mosaic descent (Judges 18:30). He was recruited for the sanctuary at Dan expressly because he was of legitimate priestly lineage (Judg 18:14-26). Likely, the greatest fault of the priests at Bethel and Dan was that they belonged to a rival faction whose hostility toward the Jerusalem priests had existed since the time of Moses, and no hostility quite matched the merciless intolerance of rival priests!

Jeroboam's golden calf was a bull symbol, known throughout the Near East as a symbol of the presence of deity. Quite likely, the bull at Bethel and Dan was an ancient symbol of El, the god of Abraham, because inscriptions from Ras Shamra mention "Bull El," as though he could have been represented by the bull symbol as well as a patriarch. By Jeroboam's time, the bull symbol of El was likely transferred to Yahweh.

Egel-yau, or "Bull of Yahweh," is a Hebrew personal name on the Samaria Ostraca, dating more than a century after the time of Jeroboam. It suggests association of the bull with Yahweh.

I think the bulls set up at Bethel and Dan represented a rival faction of Yahwism, not an apostasy to Baalism. Baalism penetrated the North a century later under Ahab. The rival faction was an old one, with a history reaching back to the wilderness wandering at Mount Sinai (Exod 32:1-6, 15-16). In the wilderness, a kind of coup was staged when Moses prolonged his stay on Mount Sinai and the bull was made under Aaron's leadership. The golden bull faction was put down by Moses, who, himself, belonged in the Ark faction, and we hear no more of the conflict until the revival of the cult under Jeroboam.

David, we recall, moved the Ark to Jerusalem, and Solomon installed it in the temple. The adherents of the old order associated with the Ark at Shiloh were alienated, as evidenced in the leadership of Ahijah of Shiloh in the revolt. Consequently, the old adherents to the Ark faction likely considered the priests in Jerusalem apostate, and the priests in Jerusalem were sure the northern priests were apostate. In any event, the sanctuaries at Bethel and Dan represented a popular return to an old form of Yahwism that was not associated with the monarchy in Jerusalem. The alienation of the North was complete when the people began making pilgrimages to Bethel and Dan, and the sad story of the disintegration of David's kingdom is told.

Chapter 9

The Clash
of Religion and Politics

1 Kings 15:1–2 Kings 11:21

	Judah	Israel
900	Asa (913–873)	Baasha (900–877)
		Elah (877–876)
875	Jehoshaphat (873–849)	Zimri (876)
		Omri (876–869)
		Ahab (869–850)
		(Jezebel and Elijah)
850		Ahaziah (859–849)
	Jehoram (849–849)	Jehoram (849–842)
	Ahaziah (842)	(Elisha)
	Athaliah (842–837)	Jehu (842–815)
825	Joash (837–800)	(Hazael of Syria) (842–806)
800	Jehoahaz (815–806)	

Israel declined to a depressing state of instability following the death of Jeroboam, and order was not restored until Omri seized power after the abortive revolution led by Zimri. Tirzah, the capital, remained a hotbed of intrigue, probably stirred by factions of prophets, and Omri built a new capital at Samaria. Extricated from the scene of plotting and constant unrest, he set about securing the state among the nations. The most significant move he made in securing the state was an alliance with Tyre that was sealed by the marriage of Jezebel, daughter of Ethbaal, to Ahab, Omri's son.

Jezebel

1 Kings 15:1–16:34

The name Jezebel tears loose from pious restraint the imagination of pulpiteers. Somehow she comes through as a spiritual seductress, the epitome of evil femininity. Chic, slim, and well-painted, the pulpiteer says, she high-heels around Ahab's palace swinging a foot-long cigarette holder, balanced on the thin edge of violent tantrum. Maybe, but to me Jezebel comes through the pages of scripture with the walk of a man. Decisive, direct, and dominating, she could have been called great anywhere but at Samaria. She got there in one of the accidents of history, and by accident she confronted her nemeses: a tough, ascetic man called Elijah who walked like a prophet of God.

The story of Jezebel's Israel begins with Omri, a commander of the army who may not have been Hebrew. Israel went into a depressing period of instability when Jeroboam died. The older order of tribal democracy was simply incompatible with dynastic stability. There was no mercenary army of professional, well-disciplined soldiers to fall back upon when revolt flared and the national army leadership became unreliable. David's kingdom had been saved twice by his mercenary forces, once during Absalom's revolt and again when Sheba led the secessionist rebellion. Solomon was made king by the mercenaries of David who beat down the national army. The northern kingdom had only a national army, however, and its dynasties changed with dizzying turnover.

Instability in Israel was fed by the prophets. Jeroboam was backed by Ahijah of Shiloh in his secession bid to set up a separate kingdom (11:29ff.). The same prophet, Ahijah of Shiloh, appeared later advocating the overthrow of Jeroboam in extremist terms. He prophesied, "Anyone belonging to Jeroboam who dies in the city, the dogs shall eat; and anyone who dies in the open country, the birds of the air shall eat" (14:11). Evidently, the prophets went to work to fulfill their prophecy, because Baasha struck down Nadab, the heir of Jeroboam at Gibbethon. As soon as he was installed as king, the house of Jeroboam was massacred, fulfilling the word of Ahijah. I take this to mean that Ahijah backed Baasha, and, most likely, the prophetic faction that followed him assisted in the coup.

Baasha was then attacked by Jehu, the son of Hanani, a prophetic spokesman, and the overthrow of his government was prophesied (16:1-

4). Baasha died a natural death (16:6), but his son Elah fell in a conspiracy that probably was led by a faction of prophets. Zimri, who may have had prophetic backing, slew Elah and overthrew the government. Omri, a professional military man who apparently was backed by his army, besieged Zimri in Tirzah. The rebel leader committed suicide when he saw that the revolt was confined to Tirzah.

Tizrah must have been a hotbed of intrigue. We know from excavations that the houses were all built on the same level, suggesting a classless society where constant plotting and conspiracy could be fanned by the volatile, ecstatic prophets. Therefore, we would not expect that Omri, once he put down his rival, Tibni, (16:22) should decide to extricate his government from Tirzah and its extremist cross-currents. He probably despaired of pleasing the prophetic leaders. Consequently, Omri purchased the hill of Samaria "for two talents of silver" (16:24) and built a new capital that he could control. Samaria quickly became symbolic of a new era of sophisticated government on the order of Solomon's kingdom half a century earlier.

Samaria was built on two levels. An acropolis towered over the lower city, which spread out on all sides. The acropolis was the royal quarter, fortified with a casemate wall built by Phoenician masons. Inside the wall was the king's palace, which housed his family and court. Shut out by the wall was the voice of dissent that may have arisen on the lower level. The two levels prophesied the end of the classless society of the old federation of tribes because Omri's system of government, as Solomon's, created a feudalistic order. An aristocracy of court favorites emerged, and the working class found itself eased into serfdom. Indeed, the constant din of prophetic agitation and dissent that had brought Israel to the edge of despair was one reason for Omri's Samaria. The clean, white masonry of the acropolis that shut out the voice of the prophet was equally disturbing. It prophesied a class inequity in Israel that would lead to injustices condemned by Amos a century later.

Omri made a series of shrewd political moves that extricated his government from the provincialism that had plagued his predecessors. Asa, king of Judah, had made a treaty with Syria during the reign of Baasha (15:16-21). Syria, which needed little encouragement to initiate border raids against Israel, waged a campaign that penetrated the Huleh basin at Dan and took north Galilee (15:20). When Omri began to reign, Syria menaced his borders on the north and east. Judah, hostile also, was occupied in repelling incursions into the Shephelah (foothills) west of Hebron by Egyptian forces (2 Chron 14:9-14).

Shrewdly, Omri made contacts with Assyria, an ominous, rising power in the East. The vigorous and brutal Asshur-nasir-pal II (883–859 B.C.) had acceded to the throne and set his face toward Syria. He was the notorious king who began a policy of calculated cruelty to keep his conquered states in subjection. One "treatment" for rebel leaders was to impale them on sharp stakes in the sun and let them die a horrible death in public humiliation. The Assyrian marched westward, overrunning the northern Euphrates valley states. On one expedition he penetrated northern Syria and "washed his weapons" in the sea. Syrian and Phoenician states bought off the invader with tribute, among which were Tyre and Sidon. Whether or not Omri paid tribute, we do not know. Assyria knew Israel for a century as "the house of Omri," suggesting that more than casual contacts were made.

The Assyrian menace neutralized Syria's threat to Omri and allowed him to extricate Israel from the impossible political situation into which it had fallen. Our information from the Bible is limited to 1 Kings 16:23-28, which gives him only passing and derogatory notice, but Omri's political activities can be reconstructed somewhat by references to him that appear in extra-biblical inscriptions. The Assyrian reference to Israel as "the house of Omri" occurs on the monolith of Shalmaneser III, which mentions Ahab's participation in the battle of Qarqar (853 B.C.). Another inscription, from Dibon in Moab, mentions the liberation of Nebo from Israel at Ahab's death, but it also indicates that Omri brought Transjordan under tribute. Thus we may conclude that Omri, free from Syrian threats because of his contacts with Assyria, secured his eastern borders by subjugating Moab.

Another significant move allied Israel with Tyre, which was sealed by the marriage of Jezebel to Ahab (16:31). Tyre had established a profitable sea trade in the Mediterranean but was threatened, like Israel, by Assyria. Thus, the treaty that bound the countries turned Israel's eyes toward the sea and strengthened the front facing Syria and Assyria. As in the days of Solomon, exports from Israel found their way to Mediterranean ports in Phoenician ships, and fine quality imports flowed into the land. Prosperity came to Israel again, although it brought with it the culture and religion of the Phoenicians, which was incompatible with the strict Yahwism of the prophetic factions. Jezebel became a part of the scene at Samaria in Omri's political move to bring material prosperity to Israel and strengthen his position against Syria and Assyria. It was an accident of history that the particular Phoenician princess given in marriage to seal the alliance with Tyre happened to be Jezebel.

The final move to secure Israel's borders was made by Ahab, who succeeded Omri (16:28f.) at Samaria. King Asa of Judah had begun a policy of moderation toward Israel when he made the alliance with Syria to ease his border troubles with Israel (2 Chron 16:1-16). Judah, it seems, was led by Asa to accept the reality of Israel. Consequently, his general policy was to abate the hostility that had exploded under Rehoboam. He concentrated on strengthening Judah internally by religious reform (2 Chron 15:1-19) and securing his own border against Egypt to the southwest. Jehoshaphat, his son, continued a policy of moderation toward Israel by concluding a marriage alliance that brought the two countries together again (2 Chron 18:1), seventy-five years after the secession of the north. Athaliah, a princess of Israel and daughter of Ahab (2 Kgs 8:18; 2 Chron 21:6), though probably not a daughter of Jezebel, was given in marriage to Jehoram, son of Jehoshaphat, to seal the alliance. The troubles between the two little kingdoms were papered over.

Omri's policies secured Israel's place among the nations, and Ahab apparently pursued a vigorous policy of strengthening the internal structure of the kingdom. Introduction of the cult of Baal Melqart from Tyre was a calculated part of Ahab's program. His palace reflected the same program. Continuous agitation by factions of prophets had brought the country to the brink of disaster. Ahab set out to emancipate Israel from what he must have considered unsophisticated provincialism. Most of the people seem to have followed him instead of the prophets. Therefore, Jezebel appeared as the evangel of a sophisticated religion and cult that would support the dynasty of Omri and stabilize the nation.

Because of her aristocratic heritage, she looked upon the simple religion of the prophets as primitive. We might, in fairness to Jezebel, attribute a kind of maternal benevolence to her in suppressing the extremist and anarchist prophets. Although her methods were direct and heavy-handed, she was probably motivated more by the social-worker spirit than we have recognized. She had the plan that would bring order into the primitive religion of Israel and stabilize the government. It would clean up those smelly prophets who wore long hair; dirty beards; and crude, woolen, odd-looking garments they never changed. I am not surprised that she got impatient with Ahab when he hesitated in dealing with Naboth because of the ancient customs of a minority of the Hebrews (1 Kgs 21:3-4).

Jezebel's aggressive championing of Baal worship was in line with a government plan to change Israel into a country like Phoenicia. This motive was evident in the building of a sanctuary at Samaria (16:32) and the importation of missionaries from Tyre who established a theological school for the training of nationals in Israel (18:19). The statement that they were "at Jezebel's table" means that they were supported by government funds. The entire strategy was implicit in the move of the capital from Tirzah to Samaria. It became painfully explicit in Jezebel's personal support of the program. Her role is memorable because she encountered a fanatically iron-willed leader of the prophetic groups called Elijah. Her overwhelming power as the queen invests the conflict with Elijah with some of the drama of David's duel with Goliath.

Elijah
1 Kings 17:1–18:46

The real flesh and blood Elijah comes to us clothed in legend. Dedicated to the ascetic calling of a prophet of Yahweh, he is depicted as a mysterious loner whose few public appearances and fewer words leave much space for the imagination to fill. We are told that he was a man from Gilead (17:1), a land of stony red hills in Transjordan that flattens out into the eastern desert. The harsh, no-nonsense discipline of a desert heritage is reflected in his character. Little is said about his past or his associates, but we may locate his company among two distinct groups.

The first group may be designated generally as the prophets of Yahweh. Elisha, who inherited Elijah's mission (2 Kgs 2:13), was associated with prophetic guilds or schools in Israel that seem to have been introduced by Samuel two centuries earlier (I Sam 9:9; 10:5ff.). We have noted that the prophets had a major role in designating rulers whom they would support, such as Jeroboam and Baasha, and that they turned against each ruler as soon as the ruler appeared to have ideas of government that were broader than theirs. The continual atmosphere of plotting and conspiracy caused Omri to remove his government from Tirzah and build Samaria. Who were these prophets of Yahweh behind Elijah, and how much support did they have?

First, the bands of prophets seem to have been organized in various communities. We read of "the company of the prophets who were in Bethel" (2 Kgs 2:3) and others "who came to Jericho" (v. 5), who came out to see Elisha. They probably lived a communal life similar to that of the Essenes at Qumran or the Christian community in Jerusalem (Acts 4:32-35). Elisha was the master of one group, evident in 2 Kings 6:1 where the "company of the prophets said to Elisha, 'As you see, the place where we live under your charge is too small for us.' " People who lived in the villages brought gifts of food for the communities of prophets (2 Kgs 4:42-44), which apparently supported them in part.

A prophet could be spotted by a mark, probably on the forehead (1 Kgs 21:41), or a uniform-like garment of hair-cloth (2 Kgs 1:8). The garment was a simple one-piece robe that could be wrapped around the shoulders and body. It was made of coarsely woven goat or camel hair, which symbolized poverty or, more specifically, the absence of possessions. This is why the prophets depended upon gifts from the people for at least part of their living. There may have been some community enterprises. Furthermore, the garment meant that the prophet was a sojourner. He did not own land nor rule over any institution. Some prophetic groups, however, were supported by the government and prophesied in the service of the king. Persons of such groups were usually called false prophets, because they would not jeopardize their living by speaking unfavorable words to the king.

For instance, when Jehoshaphat inquired of the court-supported prophets in 1 Kings 22:6ff., he knew they prophesied what they thought he wanted to hear. Consequently, the king called Micaiah, an independent prophet, to get a word that might be unfavorable but honest (22:13-23). Like the priests, the court-supported prophets seem to have been attached to the local place of worship. Evidently, they had functions beyond simply being on call to advise the king when he faced a major decision. Quite likely, they also instituted music and singing in the ritual of worship because music was a specialty of the ecstatic prophet. Singing, or more properly chanting, seems also to have been developed by the prophets.

The prophet's major function was to prophesy. 1 Samuel 9 tells the story about Saul consulting Samuel, the seer, for guidance in finding his father's asses. A seer was a diviner, one who used mechanical devices to divine the unknown. For instance, he could divine the unknown by reading the spread of a drop of oil on water in a divining cup (Gen 44:4-5) or interpreting the pattern of lines in a sheep's liver. This is called inspecting the liver (Ezek 12:21) for an answer from God to some question. Interpreting the liver was a part of the theological education of the priest, as evidenced by clay models of livers that have been found in excavations. They are marked off in sections that are labeled for the guidance of the seer.

A parenthetical observation in 1 Samuel 9:9 states that "the one who is now called a prophet was formerly called a seer." The statement obviously came from scribes who lived long after Samuel. Their reference was to the function of the prophet, who was on call to give divine guidance to anyone who needed a word from God. The prophet obtained his word from God in an ecstatic trance, however, instead of reading the liver of a sheep or the spread of oil on water. Apparently the prophetic groups at Bethel, Jericho (Gilgal, in 2 Kgs 4:38), and other places served local communities in giving out divine guidance.

A prophet sought divine guidance in individual spells of ecstatic trance (2 Kgs 3:15) or in group sessions (1 Kgs 22:1-28). When the kings of Israel, Judah, and Edom needed water for the army in a military campaign east of the Dead Sea (2 Kgs 3:4-12), they went to Elisha, the master of the prophetic guild at Bethel. According to verse 11, Jehoshaphat asked a servant, "Is there no prophet of the Lord here, through whom we may inquire of the Lord?" The servant answered, "Elisha son of Shaphat, who used to pour water on the hands of Elijah is here." Elisha was the recognized apprentice to Elijah, who waited on his master by pouring water on his hands when he washed.

"The word of the Lord is with him" (v. 12), observed Jehoshaphat. When they came to Elisha, he tried to put them off and asked, "What have I to do with you? Go to your father's prophets or to your mother's" (v. 13). The kings persisted, and Elisha reluctantly agreed to prophesy. He said, "Were it not that I have regard for King Jehoshaphat of Judah, I would give you neither a look nor a glance. But get me a musician" (vv. 14-15). When the musician played, probably on a three-stringed lute, "the power of the Lord came on him" (v. 15). He went into a trance induced by the music and prophesied an answer to the inquiry of the kings.

Elijah therefore stood out as the spokesman for these prophetic guilds that were dedicated to the service of Yahweh, their God. They were a part of the village life of the hill country in Judah and Israel and were supported in part by villagers who patronized them. In fact, they probably expected a fee for some services. When Naaman, commander of the army of Syria, consulted Elisha he brought a generous honorarium of "ten talents of silver, six thousand shekels of gold, and ten sets of garments" (2 Kgs 5:5). The way of life that they championed was simple, with probably a desert heritage. In any case, the confrontation with Jezebel brought this way of life, which she probably regarded as backward, into direct conflict with the more sophisticated urban life of the Phoenicians.

A second part of Elijah's constituency was the Rechabites who took the lead in overthrowing the house of Ahab. The Rechabites were a strict clan of Yahweh worshipers who refused to touch wine (Jer 35:2ff.) or adopt any of the conveniences of urban life. When offered wine in Jerusalem, they said: "You shall never drink wine, . . . build a house, or sow seed; nor shall you plant a vineyard, or even own one; but you shall live in tents all your days" (vv. 6-7).

The Rechabites were extremists who lived a primitive way of life that protested urbanization and the luxuries of houses, land ownership, wine, and good food—which presumably were a part of that life. Where they came from we do not know precisely, but at one time an Aramean people in central Syria worshiped a deity called Rechab and were called sons of Rechab. Possibly, the Rechabites of Elijah's time were converts to Yahwism who had a background in Syria. The fact that they seemed to be located in Transjordan where the revolt of Jehu started, along the Syrian border, suggests this probability.

It is probable also that they championed a militant kind of Yahwism that was symbolized by the chariot wheel. In fact, "rechab" means "rider," specifically of a horse, and also is used to designate the charioteer. Bidkar, Jehu's aide (2 Kgs 9:25) would possibly have been a "rechab," or personal charioteer of the commander. The chariot wheel symbol appears over the head of Jehu on an Assyrian monument that records his payment of tribute to Shalmaneser III. If this is a symbol of Yahweh for the militant Rechabites, it stands alongside the Ark as a symbol of the Yahwists who settled at Shiloh and whose symbolism was enshrined in the temple at Jerusalem. Also, it represents a northern faction alongside the golden calf faction of Yahwists who supported Jeroboam in the secession from Judah.

Support for Elijah from the militant and extremist Rechabites means that all of the moderates had gone over to Baalism. Only the prophetic guilds and Rechabites were left to champion the strict worship of Yahweh, although the fact that revolt broke out in the army reflects dissatisfaction with Ahab's policies there also. The chances of Elijah prevailing against Jezebel and her government program, which outlawed the prophetic guilds (1 Kgs 18:3ff.), must have appeared hopeless. With the populace either won over to Baalism or intimidated, the only recourse left for Elijah and his followers was revolution. The house of Ahab would have to go in a violent seizure of the reins of government.

The Victory over Baalism
1 Kings 19:1–2 Kings 11:21

A dramatic confrontation between Elijah and the Baal prophets on Mount Carmel seems to be a prelude to "the final solution" of Baalism. Mount Carmel is a picturesque hill southeast of Haifa that probably was the locale of a Baal shrine. Evidently it had been taken over by the Yahweh prophets, and the confrontation in 1 Kings 18:20-40 probably reflects a popular seizure of the shrine led by Elijah. It is related in a drama that pits Yahweh and Baal against each other in a showdown duel. Elijah, the champion of Yahweh, appears serene and confident in the presence of frenzied activity by the Baal prophets intended to arouse Baal to action. The picture of the Baal ritual is instructive, especially in view of our discussion above of the prophetic guilds.

A sacrifice was prepared by the Baal prophets, who called on the name of Baal from morning until noon. The picture we get is that of a group milling about in ecstatic confusion. A limping kind of dance was part of the ritual, probably accompanied by chanting and music (18:26). Also, the self-mutilation "with swords and lances" after their custom (v. 28) took place while they "raved on" in a sustained ecstatic trance until evening. The confrontation was won when Elijah called down "the fire of the Lord" (v. 38), which seems to have been a theophany that convinced the people that Yahweh should have their allegiance. The Baal prophets were defeated, and the shrine was restored to Yahweh.

Elijah's seizure of the Baal shrine on Mount Carmel brought down upon his head the wrath of Jezebel. Outlawed, he fled to the desert and waited for the opportunity to join a conspiracy against Ahab. He reappeared like a haunting conscience when Ahab seized Naboth's vineyard, violating the ancient laws of land tenure observed by the Yahwists.

Ahab's surprised greeting to Elijah, "Have you found me, O my enemy?" (1 Kgs 21:20), could as well be addressed to his conscience. He was aware of the traditions of the Yahwists that Jezebel roughly trod under foot. Elijah likely threw down the gauntlet to Ahab in this confrontation and retired again to the desert. His face was not seen again until the revolt was initiated.

The mantle of leadership passed from Elijah to Elisha in a dramatic vision of Yahweh as a chariot warrior (2 Kgs 2:12). Significantly, it occurred in Transjordan, in Elijah's native Gilead. Whether or not a horse and chariot actually took part in a ritual of worship, we do not know. There were ritual horses and chariots dedicated to the sun in Jerusalem over a century later. Josiah outlawed them in his reform around 621 B.C. (2 Kgs 23:11). These may have been surviving and compromised symbols of a militant Transjordan Yahweh cult that dated from the time of Elijah. In any case, the vision of the chariot warrior marked the transition of leadership to Elisha, who carried on resistance against the house of Ahab.

Some time passed during which Hazael, with the support of the Transjordan plotters, seized the throne in Damascus by slaying the ailing king, Ben-hadad (2 Kgs 8:13-15). Elisha's role in the assassination of Ben-hadad was not complimentary. Then when Jehoram, Ahab's son, was in Jezreel recovering from wounds suffered in battle with the Syrians, Elisha sent an unnamed ecstatic prophet (2 Kgs 9:11) to give blessing and support to Jehu in a conspiracy to overthrow the government.

Jehu was an army commander who seemingly shared with the ecstatic prophets a wildness that identified him when he approached Jezreel in his chariot. He was proclaimed king in Ramoth-gilead by his supporters (9:13) and forthwith set out on a reckless and headlong dash for Jezreel, across the Jordan, to slay Jehoram and seize the kingdom. The watchman saw his approaching swirl of dust and declared that the driving "looks like the driving of Jehu son of Nimshi; for he drives like a maniac" (9:20). The word translated "furiously" is the word for ecstatic prophet, which means Jehu drove like a madman, one who had taken leave of his senses and was in an ecstatic frenzy!

The military coup was swift and brutal. Jehoram came out to negotiate with Jehu and was shot through with an arrow (9:24). He died with the charge of Jezebel's spiritual harlotry ringing in his ears (v. 22). Ahaziah, king of Judah and ally of Jehoram in the war against Syria, turned and fled, but he too was overtaken by Jehu's vengeful arrow and died in Megiddo a short time later (v. 27). The account that follows was a sad memory a century later when Hosea prophesied punishment of the "house of Jehu for the blood of Jezreel" (Hos 1:4), a calamity that would overtake Israel and not just the house of Jehu. Jehu, set loose on an orgy of destruction with prophetic approval, undoubtedly went farther than anyone expected, although he was joined by Jonadab, the Rechabite, in exterminating the house of Ahab.

First, the dead body of Jehoram was thrown out of a chariot onto the land that had belonged to Naboth (2 Kgs 9:25-26). Symbolically, this evened the score with Ahab according to the blood-revenge code of eye for eye, tooth for tooth. Then Jezebel, who demonstrated cool courage when she dressed so that she could die like a queen (v. 30), was thrown from an upper window at Jezreel by her attendants (v. 33), and "some of her blood spattered on the wall and on the horses, which trampled on her." Jehu went inside "and ate and drank" (v. 34) before he gave the word to panic-stricken servants to go out and bury Jezebel. While he was inside eating, the dogs at Jezreel ate Jezebel in the court outside, "and they found no more of her than the skull and the feet and the palms of her hands" (v. 35). The desert code of revenge was satisfied, according to the prophecy of Elijah (vv. 36-37).

When Jehu climbed into his chariot again with his stomach filled and the purge on schedule, he set out to complete the slaughter. A message went out to the village elders and palace guards to show proof of their loyalty to the new regime by bringing the heads of Ahab's sons to Jezreel. A messenger arrived shortly with word that the heads of the king's sons were in baskets outside (2 Kgs 10:5-8) and the fearful leaders were standing by.

Jehu told them, "Lay them in two heaps at the entrance of the gate until the morning" (v. 8), thus allowing the elders cool their heels and fret until he was ready to deal with them. When he went out to inspect the heads the next morning, he said to the assembled leaders who had brought them, "It was I who conspired against my master and killed him; but who struck down all these?" (v. 9). He pointed to the heads and then proceeded to slay "all who were left of the house of Ahab in Jezreel" (v. 11), which included the leaders who had brought the heads of Ahab's sons as proof of their loyalty!

The purge continued with the massacre of a party of Ahaziah's kinsmen who were on their way to visit the king (10:12-15) and apparently unaware of the *coup d'état*. When he departed from the scene of the massacre, Jehonadab, the son of Rechab, met him, presumably to pledge allegiance (v. 15). Jehu asked, "Is your heart as true to mine as mine is to yours?" "It is," replied the Rechabite. "If it is, give me your hand," Jehu said, and he took Jehonadab up into the chariot. "Come with me, and see my zeal for the Lord" (v. 16).

The Rechabite rode in the chariot to Samaria and witnessed the elimination of the house of Ahab (v. 17). Then Jehu called a meeting of the people and proclaimed:

> Ahab offered Baal small service; but Jehu will offer much more. Now therefore summon to me all the prophets of Baal, all his worshipers and all his priests; let none be missing, for I have a great sacrifice to offer to Baal; whoever is missing shall not live (vv. 18-19).

When the priests and worshipers of Baal assembled, Jehu and the Rechabite went among them to see if any worshiper of Yahweh was there. Then he stationed guards outside while sacrifices were offered inside. When all was ready he ordered the guards inside (vv. 23-24). "Come in and kill them," he commanded. "Let no one escape." The Baal prophets, priests, and worshipers were hewn down and the house demolished (vv. 25-27).

Jehu's purge of Baal worship in the name of Yahweh was a national disaster. The nation was stricken a body blow that was as disabling as an invasion by a foreign power. Omri's dynasty was replaced by a madman whose perspective was so narrow that he probably never thought of foreign policy. All of Transjordan was taken by Hazael of Damascus (1 Kgs 10:32-33). Mesha of Moab had already taken the land east of the Dead Sea from Jehoram (2 Kgs 3:4-8), so Israel was confined to the west bank of the Jordan. The Assyrian representation of Jehu paying tribute to Shalmaneser III suggests that Israel became virtually an Assyrian vassal-state. The figure of Jehu, if indeed he brought the tribute, kneeling before the Assyrian is the only known representation of a Hebrew king. He probably does Israel less honor in this distinction than any other of its kings, which, in my opinion, would include Ahab also.

Chapter 10

The Poor and the Prophets

2 Kings 14–15; 2 Chronicles 26–27:9; Amos 1:1; 4–7

Judah	Israel
800 Amaziah (800–783)	Jehoash (801–786)
775 Uzziah (783–742)	Jeroboam II (786–746)
	(Amos)
750 Jotham, co-regent (750)	(Hosea)
Jotham (742–735)	Zechariah (746–745)
(Isaiah)	Shallum (745)
	Menahem (745–738)
	(Tiglath-pilesar III of Assyria, 745–727)
	(Rezin of Damascus, 740–732)
(Micah)	Pekahiah (738–732)
735 Ahaz (735–715)	Pekah (737–732)

Jeroboam II of Israel and Uzziah of Judah expanded their kingdoms aggressively, evidently with an understanding that they would not confront each other. A period of unprecedented prosperity came to the kingdoms, and no significant outside interference occurred. An internal revolution that radically changed the economic, social, and religious traditions did occur, however. A feudal type of economy supported by the royal house developed a class of wealthy landowners and merchants and a poor class of tenants and serfs. The poor rapidly lost their basic rights because they were controlled by people of wealth and influence. The religious institutions served the upper classes and secured the social system that created the poor.

Jeroboam II and Uzziah
2 Kings 14:1–15:38; 2 Chronicles 26:1–27:9

A one-room hut clung to the uneven lower slope of the city. Around its packed earth floor huddled four mud-brick walls, barely six feet high. A flat, sagging roof, plastered with mud, bowed between the walls as though it recoiled from the weather. Small, rectangular openings a foot high in the side walls answered for windows. They were packed with stones that let in restrained breezes and no light, as though an after-thought of regret had seized the occupants when they saw with windows. The only light in the room infiltrated through the door of wood scraps fas-tened to an upright pole that turned in a socket of stone. The door really shut out nothing, because it turned inward in its socket, inside the room, touching nowhere the bricks around the opening. The swinging door had no lock.

Many thousands of people in Israel and Judah lived in these one-room huts during the time of Amos and Micah. A family slept on reed mats or hand-woven rugs right on the earthen floors. When daylight came, the rugs became furniture, and the occupants sat cross-legged around a single bowl of food and had their meal. There was no privacy, no sanitation, little food, and no lock on the door. The swinging door could crash into the little family circle anytime, day or night, and admit a tax collector or landowner who could exact from the occupants their living. This person could beat the man of the house with a stick for hav-ing nothing. The man could be left trembling and cringing in the semi-darkness behind the swinging door, stripped of his human dignity and rights, anxiously wondering when a heavy foot would kick in the door again.

The swinging door with no lock is a symbol of the poor man. In fact, one Hebrew word, *dal*, is used for both. To be poor, indeed, means to have little material goods. To be poor in the sense that outraged Amos and Micah meant having no rights, no recourse to justice, no lock on the swinging door to one's person as a citizen. Without justice, any greedy official could walk over the poor man and humiliate him. He could be stripped of the substance that gave him standing before God and human-ity and thus robbed of his soul. The age that produced this kind of poor man was shaped by Jeroboam II of Israel and Uzziah of Judah in the eighth century B.C.

Little information about Jeroboam II is given in the biblical narratives, although his long reign from 786 to 746 B.C. was one of the most prosperous and powerful of any king of Israel. He was a contemporary of the equally long-lived Uzziah of Judah, who ruled from 783 to 742 B.C. Uzziah brought the first real prosperity and peace to Judah after Solomon. There seems to have been an understanding between Jeroboam II and Uzziah that they would respect their common border and not spend energy fighting each other. Both kings expanded their kingdoms in directions that would not bring them into a confrontation.

Jeroboam II recovered the northern Golan heights that had belonged to Solomon and pushed his border to Hamath and Damascus (2 Kgs 14:28). The Golan heights are a natural barrier between Syria and Israel, and whichever power commands the heights also has the other at a disadvantage. With Syria in control of the heights, all of Galilee and the Huleh basin are vulnerable under the Syrian forts. When Israel is in control of the heights, Damascus is only thirty miles from the fortresses east of the heights and has no other natural barrier to hold back a strong army. Consequently, Jeroboam II captured the heights around Dan and imposed his rule on the Syrian city-states as far east as Damascus and north to Hamath.

Also, the Transjordan land of Gilead seems to have been reclaimed, extending the kingdom at least to Mount Nebo "as far as the Sea of the Arabah" (2 Kgs 14:25). This territory had been under Israelite control during the rule of the Omride dynasty, but Mesha, king of Moab, recaptured it from Jehoram, son of Ahab. No mention is made of an alliance with the Phoenicians at Tyre and Sidon. The disaster that overtook Israel a century earlier had come about because of too close relations with the Canaanites, so Jeroboam II seems to have avoided studiously any national association with the Phoenicians.

Uzziah also expanded his kingdom radically, recovering control of the southern territory that Solomon had ruled. The copper-rich Negev was reclaimed, along with the seaport fortress at Ezion-geber (2 Chron 26:2). Excavations at Tell el-Kheleifeh, formerly identified as Ezion-geber, yielded a stamp seal of Jotham, the son and heir of Uzziah (v. 23). No merchant fleet is mentioned, so we assume that caravan traffic from Arabia across the kingdom was regulated and taxed.

In the Negev also, Uzziah put into practice soil and water conservation measures that brought much of the semi-arid marginal land under cultivation (2 Chron 26:10). Extensive surveys of the Negev reveal that more land was brought into production by Uzziah than at any other time until the Roman period. The Philistine plain southwest of Judah caught the eye of the king who "loved the soil" (v. 10). Gath, Jabneh, and Ashdod were made tributary to Judah (v. 6), enriching the treasury with taxes in kind from the rich Philistine plain.

Jerusalem, the capital, was renovated in keeping with the prosperity of the time. Towers and walls were strengthened or rebuilt (2 Chron 26:9). It is possible that a sixteen-foot wide city wall above Gihon was built at this time, set on bedrock just above the deteriorated Jebusite wall. The army also was reorganized and equipped with the latest shields, spears, helmets, coats-of-mail, bows, and stones for slinging (v. 14). New siege machines (v. 15), probably portable shelters behind which bowmen could stand and shoot their arrows at defenders on wall-towers, were constructed.

The age of Jeroboam II and Uzziah was an exceedingly prosperous one because, together, they recovered most of the kingdom of David and Solomon. This conquest had its liabilities, however. We have seen in the previous chapter the abortive effort of Ahab to bring prosperity and stability to Israel by introducing Tyrian Baalism. It was a mistake that neither of the present kings made. Instead, the strict Yahwism of Elijah and the prophetic guilds of a century earlier seem to have become sufficiently moderate to accommodate elements of the Baalism of Canaan. This is evident in several developments.

First, Jeroboam II maintained his capital at Samaria on the acropolis that Omri and Ahab built. The beautiful, hewn Phoenician masonry was added to in a rebuilding operation by Israelite masons who laid rough walls of fieldstones as was their custom. Their masonry had none of the sophistication and architectural beauty of the "foreign" masonry that had been a part of the cultural package imported from Tyre. Nevertheless, the acropolis still shut out the voice of the people on the lower terraces, and the way of life was almost the same that Jehu had overthrown in his purge of Ahab's house.

Secondly, a feudal aristocracy gathered around the court, picking up favors from the king in land and business. The land itself was tilled by Israelites who worked for absentee landowners that got rich while the workers got poorer. The problem was that the traditional clan-type social unit could not operate under the plantation-tenant system. We have noted previously that the clan-type family organization provided a measure of social security for the aged, the widowed, the afflicted, and the orphan. In a democratic society, the clan head could represent his family in court and in politics so that no great gulf in material wealth separated the people. When absentee landowners found it possible to acquire large holdings and operate them with serf-type tenants, however, the clans that became tenants had no political power and therefore little coverage by the laws of the land.

People had always had few material possessions. That was not the burden of being poor. The burden was to be dependent upon a landowner for one's bread. The older system of inherited ownership of land kept in the family at least a minimal production of food, because a few olive trees and an acre of wheat could keep a large family alive. Therefore, when the tenant lost his land, with its trees and bread, he was vulnerable to cruel abuse by heartless and greedy men. When he had no coverage of his rights by law, he was reduced to a status that was beneath the concept of humanity in the covenant.

The third development was a priestly hierarchy of Yahweh worshipers who served the king and found security in the *status quo* of the social order. Amaziah, priest at Bethel (Amos 7:10-13), is an example. He is representative of other priests and local worship places that filled a role that one century earlier had been filled by Baal worship. We are not far from the truth in saying that Yahwism had turned around almost 180 degrees since Elijah. Amos and Micah confronted a worship of God that could have gone under the name of Tyrian Baalism in Elijah's time. The pressures of material prosperity and grass-roots support of Baalism in Ahab's day brought about the change. The religion of Elijah was too rural in orientation to adapt to a prosperous urban society and retain its distinctives. When the choice was between those distinctives and prosperity, religion lost.

The changed nature of Yahwism is evident in the Samaria Ostraca, a collection of inscribed pieces of pottery that were used as records of shipments to the king in Samaria. The dockets recorded shipments of fine oil and wine, either as taxes or shares of produce from royal landholdings near the capital. A study of the places named on the Ostraca suggests that the old Solomonic administrative district produced the oil and wine. The old order of the tribal confederacy that Solomon suppressed and that brought about the secession of Israel was finally put down in the name of Yahweh. Names of people on the dockets were compounded with Yahweh, Baal, and El indiscriminately, in the same families. Thus, the sharp distinctions between Yahweh and Baal had gone the way of the old rural order of society. A new urban order had created a new kind of worship of God that absorbed much of the Baal worship that Elijah had fought at Mount Carmel.

This kind of society and religion called forth the classical prophets. Indeed, they traced their heritage and traditions from the guilds of prophets of Elijah's age, but the classical prophets were a new breed. Ecstatic behavior had given way to rational prophecy. Whatever ecstatic elements remained served to heighten the rational faculties rather than to bypass them. Consequently, we meet in Amos and Hosea, for instance, men who would be much at home in the social and religious tensions of our decade. They were appalled at the condition of the urban social order and its irrelevant religion.

Amos
Amos 1:1; 4:1–7:17

We take the measure of Amos at Bethel. He was accused of treason against Jeroboam II by the priest of the king's sanctuary. Amaziah wrote to Jeroboam II: "Amos has conspired against you in the very center of the house of Israel; the land is not able to bear all his words" (7:10).

We would expect such a charge. What king had not faced conspiracies led by prophets in Israel! If we check off the kings from Jeroboam II back to Jeroboam I, when was there *not* a prophet conspiring to overthrow the government? The conspiracy usually began as a prophecy that a new king was designated by the Lord. David was designated by Samuel, Solomon was supported by Nathan, and Jeroboam I was designated by Ahijah of Shiloh. In the eyes of the incumbent, these were the beginnings of active conspiracies to overthrow his government. So Amos was charged with conspiring against the king.

"Jeroboam shall die by the sword, and Israel must go into exile away from his land" (7:10), the report quoted Amos as saying. The prophet's response is revealing. "I am no prophet, nor a prophet's son" (v. 14), he protested. The denial of belonging to a prophetic guild was the prophet's denial of conspiring against the king. We may wonder where the prophetic guilds were. Possibly, most of the prophets supported the kingdom of Jeroboam. A certain Jonah, the son of Amittai, from Gath-hepher, prophesied the expansion of the kingdom by Jeroboam II (2 Kgs 14:25) in the tradition of the prophets of the old order, but the voice of dissent was strangely absent until Amos spoke his oracle at Bethel. What he said after denying association with a guild, furthermore, is revealing: "But I am a herdsman, and a dresser of sycamore trees, and the Lord took me from following the flock" (7:14-15).

The guild of Elisha at Bethel had received a part of its living in contributions from the people, but Amos, as the apostle Paul, supported himself. Amaziah did not believe Amos. He said, "O seer, go, flee away to the land of Judah, and earn your bread there, and prophesy there" (v. 12). Here the term "seer" is derogatory; it calls Amos a diviner and not a prophet. Amaziah implied that Amos was prophesying for bread, for a fee. He continued, "But never again prophesy at Bethel, for it is the king's sanctuary, and it is a temple of the kingdom" (v. 13).

We are confronted with a new breed of prophet, therefore, in Amos. He was not one of the sons of the prophets, a guild member; neither was he a master of a guild. Instead, he claimed to be a shepherd and dresser of sycamore who worked independently for his bread. His message was uncompromised by the need for a living. Amos had the spirit of the layman, not the professional prophet.

At least three conditions in Israel aroused the indignation of Amos. He was appalled at the social injustice of the urban way of life that had developed, as is evident in his condemnation of luxurious living in Samaria (Amos 4, 6) when the serfs who labored for Samaria were oppressed and robbed of their dignity. The prophet declared, "Hear this word, you cows of Bashan, who oppress the poor, who crush the needy" (4:1).

We are not sure how poor the serfs were. We know that tenants in Babylonia during the Persian period earned enough pay per month to buy up to three bushels of grain and two or three of dates. Garlic or leeks could be grown in garden spots. Oil from olives was used in Palestine instead of dates. We are not far from the true picture of the tenant's life in saying that he earned just enough per month to provide bread and oil for his family. There was no milk as a rule. Sweets were too expensive, unless figs and dates could be picked from the master's trees. There was no meat. Very likely the only meat eaten during the year was on the special feast days once a year.

This kind of poverty was grinding when the labor of tenants went for luxuries in Samaria. Amos preached, "Alas for those who lie upon beds of ivory, and lounge on their couches" (6:4). The tenant lived in his one-room hut and slept on a hard mat or rug on the dirt floor. He continued, "and eat lambs from the flock, and calves from the stall." Instead of having meat once a year with the tenants, the ladies of Samaria enjoyed lamb and veal, choice meat, every day of the year.

Amos went on with his description of the wealthy life:

Who sing idle songs to the sound of the harp, and . . . improvise on instruments of music, who drink wine from bowls, and anoint themselves with the finest oil (6:5-6).

With nothing to do, the idle women sat and twanged out improvised music that had no meaning, while they lolled in indecent (to Amos) sprawls on their beds. Their serfs toiled to produce the wine, but got none of it. They sacrificed to get enough oil to make their simple bread palatable, while the women of Samaria rubbed oil on their skin! The Samaria Ostraca, from the time of Amos, recorded the shipment of oil and wine from the tenants to Samaria. Amos 6:6 and the Ostraca use the same words for wine and fine oil, taking us unerringly into the social and economic situation the prophet condemned.

The perversion of justice was a second burden of Amos. We should be careful not to envision an elaborate court system with a judge, jury, lawyers, and books of law such as ours. Evidently, court was held in the city gate where the leaders of the city gathered daily to sit and talk and hear complaints that needed arbitration. Under the old rural social order, all clans would be represented in the informal sessions. With the development of a stratified society of landowners, however, merchants and bankers over against a working class, the lower class did not get adequate representation.

Amos said, "They hate the one who speaks in the gate . . . because you trample on the poor and take from them levies of grain" (5:10-11). A closed system made the law serve the interests of injustice because the poor had no ballot and no recourse to a higher court. The prophet continued, "For I know how many are your transgressions, you who afflict the righteous, who take a bribe, and push aside the needy in the gate" (v. 12). With the prophets such as Jonah, the son of Amittai, and priests such as

Amaziah at Bethel in support of the system that created inequity, the appeal to ethics and righteousness went unheeded. Both Israel and Judah had abandoned the law. "They have rejected the law of the Lord" (2:4), Amos said of Judah, and in Israel "they sell the righteous for silver, and the needy for a pair of sandals—they trample the head of the poor into the dust of the earth" (2:6-7).

Amos seemed to have been most acutely pained by the inhumanity of the social system in Israel and Judah. It was not just a violation of the spirit of the law. People who believed they were religious treated their brethren like donkeys, as though they had no soul, as if it was divinely intended that the poor should eke out a hollow existence behind the swinging doors of their huts. The plea of Amos for justice was the cry of an anguished humanitarian when he cried out more in prayer than in prophecy: "But let justice roll down like waters, and righteousness like an ever-flowing stream" (5:24). As there are no favorites when God sends the rain, the prophet said in effect, let justice like waters from the heavens fall alike upon all!

An irrelevant religion was the third concern of Amos. His indignation verged on outright anger when he looked at the religious establishment dedicated to the God of Israel. Amaziah at Bethel must have thought honestly that Amos was a revolutionary, because the institution of religion in Israel had never before prospered as it did in his ministry. Sacrifices increased in volume, evident in the prophet's taunt, "Bring your sacrifices every morning, your tithes every three days" (4:4). Interest in attending the sanctuary at the appointed times was high and by all current standards of success, the king's priests could claim an outstanding era of blessing.

Listen to the voice of dissent, however. Amos thundered, "I hate, I despise your festivals, and I take no delight in your solemn assemblies" (5:21). The very act of worship to him was a transgression of the covenant! He taunted, "Come to Bethel—and transgress" (4:4). Bethel and the sanctuary were the places to transgress the most, because every new proselyte compounded the error of an evil religious institution. In final disgust he said, "Take away from me the noise of your songs, I will not listen to the melody of your harps" (5:23).

How, we may ask, could the people of Israel, the prophets and priests, stray so far from the covenant? I think the feudal economic and social system changed the religious institution of Israel. It was a gradual change, imperceptible to people who were close to the scene. An outsider such as Amos had a much better perspective from which to see and evaluate. The trouble was that the institution of religion was gradually shaped to an inhuman social structure, and its priests and prophets propped up the structure with religion. Worship ceased to be a presentation of the self before God. It became an expression of the vanity of the worshiper. An escalation of worship therefore increased the expression of vanity!

Religion was irrelevant, and the supreme symbol of irrelevance was its institutions. Amos was very clear in his solution. He said to the people in Samaria, "The time is surely coming upon you when they shall take you away with hooks, . . . through breaches in the wall you shall leave, each one straight ahead" (Amos 4:2-3). The breaches were gaps in the city wall, pounded through the stone with siege machines, and the hooks were the pins put through lips or ears of prisoners when they were led off into captivity. The institutions of irrelevant religion would be cast upon the garbage heap of history.

Hosea
Hosea 1:1; 4:1–6:10

Seemingly, a tragic breakup of his home shook Hosea into a career of prophecy. We have no evidence that he was attached to a guild. What actually happened to Hosea's wife is not clear, which makes for much scholarly debate. Evidently, she betrayed him and went into a fling of prostitution, possibly associated with a shrine in Israel. Sacred prostitutes who plied their trade in the service of a religious shrine were always fixtures in the land. They were outlawed in reforms, but they were always back when the next reform came off. In any event, Hosea took measures to redeem his wife.

The domestic tragedy of his life shaped his career as a prophet, because he perceived that Israel had become unfaithful to its covenant with Yahweh. Therefore, he concerned himself with the spiritual adultery of Israel in paganizing Yahwism. As we observed earlier, the worship of Yahweh turned around 180 degrees between Elijah and Amos, with the result that Baalism in the time of Elijah could have been quite respectable Yahwism in the reign of Jeroboam II. Hosea's experience seems to say that sacred prostitution had also become a part of the worship of Yahweh at local shrines. The infidelity of the priests and prophets was as complete as the unfaithfulness of his wife. Therefore, Hosea came through as a prophet of responsible commitment.

The charge by Hosea against Israel is general in 4:1-2, but evidently it was leveled at priests and prophets as well as the laypersons. "There is no faithfulness or loyalty and no knowledge of God in the land." If there was no knowledge of God, pray tell us, Hosea, what was there? We know that Israel and Judah enjoyed their only great period of prosperity after Solomon during the reign of Jeroboam II and Uzziah. The sanctuaries flourished and were patronized by the king. Why was there no knowledge of God, no faithfulness?

Hosea said there was "swearing, lying, and murder, and stealing and adultery" (4:2). This leaves only five of the Ten Commandments not broken. What the affluent priests and prophets taught was evidently not the law of God. They had "forgotten" it (v. 6), or perhaps a better term would be "lost." Priorities got mixed up. An institution of religion had grown up that fed on itself, so that the prophet cried out as Amos: "The more they increased, the more they sinned against me" (v. 7). Then he went beyond Amos, "They (the priests) feed on the sin of my people; they are greedy for their iniquity" (v. 8).

Could a religious system possibly cultivate such a distortion of its heritage of faith that it fed on transgression instead of faith? If Hosea's wife went into a fling of prostitution in the service of God, I suppose her earnings turned over to the priests could be called feeding "on the sin of my people." That such was possible reveals the shocking extent of distortation (iniquity, 4:8) that had occurred. The prophet explicitly charged that "the men themselves go aside with whores, and sacrifice with temple prostitutes" (4:14). Amos spoke of the same thing when he said that a "father and son go in to the same girl" (Amos 2:7).

For Israel to come to this state of degradation was a terrible indictment of its priests and prophets, but I think Hosea found the key to the startling turnabout toward integration with Baalism. After he accused the religious leaders of feeding on the sin of their people, he observed, "And it shall be like people, like priest" (Hos 4:9). We would call this running a religious institution by consensus, based upon popularity polls. I suppose that a half century of teaching what was most popular or prophesying what pleased most people could change a religion considerably. This kind of leadership was "unfaithful," however, lacking straightness and steadfastness. It was irresponsible leadership.

Perhaps the best known quotation from Hosea is the classic summary in 6:6, where the prophet articulates the order of priorities one should have for responsible commitment: "For I desire steadfast love and not sacrifice, the knowledge of God rather than burnt offerings." Like Amos, Hosea saw no redemption for the religious institutions in Israel. He was concerned with the inner soul of leaders and people because he was an introspective man, but he reached the same conclusion that Amos reached. Speaking as the mouthpiece of God, he said, "For I will be like a lion to Ephraim, I will carry off and no one shall rescue" (5:14).

Amos and Hosea therefore took the measure of Israel, and they measured by a covenant that Israel had long since abandoned. An urban social system had created a privileged upper class that lived in luxury at the expense of a broad lower class of tenants and serfs. The unequal distribution of wealth gave rise to the classic injustices common throughout the Near East, outside Israel. Characteristic were the poor persons, poor because they had no rights under the law. Amos championed the poor and made the world aware that when people lived behind the swinging door with no lock, they still had one recourse. They could fall back upon God, who invested in humankind a dignity and nobility that deserved a better fate.

The vision of the plumbline in Amos 7:8-9 takes on a special significance in this light. Study of the fine Phoenician masonry at Samaria suggests that the masons laid their walls by trimming stones where they joined or rested on each other. No mortar was used, so a perfect fit was required. The sides were left uneven until the wall was built. Then the mason dropped a plumbline beside the wall. Working from the end along a colored horizontal line snapped on the top course with a string, the mason chipped away the wall to the plumbline, leaving a perfectly vertical, smooth-faced surface.

The prophet declared, "See, I am setting a plumb line in the midst of my people Israel. I will never again pass them by" (7:8). The line would guide the "hewer" in trimming a straight, vertical line, the meaning of "faithfulness" in Hosea 6:6. Where there was no "faithfulness," the hewer would simply chip away the entire wall. The prophet concluded, "The high places of Israel shall be made desolate, and I will rise against the house of Jeroboam with the sword" (7:9).

The plumbline was dropped in the midst of Israel about 750 B.C. It was the prophet Amos and his colleague Hosea. About 725 B.C., the hewer went to work. Shalmaneser V of Assyria led his armies into the land and put its towns and villages to the sword and torch. Samaria was beseiged three years, suffering the hell of human disintegration due to hunger and thirst. The end came about 722 B.C. when Sargon II, the new Assyrian ruler, breached the city walls with his siege machines. His annals record 27,290 prisoners led away from Samaria into oblivion. When the hewer reached the plumbline, Israel's irrelevant institutions of religion had been chipped away and lost forever.

Chapter 11

Religious Hope
and Political Disaster

2 Kings 16–25; 2 Chronicles 28–36;
Micah 2–3; Isaiah 6–7; 36–39; Jeremiah 5–8; 34–39

	Judah	Israel
735	(Isaiah and Micah)	
	Ahaz (735–715)	Pekah (737–732)
725		Hoshea (732–724)
		Fall of Samaria (722)
715	Hezehiah (715–687)	(Sargon II, 722–705)
	(Shabako of Egypt, 710–696)	
	(Invasion by Sennacherib, 701)	
700		
	(Tirhakah of Egypt,	
	co-regent, 690–689)	
675	Manasseh (687–642)	
650		
	Amon (642–640)	
	Josiah (640–609)	
	(Jeremiah)	
625	(Zephaniah, Nahum)	
	(Neco II of Egypt, 609–593)	
	Jehoahaz (609)	
600	Jehoiakim (609–598)	(Habakkuk)
	Jehoiachin (598–597)	(Nebuchadnezzar,
		605–562)
	Zedekiah (597–587)	(Ezekiel in Babylon)
	Fall of Jerusalem (587)	

The reform of Hezekiah aimed at strengthening the nation internally, while the king worked the diplomatic circuit establishing allies for a revolt against Assyria. When Sargon II was succeeded by Sennacherib in 705 B.C., the revolt began. Jerusalem was prepared.

Hezekiah
2 Kings 16:1–18:12; 2 Chronicles 28–31; Micah 2–3; Isaiah 6–7

"This same Hezekiah closed the upper outlet of the waters of Gihon and directed them down to the west side of the city of David" (2 Chron 32:30). Gihon is the spring that pours intermittently out of the base of the hill Ophel into the Kidron valley. Cavities in the limestone recesses of the spring store up water that periodically floods the cavities and pours out copiously three to five times a day. When the siphoning action empties the cavity, like the emptying of a bathroom fixture water tank, the flood subsides to a reduced flow until the cavity fills again. A tunnel from the upper slope of Jebusite Jerusalem to the back side of the spring gave Joab access to the city when David made it his capital. Hezekiah engineered a much more sophisticated and effective tunnel to bring water into his enlarged city.

> And this was the way in which it was cut through: . . . While there were still three cubits to be cut through, (there was heard) the voice of a man calling to his fellow, for there was an overlap in the rock on the right and on the left. (Siloam inscription)

The quarry workers had begun the tunnel at each end, with one party digging from Gihon and the other working from the point of exit across Ophel. They dug toward each other, meeting with "an overlap," not head-on but near enough that voices could be heard.

> And when the tunnel was driven through, the quarrymen hewed (the rock), each man toward his fellow, axe against axe; the water flowed from the spring toward the reservoir for 1,200 cubits (about 1,800 ft.), and the height of the rock above the heads of the quarrymen was 100 cubits (about 150 ft.). (Siloam inscription).
>   The rest of the deeds of Hezekiah, . . . and how he made the pool and the conduit and brought water into the city, are they not written in the Book of the Annals of the Kings of Judah? (2 Kgs 20:20)

More than anything else, Hezekiah's tunnel catches the spirit of his time. The Assyrian threat to Samaria and Judah had frightened Ahaz, the father of Hezekiah, into a vassal alliance with Tiglath-pileser III in 734 B.C.

> So Ahaz sent messengers to Tiglath-pileser . . . saying, "I am your ser-
> vant and your son" . . . Ahaz also took the silver and gold found in the
> house of the Lord and in the treasures of the king's house, and sent a
> present to the king of Assyria. (2 Kgs 16:7-8)

The surrender to Assyria was complete. Ahaz met Tiglath-pileser in Damascus and agreed to install an altar to the Assyrian gods in the temple at Jerusalem, symbolizing the capitulation of Yahweh, the God of Israel, to the gods of Assyria. (v. 10ff.). Upon his return from Damascus, Ahaz offered sacrifices upon the Assyrian altar and moved the bronze altar to Yahweh from "the front of the house" to an inconspicuous place. He ordered a great program of sacrifices on the foreign altar (v. 15). "But the bronze altar shall be for me to inquire by," he hedged.

Judah escaped the holocaust that destroyed Samaria in 722 B.C. because of its abject surrender to Assyria. Nevertheless, the humiliation of foreign domination, even to the inner sanctum of the worship of God, lay dangerously near the surface of public life. Wisely, the leaders of Judah waited for an opportune time. Hezekiah succeeded his father, Ahaz (715 B.C.), and continued paying tribute to Nineveh. He may been tutored by Isaiah, an ardent nationalist, but he waited until Sennacherib succeeded his father, Sargon II, in 705 B.C. before he made his move.

The die was cast when Hezekiah formally refused to pay tribute to Sennacherib. Pent-up nationalism erupted in a stirring demonstration of spirit that touched every facet of life in Judah. I am sure that thorough engineering for the Siloam Tunnel had already been done. The quarry workers were put to work at each end of the conduit to hasten the job, because Jerusalem knew that the Assyrian would strike as soon as he could. The city defenses were strengthened and supplies laid in.

Meanwhile, the revolt took other significant directions that betrayed long and secret planning. An embassy of Merodach-baladan, ruler of Babylon, came to Jerusalem sometime before the revolt erupted to enlist Hezekiah in a coordinated uprising that would confront Sennacherib with rebellion on many fronts. Hezehiah likely committed Judah in a secret pact because he "welcomed them (the envoys of Merodach-baladan); he showed them all his treasure house, . . . his armory, all that was found in his storehouses" (2 Kgs 20:13). Probably the prince of Babylon sent envoys to other small kingdoms in the west in his effort to enlist a coalition of armies in the rebellion. Babylon rebelled in 703 B.C., and the Assyrian army turned toward the south to put down the revolt in Nineveh's back door. Less than a year was required to bring the rebels under subjection, but it was time bought by the allies in Syria and Palestine.

Egypt also was a major party in the stirrings of revolt. During the long period of Assyrian dominating, from the reign of Shalmaneser III in the ninth century B.C., Egypt and the Israelite kingdoms enjoyed a close cultural relationship. It was occasioned by the inability of either to marshal significant resistance to the Assyrians. Egypt itself was rent asunder by feuding nobles who came to public notice briefly in the rapid turnover of the XXIIIrd and XXIVth Dynasties. Consequently, the influence of Egypt was politically insignificant, although its legendary reputation as a world power probably inspired much hope in Judah.

We see extensive evidence of the penetration of Egyptian culture in both Judah and Israel during the eighth century B.C. The ivories found at Samaria are Egyptian inspired. Craftsmen in Phoenicia probably carved the ivories, but the art work is Egyptian in origin. During this time, the seals and scarabs found in remains of cities also bear marks of Egyptian influence. Common motifs are the lotus blossom and the Egyptian standing serpent; and the rigid, stylized forms of Egyptian are characterized in much of the symbolism.

It is likely that the eyes of Israel and Judah were turned hopefully toward Egypt for a full century during the extension of Assyrian power. Both little states recognized their inability to cope with the eastern kings, so that any brief emergence of a new face in Egypt inspired unrealistic dreams of help. Within this context of constant hope but frustrated dreams we should understand the unusual Egyptian cultural influence during the eighth century B.C. It came about because the hope of Israel was fixed on Egypt more than we have recognized, not because Egypt really dominated Israel or Judah.

The inaugural call of Isaiah in 6:1ff. betrays evidence of this phenomenon. "I saw the Lord sitting upon a throne," the prophet recalled. "Seraphs were in attendance above him; each had six wings" (v. 2). Actually, the seraphim were standing above or on "it," specifically the throne, not "him." They were a part of the throne that the prophet saw. The seraphim in the vision became the attendants of the Lord, ministering to the needs of the prophet, who probably was in an ecstatic trance. Much speculation has centered on the seraphim, because almost no concrete evidence was identified before the present decade to define them. Considerable evidence now allows us to identify them and understand the symbolism in the prophet's call.

Seraphim literally means "serpents," but in Isaiah 6:2ff., the problem has been that the serpents had wings. This is no longer a problem. Carvings of serpents with wings have been found on seals and scarabs in Palestine dating to the time of Isaiah, and the serpents are always standing. In fact, the serpent is the centuries-old symbol that was found in Egypt on the crowns of pharaohs, signifying the deity incarnate in the pharaoh's office. Like the deadly and awesome cobra, the pharaoh was unapproachable and set apart. The symbol came to signify the absolute sovereignty and wholly otherness of the king. Wings were appended to the serpent simply to give it functional appendages. In Egyptian art, the number of wings varies according to the function of the serpent represented.

The Egyptian throne of Tutankhamun, popularly known as King Tut, illustrates the standing, winged serpent. The arms of the throne are formed by wings of the serpents on either side, and the serpents stand behind the arms and on either side of the sitting king. Other standing serpents are carved on the inside and outside of the throne, some with wings and some without them. We could easily conjecture that Isaiah's inaugural vision took its symbolism from this kind of throne, possibly at the enthronement of Jotham when Uzziah died. In the vision, the scene is translated into a heavenly one, with the Lord sitting upon the throne and the seraphim attending to the needs of Isaiah. The significance is that no other symbol in the Near East catches quite the same meaning of absolute sovereignty, wholly otherness, and deity that the standing serpent does. We know that these ideas of God dominated the theology of Isaiah.

Implicit in the vision of Isaiah is a hope in Egypt that the prophet himself did not share. That hope was rekindled when the Ethiopian XXVth Dynasty came to power in Egypt. Around 715 B.C., the land of the Nile was finally brought under the rule of Piankhi, who immediately began to exploit the need of small rulers in Palestine for an ally. The Ashdod rebellion of approximately 713 B.C. was probably instigated by Egypt, but Hezekiah, counseled by Isaiah who walked "naked and barefoot" in Jerusalem as a portent against Egypt (Isa 20:1ff.), wisely stood aside from the revolt. By 705 B.C., however, Hezekiah had become a leader in the revolt against Sennacherib. Against the counsel of Isaiah, he sent envoys to Egypt to negotiate a mutual assistance treaty (30:1-7), which Pharaoh Shabako (710–696 B.C.) welcomed. Long and patient diplomatic efforts therefore preceded the fateful step of open rebellion against Sennacherib.

To strengthen the internal structure of the kingdom, Hezekiah initiated an extensive reform that was both religious and nationalistic. The same social inequity that we saw condemned in Israel by Amos existed also in Judah. Micah, a village prophet from Moresheth, and Isaiah, an urban statesman-prophet in Jerusalem, both influenced Hezekiah. Jerusalem was likened to a great pagan high place by Micah (Mic 1:5-7), and Isaiah condemned the corrupt businessmen and officials who took advantage of poor people (Isa 1:23; 3:14-15). Their indignation was immortalized in graphic pictures of oppression.

"What do you mean by crushing my people," Isaiah asked rhetorically, "by grinding the face of the poor?" (Isa 3:15). He used the imagery of preparing wheat for bread. First it is pounded to crack the husks, then it is ground to extract the flour. Micah used an even more striking image: "Should you not know justice?" he asked. "You . . . who tear the skin off my people, and the flesh off their bones?" (Mic 3:2). The prophet referred to a cruel practice of the Assyrians in subjugating rebel leaders. They were tied spread-eagled to stakes driven in the ground, and their skin was literally torn in strips from their bodies. Israel abhorred this horrible form of intimidation. The same charge against the very people who resented the Assyrians and suffered under them must have stung.

Isaiah was pessimistic about reforming the nation. "The whole head is sick, and the whole heart faint," he said in resignation. "From the sole of the foot even to the head, there is no soundness in it" (Isa 1:5-6). "Ah, you who call evil good and good evil," he cried, echoing the reasons given in Genesis 6:5 for the disaster of the Flood. "Who put darkness for light and light for darkness," he continued (5:20). According to Isaiah's prophecy, the social and religious institutions were beyond reform.

The prophets and priests who supported the injustices of the social and economic system were tongue-lashed by Micah. The prophet said,

> If someone were to go about uttering empty falsehoods, saying "I will preach to you of wine and strong drink," such a one would be the preacher for this people! (2:11)

Wine and strong drink were the symbols of luxurious life, which the prophet condemned because they were supported by the sacrifice of poor people.

That Hezekiah heard the message of Micah (and implicitly, Isaiah) is evident in Jeremiah 26:18ff., when Jeremiah was threatened for prophesying the destruction of the temple. He said, "Micah of Moresheth, who prophesied during the days of King Hezekiah of Judah said . . . 'Zion shall be plowed as a field; Jerusalem shall become a heap of ruins' " (a prophecy found in Mic 3:12). Jeremiah asked, "Did King Hezekiah . . . put him to death? Did he not fear the Lord and entreat the favor of the Lord?" Hezekiah took heed to the words of Micah and the grievances he spelled out in the reforms that were initiated.

The reform touched the social structure in ways we may infer, although specific measures are not named. For instance, the centralizing of the religious cult in Jerusalem probably reflects a kind of centralized control that extended over the economic system as well. The appearance of pottery stone jars during this time with a stamped inscription on the handle, reading "(belonging) to the king," along with a place name such as Hebron has been interpreted as a standardizing of measures in tax collecting. If this is true, controls could very well have been placed on the entire economic system, analogous to the controls that brought order into the religious institutions of the land.

Religious reforms began by purging the temple of the defiling presence of foreign gods, introduced by Ahaz (2 Chron 29:5ff.). The temple was purified, the Levites were reorganized and put to work (v. 12ff.), and an elaborate ritual that was Yahwistic in inspiration was inaugurated (vv. 25-30). Outlawed in the reform were some cult objects that had become a part of the worship of Yahweh. We noted that Amos and Hosea condemned the turnabout from strict adherence to Yahweh to a syncretism that was partly Baalism. Even sacred prostitution had become a part of the worship of Yahweh in local shrines.

Hezekiah's reform outlawed first the high places that had been dedicated to Baal, then taken over in the name of Yahweh. The sacred pillars and wooden symbols of Asherah, the patron goddess of sacred harlotry, were destroyed (2 Kgs 18:4). In Jerusalem, a bronze serpent that had probably come into the temple from a Jebusite heritage was removed. Invitations went out to people in Israel, whose land had been devastated by Sargon II twenty-one years earlier, to take part in the reform (2 Chron 30:1ff.). Implicit in this reconciliation gesture to the northern tribes was also the invitation to join Judah politically in throwing off the Assyrian yoke.

The reforms served to strengthen the nation internally, as did the other measures taken, and Jerusalem was braced for a test of nerve when the Assyrian forces of Sennacherib invaded the land in 701 B.C. The last line of defense, the tunnel from Gihon to a reservoir inside the city, was completed. Hezekiah had mended his fences with Yahweh, the God of Israel in the reforms; touched all the diplomatic bases and secured promises of assistance in treaties with kings from Egypt to Tyre; and strengthened the defenses of the capital city, which symbolized the nationalistic spirit that had revitalized the nation.

The Devastation of Judah
2 Kings 18:13–20:21; 2 Chronicles 32; Isaiah 36–39

Having put down the rebellion of Merodach-baladan at Babylon, Sennacherib led his army toward the Syrian coast in 701 B.C. His strategy was to secure north Syria and the Phoenician coast before moving against the Philistine cities and Judah. Tyre, a leader in the north, was taken, and a vassal was put over the city by the Assyrian. Tyre was devastated and never recovered its glory. Other cities along the coast hastened to buy off destruction with tribute laid at the feet of Sennacherib. In the south, some cracks in the coalition appeared when Moab, Edom, Ammon, and Ashdod sent tribute also. Judah, hoping Egypt would stop the Assyrian with a confrontation in the coastal plain, held out, as did Ekron and Ashkelon.

"The officials, the patricians, and the common people of Ekron," reported Sennacherib in his chronicle, "had thrown Padi, their king, into fetters, . . . and had handed him over to Hezekeah, the Jew." The ruler of Ekron had insisted on paying tribute to the Assyrian, but a popular uprising, possibly instigated by Hezekiah (2 Kgs 18:8), overthrew him, and Hezekiah held him a political prisoner. When the Assyrians prepared to besiege Ekron, an Egyptian army showed up along the coastal road.

"In the plain of Eltekeh, their battle lines were drawn up against me," reported the Assyrian, "and they sharpened their weapons. . . . I fought with them and inflicted a defeat upon them." The chronicle then records the capture of Egyptian charioteers and the bodyguard of the pharaoh. Eltekeh was besieged and taken, after which Ekron felt the full wrath of Sennacherib.

"I assaulted Ekron and killed the officials and patricians who had committed the crime (of handing over Padi to Hezekiah)," the king recorded, "and hung their bodies on poles surrounding the city." This cruel and intimidating practice of impaling rebel leaders on sharp poles was the prototype of crucifixion, but even more brutal, because the stakes were pushed into the abdomen of the victims, or in some cases into the rectum. The other people of Ekron were either made prisoners, especially slaves, or set free. The king continued, "I made Padi, their king, come from Jerusalem and set him as their lord on the throne, imposing upon him the tribute (due) to me (as) overlord."

The return of Padi probably followed the surrender of Hezekiah, recorded in 2 Kings 18:13-18. The king of Judah "sent to the king of Assyria at Lachish, saying, 'I have done wrong; withdraw from me; whatever you impose on me I will bear' " (v. 14). Lachish was the last major city at the edge of the hills of Judah that could impede the march on Jerusalem. An Assyrian artist captured a dramatic moment in the siege of Lachish on a bas-relief discovered on the wall of Sennacherib's palace in Nineveh. The evident fate of Lachish broke the will of Hezekiah to resist.

Several earthen ramps are shown in the relief leading up to the walls of the city. Possibly the ramps were stylized and really indicate only one, like the massive Roman ramp at Masada. The ramp was necessary for the siege machines that protected the archers. They covered sappers who methodically dismantled a section of the wall for entry into the city. In the relief, the machines are penetrating the wall while defenders of the city hurl stones and lighted torches into the midst of the Assyrians. Ladders are in disarray, and bodies of wounded men are falling amid the hail of torches. Outside the city, women and children are fleeing with little bundles of belongings, walking past three naked men impaled on sharp stakes as a warning to the city to surrender.

The fall of Lachish left Jerusalem exposed to the same fate. Sennacherib boasted in his chronicle that when Hezekiah did not submit to his yoke, "Himself (Hezekiah) I made a prisoner in Jerusalem, his royal residence, like a bird in a cage." If the message of surrender reached Sennacherib at Lachish, he ignored it and besieged Jerusalem as he did Lachish and the other cities.

"I surrounded him (Hezekiah in Jerusalem) with earthwork in order to molest those who were leaving the city's gate," the chronicle reads. If he did in fact place Jerusalem under siege, this would have been the appropriate time for Hezekiah to sue for a cease-fire and agree to pay the "300 talents of silver and 30 talents of gold" required (2 Kgs 18:14). The prophet Isaiah would have been among the king's advisers counseling submission (Isa 1:5). The Assyrian claimed tribute of 800 talents of silver and 30 talents of gold, presumably collected from the temple and royal treasuries and "stripped . . . from the doors of the temple . . . and from the door posts" (v. 16).

Judah was prostrate under the Assyrian's foot. He boasted with typical exaggeration of the devastation of Judah:

> I laid siege to 46 of his strong cities, walled forts, and . . . small villages, . . . and conquered (them) by means of well-stamped earth ramps, and battering rams . . . I drove out (of them) 200,150 people, . . . horses, mules, donkeys, camels, . . . cattle beyond counting, and considered (them) booty.

With the country overrun and Jerusalem submissive, the Assyrian "took away from his (Hezekiah's) country" certain towns and gave them to loyal vassals at Ashdod, Gaza, and to Padi, restored to power at Ekron. Hezekiah had his tribute raised as a punitive measure. Sennacherib said he departed with the tribute besides certain of Hezekiah's "daughters, concubines, male and female musicians."

Much has been written about the possibility of a later campaign of Sennacherib in Judah. The biblical text is not clear and may contain telescoped accounts of two invasions that can be separated into 2 Kings 18:13-16, which agrees with the Assyrian records of the campaign in 701 B.C., and 18:17–19:37 and Isaiah 36-39, which seem to reflect another invasion. Events within the empire make plausible a second revolt in Judah around 689 B.C., when Tirhakah at the age of twenty became co-regent with his brother Shabako. Tirhakah was only nine years of age in 701 B.C., and in Nubia, not Egypt.

Babylon began a "second round" with Assyria in 700 B.C. The vassal Bel-ibni rebelled and upon Sennacherib's return from Palestine was put down and replaced by Asshur-nadim-shum, Sennacherib's son. In 693, Sennacherib's son was overthrown and killed in another coup aided by the king of Elam. This rebellion was put down also, but soon all Babylonia was in open revolt. Sennacherib moved to subdue the country again in 691 and faced a desparate coalition of Babylonians and Elamites who drove back the Assyrians. This reversal of Assyrian fortunes may have encouraged Hezekiah and his humiliated countrymen to rebel again, for their yoke of tribute was heavy.

In any case, the fires of revolt in Babylon were stamped out in 689 B.C., and Babylon was given "the treatment." The inhabitants felt the full wrath of Sennacherib in its most brutal expression; the city was destroyed and its temples defiled and left in ruins. By 688 B.C., he was free to turn again to Judah and Egypt. This time Tirhakah could have come to the aid of Hezekiah (2 Kgs 19:9ff.), and the embassy of the Rabshakeh to Jerusalem would be relevant, because the Assyrian argued with the leaders of Jerusalem to abandon Hezekiah's leadership (Isa 36:11-12). Encouraged by Isaiah, the king and his people stood firm, preferring death to further humiliation by Assyria. The army of Tirhakah and a mysterious plague (2 Kgs 19:35ff.) caused the Assyrians to withdraw. Possibly the Egyptians were driven back to their border, as Herodotus reported. He also preserved a tradition that the Assyrian army was plagued with mice that ate their bowstrings, maybe a reflection of the same disaster attributed in the biblical tradition to an angel of the Lord (19:35).

Hezekiah died soon after the Assyrians retired from Judah, and his son, Manasseh (20:21), submitted to Assyria and made peace. He was probably supported by a faction that had opposed Hezekiah's war for independence that had cost Judah its best cities, a generation of young men, and its wealth. The work of Isaiah, the great statesman-prophet, had failed to lead Judah away from the deadly game of international politics. Seemingly, he advocated a kind of isolationism that would have been practical in view of the smallness of Judah, but the constant hope in Egypt, like Israel's hope in America today, led Hezekiah into unrealistic political ventures.

Isaiah's policy was not calculated isolationism so much as a complete dedication of Judah to Yahweh that would be analogous to the prophet's own dedication. This kind of dedication—which in his case found expression in his marriage to a prophetess and giving his sons sermon topics for names (Isa 7:3; 8:1-4)—was extreme. But it would have extricated Judah from the international scene in the same way that Isaiah stood above the factional cross-currents in Jerusalem. Judah, however, would have none of Isaiah's counsel. Heady on the strong drink of nationalism, the kingdom was not ready to settle down to a monastic life in the mountains around Jerusalem.

Smoke over Jerusalem
2 Kings 22–25; 2 Chronicles 34–36; Jeremiah 5–8; 34–39

The Assyrian yoke was heavy. Judah had no choice but to endure it until the sun began to go down on Nineveh and furtive plotting in the shadows as the fringes of the empire began. A palace coup overthrew the government of Amon and took his life about 640 B.C., but level heads prevailed (2 Kgs 21:23-24) because revolt was still a dangerous risk. The assassins were executed, and eight-year-old Josiah was put on the throne. An informally organized "people of the land" ran the government. In the eighth year of Josiah's reign, Asshurbanipal died and was succeeded by his son. Revolt simmered under the surface in Babylonia, and inflexible resentment rose to the surface in the est. The elders of "the people of the land" probably began the break with Assyria by cleansing the temple of its gods and their trappings. By Josiah's twelfth year, the new king of Assyria died, and the time for open revolt seemed at hand. A vigorous reform movement that was both religious and nationalistic was begun. Judah again embarked upon the perilous enterprise of being an independent nation.

The stages in the reform movement have been related to the pattern in 2 Chronicles 34, specifically that the Assyrian gods were evicted from the temple in the eighth year of Josiah (v. 3), when Asshurbanipal died; the move to centralize the cult in Jerusalem and bring the northern tribes under control of Judah occurred in Josiah's twelfth year (v. 6); and the die was cast in a move for independence and national standing in his eighteenth year (v. 8). In any event, there was no turning back after 622 B.C. The reform movement became a complex searching out of pristine Yahwism that would infuse Judah with the vigor of David's kingdom. It was a thorough-going effort to recapture the springtime of Israel's spirit in a revival of old-time religion.

Evidence of the nationalism that gripped the reform movement peeps through the lengthy details of religious measures taken. For instance, Josiah led his army into Israel with almost the same fanatical arrogance of a Jehu. The annals read,

> Moreover, the altar at Bethel, the high place erected by Jeroboam son of Nebat, . . . he pulled down that altar along with the high place. He burned the high place, crushing it to dust. . . . Josiah removed all the shrines of the high places that were in the towns of Samaria, . . . he did to them just as he had done at Bethel. He slaughtered on the altar all the priests of the high places who were there, and burned human bones on them. (2 Kgs 23:15, 19-20)

Excavations at Shechem in 1962 possibly uncovered some evidence of Josiah's reform among the "towns of Samaria." Carefully uncovering the ancient remains in Field IX, a supervisor came upon the ruins of a mud-brick walled house. The walls enclosed a thick ashy layer that covered the floor and objects lying directly on it. When the ashes were examined, artifacts pointing to a sudden and violent destruction came to light. Slingstones, a spear head, broken pottery on the floor, and an overturned grinding stone suggested the sudden violence that hit the area. The proximity to the temple and Baal high place and a seventh-century B.C. destruction date point accusingly toward Josiah as the destroyer.

Two directions were taken in the reform of religion in Judah. A lawbook was discovered in cleansing the temple (2 Kgs 22:8), which seems to have contained at least the core of the present book of Deuteronomy. The document apparently derived from the reform of Hezekiah either as a book produced during the reform or a kind of memoir that interpreted Hezekiah's reform written during the reign of Manasseh. An inquiry was made of Huldah, a prophetess, for authentication of the lawbook (v. 14ff.), apparently to ascertain whether it had been the basis for the previous reform. Satisfied with her report, the king's advisors immediately began to implement the measures articulated in the book, making it a guide for the reform. The first direction taken in the reform was to anchor it to the law traditions that were believed to go back to the founding of the nation. The second direction was to carry the movement toward centralization of the worship of Yahweh begun by Hezekiah to its fulfillment as a demonstration of faith.

The ancient traditions of the entry into Canaan, the settlement, the period of the Judges, and the early monarchy were collected and reviewed. Israel's history was reinterpreted in the light of the need for absolute loyalty to Yahweh in the seventh century B.C., and pivotal events of the past were made to preach the rewards of obedience. We have noted that the ancient accounts of the capture of Jericho and 'Ai were two events that were picked up and made exemplary of the theology of the seventh century B.C. Jericho fell to Israel without a battle because Israel had faith in God. Achan's disobedience sabotaged the expedition to capture 'Ai, but when Achan was eliminated from the camp of Israel, the city of 'Ai fell to Joshua. History was recounted and elaborated with details added hundreds of years later by preachers of reform, the traditions of which we have in the present scriptures.

Events that occurred in the time of the Judges were interpreted in a more or less rigid pattern of "obedience equals success; disobedience equals failure." When Israel forsook the Lord and served Baal, the anger of the Lord was kindled. God gave the people over "to plunderers, who plundered them, and he sold them into the power of their enemies round about" (Judg 2:13-14). When the people repented and cried out to the Lord, however, God raised up saviors who delivered them from the hand of the enemy (3:9-11). Thus, disobedience brought strict retribution in the form of oppression. On the other hand, obedience brought deliverance and national prosperity. Consequently, the preaching in Josiah's reform was a condemnation of any deviation from the lawbook.

The prophetess Huldah said,

> Tell the man who sent you to me, Thus says the Lord, I will indeed bring disaster on this place and on its inhabitants—all the words of the book that the king of Judah (Josiah) has read. Because they have abandoned me and have made offerings to other gods, . . . therefore my wrath will be kindled against this place, and it will not be quenched. (2 Kgs 22:15-17)

When these words were brought to King Josiah, he called a meeting of his people "small and great; he read in their hearing all the words of the book of the covenant that had been found in the house of the Lord" (23:2).

Repentant of his disobedience through ignorance of the lawbook, "the king stood by the pillar and made a covenant before the Lord, . . . to perform the words of this covenant that were written in this book" (2 Kgs 23:3). There followed a vigorous purge of all pagan elements that had crept into the worship of Yahweh (vv. 4-14) that were symbols of Israel's disobedience. Josiah's example of strict obedience to the law set the pattern that was to be followed; and where it was not readily accepted, the king imposed it by force upon the inhabitants (vv. 15-18). He left no stone unturned in obeying the strict letter of the law. He believed with his advisers that he was at the same time securing the nation against disaster.

Evidence from excavations suggests that Josiah's reform did not have widespread support among the people. At Tell en-Nasbeh, probably biblical Mizpah, images outlawed in the reform were found in almost every house! Tombs used until the end of the monarchy continued to have figurines and images placed in them. One reason for the weakness of support for the reform may have been the radical measures taken to centralize worship in Jerusalem. The local places of worship, patronized from the earliest memory of the inhabitants, were outlawed. Evidently, local priests were invited to take positions in Jerusalem, but many refused and instead "ate unleavened bread among their kindred" (2 Kgs 23:9). The Jerusalem priesthood probably would have placed them in second or third class roles, which was unacceptable. Consequently, the reform seems to have enforced external measures upon the people that were never really accepted. It lived mainly in the driving presence of Josiah, which proved to be a precarious existence.

The prophet Jeremiah may have supported the reform at first, but he soon became disillusioned with the irrelevance of its religion. The prophet asked scornfully, "How can you say 'We are wise, and the law of the Lord is with us?' when . . . the false pen of the scribes has made it into a lie?" (Jer 8:8). Jeremiah seemed to question the interpretation that the scribes put on the ancient traditions. With their rigid *quid pro quo* theology that obedience brought reward and disobedience brought punishment, they were vulnerable. His voice of dissent therefore should be taken seriously because it represents a difference of opinion on a major issue within the biblical traditions. The prophet was certain that those who preached the reform were not walking in "the ancient paths" (6:16), and he scorned the security they preached as the reward for obeying what was found in the lawbook. The prophet cried, "They have treated the wound of my people carelessly, saying 'Peace, Peace,' when there is no peace" (6:14).

Further observations may be made about the reform in the light of the international situation on the one hand and the prophet Jeremiah on the other. An ominous feeling of approaching disaster weighed heavily upon the Near East in the seventh century B.C. Political and religious leaders faced a world that was looking into the sunset of its existence. The old patterns of government and religion were breaking up, and uncertainty about what would supplant them gripped thoughtful people from Babylon to Egypt.

Babylon had a revival of "the old-time religion" in the next century and enjoyed a brief rebirth of the spirit that we call "Neo-Babylonian." The towering ziggurat at Babylon was restored to its ancient glory, and Babylon basked for awhile in renewed power before the end came around 539 B.C. It is not surprising, therefore, to find in Judah a similar response to the same foreboding that characterized the age. Josiah programmed his reform with the promulgation of a second law: "Deuteronomy."

The reform reached back into Israel's heritage for the vitality that had characterized the pioneer days. That vitality, we should note, looked different from the perspective of five centuries later than it did in its own time. To the reformers, it seemed to be the security the nation needed. Our second observation, then, is that the security found in the reform was an illusion. I think Jeremiah underscored the futility of looking for national security in a revival of religion, because a revival grasps for something out of the past to meet today's problems. It evades coming to grips with the issues that make the world situation ominous in the first place.

Josiah's reform was killed by one Egyptian arrow at Megiddo. The king attempted to intercept Pharaoh Neco who was going to the aid of Assyria in the north (2 Kgs 23:29). Babylon had Assyria reeling toward Carchemish, following the sack of Nineveh in 612 B.C. Josiah recklessly overestimated his power, possibly under the false security infused by the reform, and he was brushed aside by the Egyptian army. "His servants carried him dead in a chariot from Megiddo, brought him to Jerusalem, and buried him" (23:30).

Judah rapidly fell a victim of the chaotic world situation. Zedekiah, who was put on the throne by Babylon, placed his hope in Egypt, misjudging that Babylon was the rising power with which to be reckoned (2 Kgs 24:18-20). Jeremiah rightly saw the need to come to terms with Babylon, but he was not heard by the king (Jer 38). Consequently, it was only a matter of time until Babylonian armies tramped the long road to

Judah to stamp out Zedekiah's rebellion. In 589 B.C. they came. According to the annals,

> In the ninth year of his (Zedekiah's) reign, . . . King Nebuchadnezzar
> Babylon came with all his army against Jerusalem, and laid siege to it;
> . . . so the city was besieged until the eleventh year of king Zedekiah.
> (25:1-2)

Judah came slowly but surely under the stranglehold of the Babylonian army. Cities were shut up and guarded, so the people would break under thirst and hunger. Communication was by runners, who slipped through enemy lines, or by smoke signals. The smoke signals that Jerusalem saw for two years told mainly of the devastation of the land. Little columns from burning villages rose straight up like fires from an altar. At about 2,000 feet, the wind from the Mediterranean bent the column due east, like the flattened head of a standing cobra, and blew its message of destruction into the face of Jerusalem. Zedekiah, shut up in the city, sought counsel. Where, he asked, was Egypt?

The Egyptians came, and the siege of Jerusalem was lifted momentarily (Jer 37:5), but Jeremiah sent his counsel to the king that the relief was temporary (v. 7). The Egyptian would show his face to Jerusalem to reassure Zedekiah and frighten the Babylonians, but he would not risk Egypt for Jerusalem. Jeremiah warned, "And the Chaldeans shall return and fight against this city; they shall take it and burn it with fire" (v. 8).

The king wavered between the counsel of one faction and another. His heart was with the pro-Egyptian faction, but he halfway believed the group represented by Jeremiah's pro-Babylonian position. When Jeremiah attempted to leave the city during the interval of Babylonian withdrawal to go to his village of Anathoth about two miles away, he was seized by the king's guards (Jer 37:11f). "You are deserting to the Chaldeans," the sentry charged (v. 13). "That is a lie," the prophet protested. "I am not deserting to the Chaldeans" (v. 14).

Confined to the guard house, Jeremiah waited out the siege a prisoner of the king. Zedekiah secretly sought the prophet's advice (37:17), but he remained pro-Egyptian publicly, because any move to make peace with Babylon would likely have brought on his assassination by the army. When the prophet persisted in his dissent, the pro-Egyptian princes regarded him as a traitor. They clamored, "This man ought to be put to death because he is discouraging the soldiers who are left in this city" (38:4).

Meanwhile, the army that was posted in the hills of Judah fought on but received conflicting reports. A message from an outpost commander to his superior at Lachish, found written on a piece of broken pottery, takes us into the same chaotic situation that the book of Jeremiah reports. The letter reads, "Behold, the words of the princes are not good, (but) to weaken our hands and to slacken the hands of men who are informed about them" (Lachish Ostracon VI). Jeremiah's dovish attitude toward Babylon was shared by princes in the king's court also, but they were outvoted by the hawks who looked for help from Egypt.

The help did not come. Egypt retired in the face of war with Babylon, leaving Jerusalem exposed to the wrath of Nebuchadnezzar. Smoke again rose from the cities and villages, and the west wind blew it into the face of Jerusalem. Outpost after outpost fell. The lonely commander sent a terse communique to Lachish. He said, "And let my lord (the superior officer) know that we are watching for the (smoke) signals from Lachish, . . . for we cannot see Azekah" (Lachish Ostracon IV). The same information is reported in Jeremiah 34:6-7:

> Then Jeremiah . . . spoke . . . to Zedekiah . . . , when the army . . . of Babylon was fighting against Jerusalem and against all the cities of Judah that were left, Lachish and Azekah; for these were the only fortified cities of Judah that remained.

Our eyes are spared the destruction that sent up Jerusalem in smoke in 587 B.C. Its signal, however, was the unwritten communique to history that Josiah's reform had failed. Tumbled stones strewn down the slopes of the city of David that were uncovered in 1962 tell the same story. The illusion that national security could be bought with a religious reform was shattered as Jeremiah had prophesied. Zedekiah, however, was not spared the sight of destruction. He watched his city burn. Fleeing toward Jericho, the smoke of Jerusalem followed him like a relentless avenger, and he was captured. His sons were put to the sword "before his eyes," the scribe wrote. Then the king of Babylon "put out the eyes of Zedekiah" and led him away to Babylon (Jer 39:6-7).

Chapter 12

Exile and the Lonely City

2 Kings 24:10–25:30; Jeremiah 29; 40–44
Lamentations 1–5; Ezekiel 1–19; Psalm 137

600	Babylonia dominates Near East
597	First deportation from Jerusalem, by Nebuchadnezzar
	(Ezekiel in Babylon)
587	Third deportation by Nebuchadnezzar
	(Jeremiah taken to Egypt)
575	Exiles in Babylon and Egypt
562	Jehoiachin freed by Evil-Merodach
	Nabonidas (556–539)
550	Cyrus of Persia (550–530)

About 4,600 of the leading citizens of Judah were carried away to Babylon in three deportations: 597, 587, and 582 B.C. Many of the people integrated with the Babylonian way of life within a century and provided an economic base of support for the restoration of Jerusalem under Ezra and Nehemiah. Jehoiachin, the captive king, was kept under house arrest in Babylon. Records of the issue of rations to him indicate that he was still regarded as the legitimate king even while the vassal Zedekiah ruled. A core of priestly and prophetic leaders mourned the destruction of Jerusalem and sang the songs of Zion in exile.

By the Waters of Babylon
2 Kings 24:10-16; 25:8-21
Jeremiah 29; 40–41; Ezekiel 1–19; Psalm 137

Ezekiel worked with absorbed concentration on the soft, wet face of a mud brick. The flattened end of the wood stylus fashioned a brittle line of small, straight impressions. Slowly, two enclosures (which represented

Jerusalem) took shape on the brick: a rectangular one on the upper end, abutting a narrow, elongated one connecting on the lower end. Passersby probably watched him work and then walked away shaking their heads in silent pity for the man. Others stayed and watched. Their mumbled conversation tried to read the artist's mind and anticipate his next line, but he worked on, hearing only the silent instructions that had commissioned his work of art:

> Take a brick and set it before you. On it portray a city, Jerusalem; and put siegeworks against it; . . . set camps also against it and plant battering rams against it all around. (Ezek 4:1-2)

This command was the classic siege method, graphically preserved in the Herodian remains at Masada in Israel today. The encircling wall and camps where the besieger waited for his victims to break down from hunger and thirst were terrible psychological weapons. Every morning when he looked out from the city, the siege wall and enemy camps implied "no escape," and every night when he went to bed, he knew the end was one day nearer. The command continued, "Then take an iron plate and place it as an iron wall between you and the city" (Ezek 4:3).

A bearded onlooker discovered the key to Ezekiel's strange preoccupation with the mud-brick. The city was shaped like Jerusalem, and the bank of earth around the brick was a siege wall. The man was pantomiming a siege of Jerusalem! Furthermore, the iron plate symbolized the disengagement of Yahweh from Jerusalem. God would allow the city to fall. There would be no ninth hour deliverance such as the one that occurred in the days of Isaiah when Sennacherib's second siege of the city was lifted and Jerusalem was spared.

Jerusalem indeed fell before the Babylonians three times. The first capture occurred on 16 March 597 B.C., when Jehoiachin surrendered to Nebuchadnezzar rather than see the city burned. We have two accounts: one Babylonian from the royal chronicle, and one from 2 Chronicles 36:10:

Babylonian Chronicle

> In the seventh year (of Nebuchadnezzer) in the month Kislev, the king of Accad . . . beseiged the town of Judah (Jerusalem), and on the second day of the month Adar (16 March), he took the town and made the

king (Jehoiachin) prisoner. He chose a king after his own heart (Zedeki-ah) and took much tribute from him.

2 Chronicles 36:10

In the spring of the year King Nebuchadnezzar sent and brought him (Jehoiachin) to Babylon, along with the precious vessels of the house of the Lord, and made his brother Zedekiah king over Judah and Jerusalem.

Because the city surrendered, the slaughter of its inhabitants was not great, but the largest deportation to Babylon occurred. Jehoiachin and his family were led away, along with the leading intellectuals, political leaders, religious officials, businessmen, and merchants. The cream of Judah's leadership was skimmed off and taken to Babylon where they could not instigate revolts, and Zedekiah agreed to become a vassal to Babylon. Very likely, Ezekiel was in the sad band of exiles that trudged on foot, with older people and children riding in two-wheeled carts, the thousand miles to Babylon. The royal family was kept under a kind of house arrest in the capital while the others were sent into the provinces, evidently in the Nippur area. In fact, they probably established the settlement of Tel Abib (namesake of modern Tel Aviv) on the Chebar canal.

A second and smaller deportation occurred when Jerusalem was sacked in 587 B.C. The populace endured the wrath of Nebuchadnezzar that time because of Zedekiah's treacherous revolt in league with Egypt. Zedekiah's punishment was representative of the cruel fate of leaders who would normally be deported. A total of seventy-one top leaders—including the chief priest, the top general of the army, the king's cabinet members, and sixty members of "the people of the land"—were executed at Riblah in Syria (2 Kgs 25:18-11). The rest of the upper-level leadership, along with people who had deserted to the Babylonians, was carried into exile (v. 22). Finally, a third deportation occurred when the assassination of Gedeliah was avenged in 582 B.C. (2 Kgs 25:22-26; Jer 40-44). Fearful leaders who survived the abortive revolt fled to Egypt. Although the narratives are silent about a deportation to Babylon, Jeremiah 52:30 gives a total of 745 persons deported in the twenty-third year of Nebuchadnezzer (582 B.C.).

The total number of deported Hebrews was probably much smaller than the number left in Judah. Jeremiah 52:28-30 lists three deportations:

in 597, 587, and 582, with a total of 4,600 persons in all. This is a smaller number than that given in 2 Kings 24:14, where 10,000 captives are reported taken away in 597 B.C. If Jeremiah's totals include men only, which does not seem warranted because he gives a total number of "persons," the two traditions may be brought near agreement. Quite likely, the 10,000 of 2 Kings 24:14 is a general estimate, while the numbers in Jeremiah 52:28-30 are more accurate. In any case, this represents a small minority of Judah, but the best leadership of the kingdom. Therefore, we can expect that spiritual and intellectual leadership of the Jews would eventually emerge out of Babylon, rather than in present-occupied Judah.

Two archaeological finds in Babylonia indicate the status of the Jews in exile. First, a collection of inscribed clay tablets, the Jehoiachin Tablets, was discovered by Robert Koldewey in the palace of Nebuchadnezzar. Cached in a vaulted underground building associated with the palace, the tablets were records of rations issued by the royal "oil purveyor." Monthly rations of food, particularly oil and sesame, were issued to King Jehoiachin of Judah. The records cover a period between the tenth and thirty-fifth years of Nebuchadnezzar's reign, which would be between 595 and 570 B.C. Jehoiachin had been taken to Babylon in 597 B.C., when Zedekiah was made ruler by Nabuchadnezzar. The tablets cover the period between the third deportation, when Gedeliah was assassinated in 582 B.C., and the accession of Evil-merodach in 562 B.C. (2 Kgs 25:27), when the biblical traditions are silent about the exiles in Babylon.

Reference in the tablets to Jehoiachin as king of Judah has been taken to mean that he was regarded in captivity as the legitimate king. Zedekiah was an usurper. Quite likely, Jehoiachin's legitimate title was recognized by the Jews in captivity as well as by the Babylonians. Ezekiel's prophecy was dated "in the fifth year of the exile of King Jehoiachin" (1:2), or during the reign of Zedekiah in Jerusalem. Also, even in Judah, Jehoiachin was still the legitimate king during Zedekiah's reign. Three impressions of a seal inscribed with the legend "To Eliakim steward of Jaukin" have been associated with Jehoiachin. Eliakim was the overseer of crown property maintained in Judah by the exiled king, who was expected to return in a prophecy by Hanniah:

> I (the Lord) will bring back to this place (Judah) Jeconiah (Jehoiachin) . . . and all the exiles from Judah who went to Babylon, . . . for I will break the yoke of the king of Babylon.

The prophecy was false, but it indicated a faction loyal to Jehoiachin that remained in Judah.

Furthermore, the tablets indicate that the captives from Judah were mixed with captives from other lands in a way reminiscent of the inter-racial mixture of slaves in Egypt prior to the Exodus. One scholar has identified Philistines from Ashkelon, Phoenicians from Tyre and Byblos, Egyptians, Elamites, Persians, Lydians from Asia Minor, and others. Gathered around the Tower of Babel prototype in the walled city of Babylon was a mixture of peoples whose only common element was sub-mission to Nebuchadnezzar. It was a humiliating experience for the proud aristocrats and royal families. The Jews, for instance, kept their eyes turned toward Jerusalem because, to them, Jerusalem was at the center of the universe. Yahweh had said "This is Jerusalem; I have set her in the center of the nations . . . all around her" (Ezek 5:3). But they were oppressed by a people just as proud, who put Babylon right in the middle of their map of the universe.

A second discovery of inscribed clay tablets, the archives of the Mur-ashu banking family in Nippur, indicates a state of prosperity for many Jews a century after the exile. The deported Hebrews settled at Tel Abib on the canal Chebar (Ezek 3:15) and at other places named in Ezra 2:59 and 8:15 whose locations we do not know. The canal Chebar was in the rich, irrigated agricultural area of Nippur. Many of the Jews did not hang their harps on the willows and weep for Zion; they engaged in farming operations financed by the Murashu company. By the fifth century B.C., many Jews were integrated with Babylon in business and culture, as Jere-miah 29:5-8 advocated. These were likely the ones "who were around the exiles Ezra gathered to return to Judah," the ones who "aided them with silver vessels, with gold, with goods, with animals, and with valuable gifts" (Ezek 1:6). They sent money back to devastated Judah but stayed in Babylon where there was more money to earn.

In spite of the integration of many Jews into Babylonian life, a dedi-cated religious leadership longed for the restoration of Jerusalem. Ezekiel was the most outstanding of the prophets until the exilic Isaiah sang his immortal prophecy of deliverance (Isa 40–55). We cannot explore the prophecy of Ezekiel in detail, but we should note that he was at home in Babylon among the exiles. His message and medium were distinctly col-ored by his environment, although his obsession was with Judah and Jerusalem. He was among the devout ones who gathered on the sabbath to mourn the humiliation of Zion and refused to sing the "songs of Zion" in a strange land (Ps 137:1-3). To sing the sacred psalms on unclean soil would have been an affront to God.

The complex and unusual symbols that Ezekiel used in his prophecy, for instance, are understood best in the context of art and ideas indigenous to the Mesopotamian Valley. His vision of the throne chariot of Yahweh made use of winged beasts, four-faced creatures, animals with human heads, or creatures with animal heads and the bodies of men. Some of the symbols have come into Christian art from their pagan background through Ezekiel. No painting or bas-relief that we know contains all of the complex details in the vision of the storm chariot, but the details carry their native meaning, translated into attributes of Yahweh.

One part of the vision, for instance, may be compared with an enameled portrayal of the Assyrian god Asshur. The work of art was in full color on the palace walls at Asshur in ancient Assyria. Ezekiel described his vision in 1:26-28.

> And above the dome over their heads there was something like a throne, in appearance like sapphire (lapis lazuli, which is blue); and seated above the likeness of a throne was something that seemed like a human form. (v. 26)

Could the sky be thought of as "something like a throne"? In view of the attributes of Asshur in the drawing and Yahweh in the prophet's description, I think it is conceivable.

The prophet continued, "Upward from what appeared like the loins, I saw something like gleaming amber, something that looked like fire enclosed all around" (v. 27). The actual colors of the wings were bronze alternated with blue, and the arms and chest were light bronze against the background of darker bronze flames encircling the head. Bronze and blue symbolized the sun and the sky, and the wheel of radiating flames was the sun.

Ezekiel further described his vision: "And downward from what looked like the loins, I saw something that looked like fire, and there was a splendor all around" (v. 27). Yahweh was illuminated against a background of the sun, symbolizing the God of the sun, which the Assyrians claimed for Asshur. He continued,

> Like the bow in a cloud on a rainy day, such was the appearance of the splendor all around. This was the appearance of the likeness of the glory of the Lord. (v. 28)

The bow in the hands of Asshur was the rainbow. It became a wheel of fire encircling the sun, which was the inner wheel. Asshur was the weather god, symbolized by the outer wheel, and god of the sun, indicated by the inner wheel. The loop at the top united the two into a composite. He was thus the god of life, fertility, and justice to the Assyrians. Likely, the revelation that overwhelmed Ezekiel was his first awareness that Yahweh, in a foreign land, was the true god of the storm and the sun, not Asshur nor the Babylonian gods. But the revelation came to him clothed in part by the contemporary symbols that people in Babylonia understood.

In the Land of Egypt
Jeremiah 42–44

Seemingly, Judah had an unusual hope in Egypt for at least the last century of its turbulent existence. During the last 100 years before 582, when the nation polarized around pro-Egyptian or anti-Egyptian factions, political refugees probably fled to Egypt. Others who became fearful in the last days of the kingdom would have found a natural haven in the land of the Nile. A sizeable group fled after the assassination of Gedeliah in 582 B.C. to Egypt, taking Jeremiah against his wishes (Jer 43:5-7). They settled a refugee village at Tahpanhes on the coastal road into the Nile delta. Jews dwelt at Migdol, probably farther south along the eastern frontier. Others were found at Noph, or Memphis, which is near modern Cairo, and in the land of Pathros, somewhere along the upper Nile valley.

Thus, settlements in varying stages of integration with Egyptian life were found in the land of Egypt. Because they were made up of various groups of dissidents, they probably had little communication with each other. Isaiah 19:19 refers to "an altar to the Lord (Yahweh) in the center of the land of Egypt," implying the existence of established worship places where the Jews had no intention of returning to Judah. Josephus referred to a letter from Onias to Ptolemy Philometer (181–145 B.C.) that reports: "In various places inhabited by our people (the Jews), I have found almost everywhere sanctuaries after an improper manner so as to set one another at variance." The Jews in Egypt, who fled there on their own initiative, seem to have had little concerted ambition to return and build Jerusalem again. They made for themselves a new life, complete with places to worship Yahweh. One such place, settled before the fall of Jerusalem in 587 B.C., was at Elephantine, under the shadow of the present Aswan Dam in upper Egypt.

A colony of Jewish mercenaries probably settled on the island of Elephantine, in the Nile River, at the southern frontier adjoining Nubia. A corpus of papyrus documents that were purchased piecemeal in Cairo between 1906 and 1911 proved to be from the Jewish settlement. They give a contemporary glimpse of this independent and permanent village during the fifth century B.C., when Judah was being resettled by Nehemiah and Ezra. The village could have served the purpose of border kibbutz villages in Israel today. It was a civilian military unit guarding the southern frontier, but normal life was pursued in agriculture, commerce, and crafts. The papyri indicate that villagers intermarried with Egyptians, and that they did not know the extreme measures of the reform of Josiah in their practice of religion.

A temple and priesthood were devoted to Yahweh at Elephantine. The temple was standing in 525 B.C., and we learn of it because local Egyptians burned it to the ground in the fourteenth year of Darius II, around 410 B.C. They were incited by rival priests of the neighboring temple of Khnub, who bribed the local Persian governor, Widrang, to turn a blind eye to their activity. The conflict with the local Egyptian priests seems to have been political, not religious. One papyrus mentions that on the accession of Darius II (423 B.C.), the Egyptians staged an abortive revolt against Persian rule. The Jewish colony remained loyal to the Persians, however, incurring the wrath of local nationalists. Sacking of the Jewish temple in 410 B.C. was likely reprisal for Jewish loyalty to the Persians.

The temple reflects a paganized Yahwism that may reflect the kind of religion found in Judah and Israel before the "Deuteronomic" reforms of Hezekiah and Josiah. Yahweh, the God of Israel, was worshiped, but names compounded with Yahweh represent a compromise of strict orthodoxy. One of the names, "Anathyahu," is a combination of Yahweh and Anath, a fertility goddess of the Canaanites. The priests did not regard themselves as estranged from Israel, however. Appeals for contributions to help rebuild the temple went out to Delaiah and Shelemiah, sons of Sanballat at Samaria, and to Johanan, the high priest in Jerusalem. The letters reflect no awareness of the sharp religious differences between Jerusalem and Samaria in the fifth century.

Life in the Jewish community was not significantly different from that of the Egyptians. There is the case of an Egyptian family of a mother and three sons who were slaves of the Jews. When the estate of the owner was divided, two older sons were divided between brothers among the heirs, and the woman and younger son were unallocated. The slaves were branded on the arm with a mark and the name of the owner. Other cases related in the papyri reflect steep profits reaped by the Jews in money-lending. Loans were given on the security of property, goods, food, or slaves. Interest on loans amounted to as much as 60 percent of the principal, and when it could not be paid regularly, the interest was added to the principal and compounded. Persons who made loans accumulated debts that were inherited by their heirs, which probably accounts for the Egyptian slaves referred to above. The Jewish community at Elephantine, in the land of Egypt, did not mourn the destruction of Jerusalem, nor did it long to return to Zion.

Jeremiah's last days were spent among the exiles in Egypt. He continued to prophesy, but his messages condemned the faithless in Egypt in the same terms that he had condemned them in Judah. "I will punish those who live in the land of Egypt, as I have punished Jerusalem" (Jer 44:13), the prophesy proclaimed in the name of Yahweh, "so that none of the remnant of Judah who have come to settle in the land of Egypt shall escape or survive or return to the land of Judah" (v. 14). The prophet continued, "All the people of Judah who are in the land of Egypt shall perish by the sword and by famine, not one is left" (v. 27).

We do not know what happened to Jeremiah. Most likely, his last days were days of depression and despair because he remained pro-Babylonian in the midst of the pro-Egyptian refugees from Judah. We can only imagine the slow death of his spirit as he met only rebuff and hostility among his countrymen who had not only abandoned Judah, but also had abandoned the hope invested in Jerusalem.

Jerusalem, the Lonely City
Jeremiah 40:11-12; Lamentations 1–5

When war came to Judah, the people in villages and towns fled to the hills on foot, as they have always done. A picture forever imprinted in my memory is the description of refugees fleeing before the Israeli army during the Six-Day War. A force composed of forty massive tanks broke into the West Bank on Tuesday, 6 June 1967, and started a mad dash at top speed from Jerusalem to Shechem. Forty tanks traveling at 30 m.p.h. shook the ground and created a deafening roar. Gunners in the turrets turned their machine guns at the upper floors of houses and pelted the walls and windows with bullets, knowing that people huddled in cold fear in the basement rooms. The intimidation was complete.

On Wednesday morning, 7 June, a man who lived at a village between Ramallah and the Jordan Valley looked into the dawn and saw a terrifying sight. Fifty thousand people were milling and scrambling across the rocky hills, headed for a hiding place with such belongings as they could carry. This particular man fled down the Wadi Auja with his family and relatives and found refuge in a cave. Seventeen people lay in the cave, which was a Roman tomb I had excavated in 1966, for two nights and a day. They were cold, hungry, thirsty, and scared. On Friday, the man's wife said "If I'm going to die, I had rather die in my house than in this wretched cave!" He decided to venture back to the village, which he did. It was as silent as the tomb had been. When he met soldiers and learned that the village was undamaged and its people were free to return, the trek back out of the wasteland of the West Bank began.

The same kind of flight by villagers occurred when the Babylonians invaded the land in 589 B.C. I suspect the hills and valleys were covered with the fleeing civilian population. Some people went to Egypt, some fled south into the Negev, and some trekked east across the Jordan. Jeremiah 40:11-12 narrates,

> When all the Judeans who were in Moab and among the Ammonites and in Edom and in other lands heard that the king of Babylon had left a remnant in Judah, . . . then all the Judeans returned from all the places to which they had been scattered and came to the land of Judah.

There was another brief disturbance and dislocation after Gedeliah was assassinated, but many of the peasants returned to their villages. These people readily adjusted to changed circumstances anyway because they were oppressed by whatever government ruled over them. The Babylonians had left their villages in smoldering ruins, but mud-brick huts were quickly and inexpensively built and required no special skill.

Consequently, the "poorest of the land" left by the Babylonians to "be vinedressers and tillers" (2 Kgs 25:12) probably numbered more people than most scholars allow. The cities were desolate, however, especially Jerusalem. "How lonely sits the city," the lament begins, "that once was full of people!" (Lam 1:1).

The temple was burned and wrecked by the Babylonian soldiers. Because it was a focal place where intrigue and plots were born, the full wrath of the Chaldeans struck it. In 100 years of excavations at Jerusalem, not one stone nor artifact has ever been discovered that can be directly associated with the first temple. Nevertheless, the site remained a holy place during those dark years in Jerusalem when the scribe's pen was still. Devout worshipers of Yahweh continued to make pilgrimage to the lonely city, as Jeremiah narrated before his departure:

> On the day after the murder of Gedaliah, before anyone knew of it, eighty men arrived from Shechem and Shiloh and Samaria, with their beards shaved and their clothes torn, and their bodies gashed, bringing grain offerings and incense to present at the temple of the Lord. (41:5)

The lower city, where David had lived, was a ruin. Ashes and broken pottery lay on the plaster or packed earth floors under collapsed roofs and walls. Weeds grew up among the walls and debris, leaving little cavities where mice and vipers could make their hidden nests. Owls flitted about over the ruins at dusk, looking for an unsuspecting mouse, and jackals haunted the ruin, slinking furtively among the weeds and "hewn stones" that blocked the ways, that made the "paths crooked" (Lam 3:9). Buried under the rubble were the scattered bones of the fallen, "their skin shriveled on their bones" (4:8), a horrible witness to the horrible last days when "the hands of compassionate women . . . boiled their own children" (4:10).

Jerusalem the golden became a symbol of shame. We enter with difficulty the emotional arena of the Jewish soul in its attachment to the city of David. To the devout, it was more than a place. It was the navel of the earth attached to the umibical cord of divine favor. Created by David and his heirs, Jerusalem was the Jew, though not a Jew in the same sense anywhere else on earth. Therefore, Jeremiah sat down and wept by the waters of Babylon and mourned because "the Lord has trodden as in a wine press the virgin daughter Judah" (Lam 1:15).

The mice nested in the stones darted among the ruins of his soul. Jackals haunted the tangled, weed-infested open spaces where the beautiful structure of Jeremiah's air-tight theology had stood. Swinging in the wind with its lock ripped off was the door of his faith that had been so secure. Silent and subdued, with "no one to help" (Lam 1:17), he sat like the lonely city, hearing only the eerie swish of owls as they sailed through windowless openings and swinging doors.

Chapter 13

A New Order

Isaiah 40–55; Ezra 1–10; Nehemiah 1–13;
Haggai 1–2; Zechariah 1–14; Malachi 1–4.

550	Cyrus of Persia (550–530)
	Ministry of the Prophet of the Exile
539	Fall of Babylon to Cyrus of Persia
	Edict of Cyrus (538)
537	Shesh-bazzar leads first return to Judah
	(Zerubbabel)
520	Rebuilding the temple (520–515)
	(Haggai and Zechariah)
475	(Malachi)
450	Nehemiah
410	Jewish temple at Elephantine destroyed
400	Ezra's reform (397)

The prophetic herald of good tidings aroused the despairing exiles to hope of a second Exodus, this time from Babylon. He preached that Yahweh was the only sovereign Lord of the universe, and that nations were on the verge of being shaken up so that the chosen people could return and rebuild Jerusalem. Cyrus of Persia was designated the "anointed" of the Lord who would deliver Israel from bondage. Indeed he shook up the nations and, between 559 and 539 B.C., became the undisputed ruler of the Near East to the borders of Egypt and Greece. A polity of repatriation was proclaimed in 538 B.C., and the first band of exiles started out for Jerusalem with Shesh-bazzar as leader around 537 B.C.

The Herald of Good Tidings
Isaiah 40–55

The prophet Isaiah broke the silence of the long, lonely night of the exile, proclaiming good news given to him by "a voice": "Comfort, O comfort my people. Speak tenderly to Jerusalem, and cry to her that she has served her term, that her penalty is paid" (40:2). He was a prophet of the new generation. For the first time, we hear words of comfort instead of condemnation and words of hope for a prophet's contemporaries.

The voice continued: "In the wilderness prepare the way of the Lord, make straight in the desert a highway for our God" (40:3). The prophet's message unfolded in this two-fold announcement of "good tidings." The devout Jew was about to be delivered from the bondage in Babylon in a second Exodus; and ruined Jerusalem would be rebuilt to reunite the Jews and their holy city, the emotional significance of which only Jews can fully understand. Therefore, the message became almost ecstatic: "Lift up your voice with strength, O Jerusalem, herald of good tidings, lift it up, do not fear, say to the cities of Judah, 'Here is your God!' " (v. 9)

Ezekiel, we recall, saw in the vision of the storm chariot a revelation of the sovereignty of God over Babylon and the nations. The prophet of the second Exodus saw Yahweh as supreme over nations and history. Isaiah declared, "It is he who sits above the circle of the earth, and its inhabitants are like grasshoppers" (40:12). In the Canaanite pantheon, El sat on the throne above the circle of the earth. El was the supreme deity, ruler over all subsidiary deities. The prophet affirmed the supremacy of God in such ecstatic poetry that one feels it had just come as a revelation.

He continued to describe God: "who stretches out the heavens like a curtain and spreads them like a tent to live in" (40:22). Yahweh is the Lord of nature, the storm-God, as Ezekiel learned, and God of the sun. "Who brings princes to naught," he preached, "and makes the rulers of the earth as nothing" (v. 23). Yahweh is both sovereign of the domain of the nature deities and the Lord of history.

We recall that the Babylonians believed that Marduk, their deity, possessed the Tablets of Destiny, which gave him authority to program the events of history according to his purposes. The prophetic spokesman of the bedraggled captive Hebrew people now claimed this prerogative for their God. It was the doctrine of predestination, pre-Israelite in origin and concept, but nevertheless claimed for Yahweh. The Hebrew God programs history to serve divine purposes, as would be demonstrated in the second Exodus. To get the captives free for a triumphant return to Jerusalem, Yahweh would reshuffle the nations of the earth. Kingdoms great and small would be moved about as in a cosmic chess game to allow one little pawn to move.

"Scarcely are they (the rulers of the earth) planted, . . ." the prophet said, "when he blows upon them, and they wither, and the tempest carries them off like stubble," (40:24). "He gives power to the faint," he continued, encouraging his subdued people, "and strengthens the powerless" (v. 29). Furthermore, "Those who wait for the Lord shall renew their strength, they shall mount up with wings like eagles" (v. 31).

When we consider the setting in which the prophetic message was spoken, it sounds simply audacious. A spokesman for one minor captive people, a few thousand among possibly 20,000,000 in Babylonia, claimed that his God would gather up all the princes of the earth like a handful of cards and deal them out again! And the new deal would be solely to allow the few thousands of Hebrews to return and rebuild their holy city! Yahweh could do this great deed because Yahweh is "the creator of the ends of the earth" (40:28).

"Is there any God besides me?" the prophet asked rhetorically for Yahweh. Then he answered, "I know not one" (44:8). All of the gods of the princes of the earth are illusions because a craftsman creates them. A man cuts down a tree, burns half of it for fuel and says, "Aha, I am warm," then he fashions an idol with wood from the other half (vv. 14-16). The princes of the earth who fall down before the block of wood are deluded (v. 20), because their gods are powerless before Yahweh.

Evidently, the prophet's message was not believed by all of the exiled Jews because he gave them a lecture in theology. "Listen, you that are deaf," he exhorted, "and you that are blind, look up and see" (42:18). Then he explained that Israel was not run over in Judah because the kingdom accidentally got caught in front of Nebuchadnezzar's chariot. Judah's devastation was programmed in heaven as a part of a larger divine purpose.

"Who gave up Jacob to the spoiler?" Isaiah asked. "Was it not the Lord (Yahweh), against whom we have sinned?" (42:24). The Exile was therefore a historical purgatory, where Israel would pay for its iniquity. The herald cry of good tidings, we remember, was that the "warfare" of Jerusalem had ended. A more accurate translation is "time of service," specifically in the purgatory of Babylon because of its transgressions against Yahweh. But the prophet lectured his people; Israel had been purged of its iniquities and redeemed. The idea of redemption evoked an ancient Near Eastern custom of retaining rights to property that enabled a person to claim it when he paid the mortgage or other costs that had accumulated against it. Therefore, the prophet proclaimed in behalf of Yahweh: "Do not fear, for I have redeemed you, I have called you by name, you are mine." (43:1)

The theology of Israel's redemption is profound and therefore much discussed in many books. It evolves around a suffering servant who is Israel in Isaiah 40–55, except in four "servant poems" (Isa 42:1-9; 49:1-6; 50:4-9; 52:13–53:12) where the servant seems to be an individual. The individual is called Israel in 49:3 but is not national Israel. The servant cannot be identified with any contemporary historical individual. Actually, the servant seems to be an individual who is representative of ideal Israel, a corporate figure that may fluctuate between one and many. He is a faithful remnant who will "restore the survivors of Israel" (49:6) in rebuilding Jerusalem, but he is also an individual who makes himself a sin offering for his people (53:10). The servant as remnant and idealized individual satisfied the theological requirements for redemption and prepared the way for a historical second Exodus, this time from Babylon.

An immediate purpose of the theology of the suffering servant was to invest the suffering of the Babylonian exiles with purpose. The people who sat "in darkness" (42:7), in the anonymity of a captive minority group, needed purpose. They needed a vision of the great pattern of God's purposes in history and divine summons to a role in those purposes. Without this call to greatness, there could be little hope of resurrecting their spirit for a second Exodus. The prophet therefore quoted the summons: "I am the Lord, I have called you in righteousness, . . . I have given you as a covenant to the people, a light to the nations" (v. 6).

Informed with purpose, the people who sat down and wept by the canal Chebar put off their garments of mourning, for the prophet had set their feet in the highway of God's purposes. He had prepared a way in the wilderness of their despair; he had built a highway in the desert of their dreams. They waited, like track runners on their starting blocks. We can almost feel the tensing of muscles, the slow focusing of the eyes straight ahead, the silent concentration as they listened for the herald cry: "Go out from Babylon, flee from Chaldea" (48:20).

The Second Exodus
Isaiah 45:1-13; Ezra 1:1-4; 6:3-5

An unusual "messiah" appeared on the scene to initiate the exodus from Babylon. For the first time in biblical traditions, a foreigner was "anointed" to be an instrument of the divine. We should expect a development like this, however, because the prophet had drawn a picture of the world scene with Yahweh controlling the events of history.

The foreigner was Cyrus of Anshan (Isa 45:1), a man of the Pasargadae tribe on the Iranian plateau. In 559 B.C., he succeeded his father, Cambyses, and became king of Persia. Bound by vassal treaty to Astyages, king of Media, he indeed ruled over a small kingdom. Within twenty years, however, or by 539 B.C., Cyrus had overrun the entire Near East, with the exception of Egypt. His meteoric rise to power kindled a variety of emotions among people. The exiled Jews looked upon him as a deliverer, sent by Yahweh to strike from them the bonds of captivity, but the Babylonians did not share their opinion of the Persian.

The sophisticated Babylonians regarded Cyrus as a provincial upstart. He was indeed of nomadic heritage, and his kingdom was made up in part of desert tribes. Therefore, humiliation must have been the result when circumstances pushed Babylon into an alliance with Cyrus. King Nabonidas of Babylon wanted Haran in north Syria, and the only way he could take it was to join Cyrus in war against the Medes. A vision recorded by a Babylonian chronicler betrays Nabonidas' view of Cyrus.

Marduk, patron deity of Babylon, ordered the king in a vision to restore his sanctuary at Haran. The king protested that the Medes surrounded Haran and were fearfully strong. "The Mede of whom you are speaking," Marduk said in the dream to Nabonidas, "he himself, his land, and the kings who march at his side are not!" Marduk therefore reassured Nabonidas that the sun was setting on the king of Media and his domain. "When the third year comes," Marduk continued, "the gods will cause Cyrus, his little slave (i.e., vassal king to Media), to advance against him with his small army. He will overthrow the wide extending Medes."

The message of Marduk reflects Babylonian disdain toward Cyrus, but with recognition that he looked like a man of destiny. In fact, the overthrow of Media, long a rival of Babylonia, would have pleased the vanity of Nabonidas and at the same time allowed him to take Haran into his kingdom. He saw Marduk, his god, guiding him in the alliance with

Cyrus and therefore working events to his benefit. When the revolt of Cyrus began, Nabonidas left his son, Belshazzar, in Babylon and marched north to seize Haran. Meanwhile, Cyrus battled the main forces of the Medes and eventually won when a Median general, Hapragus deserted and brought his army over to the Persian. Astyages, king of Media, led a second army against Cyrus, but it mutinied and handed the king over to Cyrus. Media therefore became the first major addition of Cyrus' kingdom, in 550 B.C., and Haran went to Nabonidas as a prize of war.

Cyrus' victory over Media gave him claim to a large part of the Assyrian empire, which had been taken jointly by the Medes and Babylonians. A conflict with Babylon was therefore inevitable, because the reason for the alliance was ended. Marduk did not look that far into the future when he bade Nabonidas make an alliance with Cyrus! The Babylonian did not need divine guidance to perceive the sudden shift in international power, however. He found states to campaign against in the desert kingdoms of Edom and Arabia. Tema, an oasis in the Arabian desert, was captured in a strange expedition whose objectives are puzzling.

Some documents from this period tell of caravans delivering food to the king at Tema, likely the home of a royal residence! Babylon was left in the care of Belshazzar, his son. In fact, Nabonidas developed quite an interest in archaeology; and his preoccupation with ancient temples and ruins diverted most of his time away from administering the state. During this period Cyrus overran Asia Minor, capturing Lydia and its capital, Sardis.

Babylon was left alone to face "the little slave" who ruled an empire reaching from the Indus valley in the east to the Greek mainland in the west. Nabonidas, the king, spent his time at Tema in the desert; and Babylon was ruled by Belshazzar, his son. The priests of Marduk were alienated by Nabonidas' reforms, which sought to return to "the ancient paths." Probably during this time, after 547 B.C. and before Cyrus marched against Babylon, Cyrus was hailed as the Lord's anointed by the prophet of the exile. The Jews waited with delight for the overthrow of Belshazzar, the priests of Marduk were fed up with the reforms of Nabonidas, and the population was apathetic toward indifferent rulers. When Nabonidas gathered up local gods and carried them to Babylon for the "protection" of the capital against the Persians, the population turned hostile.

By the end of August 539 B.C., Herodotus reported, "The gods of Akkad (Babylonia), all who are above and below the earth, were entering into Babylon." This seems to reflect Isaiah 46:1-2, where the prophet stood on the sidelines and jeered the game that Nabonidas was calling against Cyrus: "Bel bows down, Nebo stoops," he seemed to mock, staggering along as though he carried one of the heavy idols, "their idols are on beasts and cattle."

Then turning in front of his Jewish cheering section, he called out through cupped hands to the Babylonians: "These things you carry are loaded as burdens on weary breasts." Reminiscent is the biting satire on idols in Isaiah 44:9-20. Idols are nothing, the prophet said there, and all who depend upon idols are deluded; they feed on ashes!

A battle at Opis on the Tigris River in October 539 B.C. broke the resistance of the Babylonians. Nabonidas fled his capital, and on 13 October 539 B.C., Gobryas led the army of Cyrus into Babylon without a battle. A tablet written by Nabonidas at Urak on 14 October suggests that he had not learned of the fall of his capital! Actually, there was no perceptible change of pace in the capital. By 26 October, the scribes were dating their records by the reign of Cyrus. The Persian's own account of the capitulation reflects the attitude of priests and the man in the street, with due allowance of course for Persian propaganda.

"A weakling had been installed as the *enu* (ruler) of his country," the chronicle relates. "The correct images of the gods he removed from their thrones, imitations he ordered to place upon them." We can see behind the scene a priest who had been offended by Nabonidas dictating to the scribe. "Daily did he blabber (incorrect prayers)," it continues. "The worship of Marduk, . . . he changed into abomination."

Then the complaint of the population emerges in the chronicle: "He (tormented) its (inhabitants) with corvée-work without relief; he ruined them all." Because of the complaints against Nabonidas, Marduk—the god of Babylon—became angry and departed from "their region." But he looked back and saw "the sanctuaries . . . in ruins and . . . the inhabitants . . . like living dead, . . . and he had mercy upon them," the chronicle narrates. A desolate and despairing situation not unlike that of the Jewish exiles gripped all of the nation.

"He (Marduk) scanned and looked through all the countries," the account continues, "searching for a righteous ruler willing to lead him (Marduk)." This is a reference to leading Marduk in the annual new year procession in which his supremacy was acknowledged and the king's designation by the gods was reaffirmed. "(Then) he pronounced the name of Cyrus," the chronicle goes on, "king of Anshan, (and) declared him to be(come) the ruler of all the world." To the Babylonians who opposed Nabonidas and the priests of Marduk who had been disenfranchised, Cyrus was the "anointed" of Marduk who would restore them to power.

The entry of Cyrus into Babylon "without any battle" was brought about by Marduk, who delivered Nabonidas, captured probably at Urak, "into his hands." "All the inhabitants" bowed to Cyrus and kissed his feet in subjection. "As a master through whose help they had come (again) to life from death," the scribe wrote, "they greeted him." A similar attitude was expressed by the prophet of the exile. "For the sake of my servant Jacob, and Israel my chosen, I call you (Cyrus) by your name." "I surname you," he prophesied candidly, "though you do not know me" (45:4).

The whole scene of Cyrus' entry into Babylon and his triumphant reception by the Marduk priesthood was looked at by the exiled Hebrews as their own little party that Yahweh arranged. In Babylon there was much pageantry and jubilation by the inhabitants when Cyrus was hailed as a deliverer, but the Jews waiting out in the province near Nippur viewed the whole affair from the perspective of what it meant to them. Cyrus, the focal figure in all the pageantry, whose feet were kissed and whose name was extolled, was actually doing all of this because Yahweh "grasped" his right hand, though Cyrus was unaware of Yahweh or the Jews. "I arm you," the prophet said of Cyrus in behalf of his God, "though you do not know me." (45:5).

Cyrus issued a proclamation immediately, ordering the return of "all the gods of Sumer and Akkad whom Nabonidas had brought into Babylon." Nabonidas had alienated much of the populace by seizing these gods in the first place for the "protection" of the capital. The proclamation was, therefore, a shrewd political move. "I returned to (these) sacred cities on the other side of the Tigris," he reported, referring to vassal cities that had been subject to Babylon, "the images which (used) to live therein and established for them permanent sanctuaries." The repatriation of gods in Babylon was followed by a return of the gods of captive peoples also. "I (also) gathered all their (former) inhabitants," he said, "and returned (to them) their habituations."

Captive peoples as well as their gods were repatriated as a general policy of the Persian. The exiles from captive states were probably the top leadership, like that of Judah. Consequently, the restoration of this leadership, along with authority to rebuild their sanctuaries, was a shrewd political move that reminds us of David's shrewdness in dealing with the house of Saul. It put the restored leadership in debt to Cyrus, and at the same time restored a sound economic and political base in subject states that could yield heavy taxes for the Persian king. The repatriation policy reflects a dimension of the Persian that explains in part his incredible rise to power over the Near East from Persepolis to Lydia in a scant twenty years.

The edict of Cyrus set free the Jewish exiles also. Long years of despair turned to a year of hope in 538 B.C. when the proclamation of Cyrus was heralded through the kingdom and "put in a written edict" (Ezra 1:1), probably a reference to the specific permit implementing the general policy. The Jews still looked at events, however, in terms of their own interests, so the proclamation was reported as though Cyrus was issuing it in the name of Yahweh for the few thousand Jewish exiles. The proclamation begins,

> Thus says King Cyrus of Persia, "The Lord (Yahweh), the God of heaven, has given me all the kingdoms of the earth, and he has charged me to build him a house at Jerusalem, in Judah. Any of those among you who are of his people, are now permitted to go up to Jerusalem, . . . and rebuild the house of the Lord." (vv. 2-5)

We recall that the prophet said in behalf of Yahweh, " I surname you (Cyrus), though you do not know me" (Isa 45:4); and "I arm you, though you do not know me" (v. 5). Cyrus himself did not mention the Jewish exiles in his chronicle. Therefore, the special proclamation in Ezra 1:2-4 most likely is based upon the specific permit issued to the exiles by the king's scribes authorizing them to return to Judah. This permit seems to be reflected in Ezra 6:3-5 and would be implementation of the general repatriation policy.

The exiles had been inspired by the prophetic summons to prepare to "go forth from Babylon," and we should assume an atmosphere of expectancy as Cyrus took over the land. The royal herald announced the king's policy in the cities and provinces, and someone, probably Shesh-basser, a son of Jehoiachin, applied for permission to return to Judah. An unknown scribe issued the permit, and Shesh-bazzar was put in charge of the second Exodus.

A Day of Small Things
Ezra 1:5–6:22; Nehemiah 7:5-73;
Haggai 1–2; Zechariah 1–14

The exodus from Babylon, spoken of in such stirring words by the prophet of the exile, was less than spectacular. Shesh-bassar, a man in his sixties, recruited a hard core of the faithful for the thousand-mile trek back to Judah. It was not an attractive undertaking from a purely practical standpoint. First, the journey over land was wearing, especially on older people. Most of the thousand miles would have to be walked. Second, the rich, irrigated land in the Euphrates valley was much more productive than the arid and rocky hills of Judah. Third, a second generation of Jewish exiles had grown up in Babylon, and they would be much more attached to life there than to strike out for the distant province of Judah to rebuild a temple they had never known.

Shesh-bazzar had some difficulty recruiting a sizeable group to begin the long trip back home. People who stayed behind paid the expenses of those who returned to Judah (Ezra 1:4). According to Josephus, many of them stayed behind because "they were not willing to leave their possessions." Actually the Jews were not slaves in Babylon, and the incentive to return to Judah was religious. Consequently, the initial party that set out in 537 B.C. was likely a small group consisting mainly of older people who wanted to be buried in Judah and a core of the *Hassids* who were oblivious to the comforts of the world around them. The group of families listed in Ezra 2 and Nehemiah 7 probably returned at a later time, with Zerubbabel, a grandson of Jehoiachin, not with the initial party.

The temple ruins drew the first party back to desolate Judah, so the initial focus of interest was there. Ezra 5:16 credits Shesh-bazzar with laying "the foundations of the house of God," but little more than regulation of worship was done until the prophets Haggai and Zechariah arrived and began preaching a building program about 520 B.C. The first years were hard ones, because the type of person who responded first to the summons was probably more at home reading the sacred traditions than he was at farming. The book of Haggai speaks of crop failures (1:9-11) and natural disasters of blight and hail (2:17), reflecting inexperience in trying to wrest a living from the reluctant soil of Judah as much as the transgression of not completing the temple. There was not adequate food nor clothing (1:5), which suggests that the initial party had to be rescued by the larger group that came with Zerubbabel some time later.

Trouble with the local population seemingly plagued the newcomers to Judah from the time they arrived. The first problems probably arose when Shesh-bazzar's group occupied the temple site. Local Jews would have been forced to submit to new regulations to worship there. On top of this was the undisguised feeling of religious superiority over the local people who came to worship, evident in a later prophecy of Haggai: "If one carries consecrated meat in the fold of one's garment," the prophet asked the priests, "and with the fold touches bread, or stew, . . . or any kind of food, does it become holy?" "No," the priests replied, meaning that careless handling of the "consecrated meat," ritually clean because it was selected and prepared according to the rigid rules of the priests, polluted it. "So it is with this people, and with this nation before me," the prophet said in the name of Yahweh, "and so with every work of their hands; and what they offer there is unclean" (Hag 2:12-14).

The newcomers, evidently from the time they arrived, considered themselves holy because they observed the strict regulations that their scribes had prepared on the basis of the ancient traditions. To associate with the local inhabitants who neither knew nor practiced their rules for keeping ritually clean made them unclean. They disdained the local people, which did not further good relations in the community. Also, the newcomers claimed ancestral holdings of land when they arrived in Judah. Houses and land had been abandoned in the wake of deportations to Babylon, and local peasants who straggled back seem to have moved into the abandoned houses. A messenger is reported to have fled Jerusalem and reported to Ezekiel that the city had fallen about two years after the city was sacked. Evidently, he brought his report from the local people: "Abraham was only one man, yet he got possession of the land," they had said; "but we are many; the land surely is given to us to possess."

They considered the land theirs after holding it almost a lifetime, specifically up to sixty years. The leaders who returned from Babylon claimed possession of what had belonged to their ancestors, so we would expect tension and hostility to mount. The local people probably had support from the Samaritans, who also resented the sudden intrusion of outsiders into what had been a part of the province of Samaria.

Cyrus or his successor, Cambyses, apparently reorganized the land into administrative districts that created a province of Judah with Jerusalem as its center. The Babylonians had simply annexed Judah to the province of Samaria in 587 B.C., so the creation of a rival province out of a part of Samaria antagonized the Samaritans. They vented their wrath upon the Jews in Jerusalem, as we shall see, when the province was created by the Persians for security reasons from their point of view. The returned leaders of Judah would be pro-Persian, whereas local people who knew the Persians only as harsh tax collectors would have no particular loyalty to the king.

Zerubbabel replaced Shesh-bazzar as the "governor" of Judah sometime between 537 and 520 B.C. He led a large group of exiles from Babylon, listed in Ezra 2 and Nehemiah 7, although the infusion of his band did not put much life into the dispirited community. Joshua, the son of Jozadak, was in charge of temple worship, but he still had no temple! Work had come to a halt because of adverse economic conditions and interference by the local people, instigated by the Samaritans. The local people had offered to help build the temple, but Joshua declined the offer, saying, "You shall have no part with us in building a house to our God; but we alone will build to the Lord" (Ezra 4:3). "Then the people of the land discouraged the people of Judah," the chronicler wrote, "and made them afraid to build, and they bribed officials to frustrate their plan." (vv. 4-5).

The restoration of Judah was at the point of failure by 520 B.C. Hostility, harassment, subversion, and economic hardship had been the lot of the faithful returnees for eighteen years. The encouraging words of the prophet in Babylon had promised much, but there had been no mad rush of Jews to Judah. Cyrus had not been converted to Yahweh, and his tax collectors exacted their harsh tribute from their living. There were no signs on the horizon that even Yahweh was aware of the despair and grinding poverty of the people. Among the chosen people, there was a deep conflict between the impractical idealists who controlled Jerusalem and the practical compromisers in the villages. The ranks of the returned community were most likely purged of all who were not rigid idealists by the ruthless discipline of circumstances.

A flurry of revival excitement occurred during the year 520 B.C., when the prophets Haggai and Zechariah began preaching an imminent breakthrough in the tight economic and political situation in Judah. Haggai, in particular, seems to have been a separatist. We have noted that he regarded the people of the land as ritually "unclean" (2:12-14), and he urged the returned exiles to separate from them. Coupled with the call for complete dedication to the Lord was also a challenge to complete the temple as a demonstration of their faithfulness (1:3-6).

The prophet laid down a hard line for the faithful of Judah, and they "feared" before the Lord (Hag 1:12). In part, his preaching intimidated them into resuming work on the house of the Lord, but in part he inspired them with visions of a messianic breakthrough when Yahweh would again reshuffle the nations and set Zerubbabel at the head of kingdoms as the divine viceroy (2:21-24). He would be the "signet ring" of Yahweh, stamping the authoritative signature of the almighty upon the administration of the world kingdoms. Zechariah, younger and more sensitive than Haggai, promoted the building of the temple (Zech 1:16) and "aliya," or emigration from Babylon (2:7). His cryptic visions inspired the enlightened of Judah, but probably left cold the peasant who plowed the rocky hills around the holy city.

A day of rejoicing came in 515 B.C. The completed temple was dedicated amid extravagant festivities (Ezra 6:16-17), and the passover was celebrated. The first part of the prophetic program of Haggai and Zechariah was fulfilled, but the messianic hope they had preached was deferred. The enthronement of the kingdom of David over all the nations, with Zerubbabel being the "signet ring" of Yahweh, did not happen. In fact, Zerubbabel possibly was removed by the Persians and executed on suspicion of treason, traceable to the messianic hopes invested in him by the prophets.

A New Order
Ezra 7–10; Nehemiah 1–7:4;
8:1–13:31; Malachi 1–4

The silence that hid Judah from history for a half century after completion of the temple was abruptly split by the strident voice of a prophet. Priests at the temple offered "blind animals in sacrifice, despising "the table" and the "name" of Yahweh (Mal 1:6-8). Laymen robbed God by withholding their tithes (3:8-9), depriving the priests of "food in my (Yahweh's) house" (v. 10).

The prophets challenged the people to put God to the test in bringing the full tithes. This suggests a general feeling in the community that it did not pay to observe the rigorous laws of the faithful. Malachi reiterated that it would pay. On behalf of Yahweh he said,

> Put me to the test, see if I will not open the windows of heaven for you, . . . I will rebuke the locust for you, so that it will not destroy the produce of your soil. (3:10-11)

The morale of the community was indeed low. Under pressure of naked want and disillusionment with the prophetic promises, post-exilic Judah had taken on the character of the people of the land. Ideals of the returned leaders had gradually succumbed to the strangling siege of poverty and hostility. Again the prophet enumerated the old spiritual pitfalls of Canaan: sorcery, adultery, deceit, oppression of the weak (3:5). These were pitfalls for the have-nots, as they were for the wealthy in the days of Micah. The time had come for strong leadership to emerge; the community was in danger of being absorbed into historical anonymity. Nehemiah, a politician, and Ezra, "the scribe," helped Judah find its soul and set its feet back in the paths of history.

Nehemiah, a high official in the court of Artaxerxes I (465–424 B.C.), received a report that "the survivors (in Jerusalem) . . . are in great trouble and shame; the wall of Jerusalem is broken down, and its gates have been destroyed by fire" (Neh 1:2-3). Seizing upon the need of the king for a strengthened presence in Judah, Nehemiah obtained authority to go to Jerusalem and repair its walls with wood and materials from the king's forest in Lebanon (2:7-8). He set out for Jerusalem about 444 B.C. with a royal escort, paid his respects to the governor of the Fifth Satrapy of which Judah was a province, and proceeded to his destination (2:1, 9-11).

Upon arrival, Nehemiah secretly inspected the ruins of Jerusalem at night (Neh 2:12ff.). The debris on the east slope above Gihon was scattered to the base of the hill, so that "there was no place for the animal I was riding to continue" (v. 14). Nothing had been done since the Babylonian soldiers dismantled the city walls a century and a half earlier. We know now from excavations at Jerusalem during the twentieth century (1961–1967) that Nehemiah proposed (v. 17) a reconstruction of only the top of the hill above Gihon. The tangled slopes on the sides of the hill were left in ruins. A work force from the families of Judah was recruited to rebuild the walls, with specific sections assigned to family groups (3:1-32), and the crest of the hill was enclosed.

The rebuilding was made difficult by the mass of stones (Neh 4:10) that covered the city. We almost get a picture of people laying up stones in openings between ruined house walls in the rush to complete the task and shut out the taunting enemies of Jerusalem (v. 7ff.). If the wall was completed in fifty-two days (6:15), it was likely more symbolic than strong. A wall authorized by the king of Persia would be effective, however, even if it were symbolic, because its integrity would be guaranteed by the king. A strong wall could have been built over a longer period of time, however, because Josephus reports a total building period of two years and four months. A section of wall on the east edge of the hilltop was identified in 1962 as Persian period construction, and it was a carefully fitted, strong wall of hewn stones. This type of wall would require more than fifty-two days for construction.

As governor, Nehemiah sought to revitalize the economy of the small province. Not more than 50,000 people lived in the vest-pocket state, so the Persian quota of taxes was oppressive. Herodotus reported a tribute fixed at 350 talents of silver for the Fifth Satrapy. If we calculate the weight in "light" talents of about 70 pounds, it totals 24,500 pounds of silver. The assessment on Judah would be oppressive; it was well-nigh impossible to obtain any silver with its meager resources. Consequently, we hear the cry to the governor: "We are having to borrow money on our fields and vineyards to pay the king's tax," some of the people said (Neh 5:4). "We are having to pledge our fields, our vineyards, and our houses in order to get grain during the famine," others said (v. 3). "Some of our daughters have been ravished, and our fields and vineyards now belong to others," some complained (v. 5).

Nehemiah rebuked the nobles and officials for "taking" excessive interest (Neh 5:7). Presumably, these were the "faithful" who controlled the temple and Jerusalem. They exacted from the "unclean" money, land, even sons and daughters for slaves in exchange for money to pay taxes and buy food. Nehemiah ordered the restoration of property to owners and cancelled interest on loans (vv. 6-13). Then he took a pledge from the officials and priests that they would no longer bleed the lower classes of their meager belongings. As an example, Nehemiah cancelled the governor's tax, which was in addition to the royal taxes, for a period of twelve years (vv. 14-18). Political and economic order was restored in Judah, leaving only the need for religious reform.

This need was most evident in Nehemiah's second term as governor when he found the Sabbath desecrated (Neh 13:15) and the temple in disarray (vv. 4-9). One emotional scene occurred when the aristocratic governor met children of marriages between Hebrews and "foreigners" in the land (v. 23). He discovered some who could not even speak Hebrew, which threw him into an uncontrollable rage. "I contended with them and cursed them," he said, "and beat some of them and pulled out their hair." (v. 25).

Then Nehemiah discovered that a son of Jehoiada, of the priestly family of Eliashib, had married a daughter of Sanballat, the bitter foe of Jerusalem. "I chased him away from me," he reported, meaning probably that he sent him to Samaria. Nehemiah obviously was not the man to lead in a religious reform, but the right man soon appeared—if not while Nehemiah was thrashing about in anger and frustration, then very soon afterward.

Ezra the scribe, called by one scholar the Minister of State for Jewish Affairs, came to Jerusalem to regularize worship and set the norm for the religious community. He had legal authority to carry out his commission, for he was "sent by the king"; and the blueprint for the task was "the law of your God, which is in your hand" (Ezra 7:14). The law was, of course, the Torah, but it was the tradition that had been kept and interpreted in Babylon. Therefore, Ezra brought the Babylonian tradition and with legal authority imposed it upon all who worshiped at the temple in Jerusalem. Perhaps the nature of his commission made him look severe and merciless in hewing to the letter of his law. In any case, however, it is not difficult to see in Ezra a kind of ecclesiastical dedication to his understanding of Yahweh, but one-sided in his outlook, as though he never heard a word from anyone other than himself.

One of the first steps in Ezra's reform was to establish the law as his authority. We read of a great convocation in an open square "before the Water Gate" (Neh 8:3ff.). The memoir relates, "He read from it (the law of Moses) . . . from early morning until midday, . . . and . . . (he) stood on a wooden platform that had been made for the purpose" (vv. 3-4). The reading was interpreted to the people "so that the people understood the reading" (v. 8).

Upon hearing the law and perceiving its meaning, presumably for the first time in their lives, the people wept in penitence (8:9). They were ministered to by the Levites, who instructed in the law the next day, and prepared for celebration of the Feast of Tabernacles (v. 11ff.). This measure established the law brought by Ezra as the norm, accepted by all who participated in the fall festival.

A second step in the reform was to deal decisively with the problems that Nehemiah had railed against. Ezra is pictured in a state of shock also, closeting himself in the "chamber of Jehohanan . . . where he spent the night" fasting and "mourning over the faithlessness of the exiles" (Ezra 10:6). The returned exiles had become "the people of the land" in practice, something Ezra found incredible. He called another convocation, giving the people only three days to put aside whatever they were doing and go to Jerusalem (vv. 7-8). When they straggled into Jerusalem, they all "sat in the open square before the house of God, trembling because of this matter and because of the heavy rain" (v. 9).

"You have trespassed and married foreign women," Ezra accused the congregation, as they sat trembling in the cold rain. "Now make confession to the Lord . . . and do his will; separate yourselves from the people of the land and from the foreign wives" (Ezra 10:10-11). "It is so; we must do as you have said," they responded. "But the people are many, and it is a time of heavy rain; we cannot stand in the open" (vv. 12-13).

Someone suggested that a committee be appointed to deal with the matter of implementing the separation from foreign wives (Ezra 10:14). Ezra approved when the returned exiles voted for the suggestion. Each case was investigated as it came before the appointed group, and within three months (vv. 9, 16) "they had come to the end of all the men who had married foreign women" (v. 17). The reform ended when the people came together again and entered into a "curse and an oath" (covenant) "to walk in God's law, which was given by Moses" (Neh 10:29); to abstain from mixed marriages (v. 30); to keep the sabbath day holy (v. 31); to support the temple and its priests with an annual tax of "a one third of a shekel" (v. 32); and to "forego the crops of the seventh years and the exaction of every debt" (v. 31). The abuses that provoked Nehemiah to anger (13:15-29) were thus corrected in Ezra's reform.

Ezra's mission, apparently a short one, succeeded in gathering up the people of Israel who would build their lives around the strict letter of the law. Those who would not make the commitment were excluded from the community and its worship. Perhaps someone such as himself, who could make harsh decisions and evidently not be perturbed, was the kind of leader Judah needed. He loomed in the traditions of Judaism as a kind of second Moses, because he did in fact mediate a second covenant. It is the basis of law and order that we find in Judaism of the first century A.D., and it laid a non-nationalistic foundation that could survive the loss of the state and the temple. Thus it was said, "Ezra would have been worthy of receiving the Torah for Israel, had not Moses preceded him," (Sanhedrin 21b). Indeed, Ezra initiated a new order, but it was not the order that produced Jesus of Nazareth.